D0422474

LIVING IN TIME

LIVING
· IN ·
TIME

The Poetry of
C. Day Lewis

ALBERT GELPI

New York • *Oxford*

Oxford University Press

1998

HOUSTON PUBLIC LIBRARY

R0l134 2l757

Oxford University Press

Oxford   New York
Athens Auckland Bangkok Bogota Bombay Buenos Aires
Calcutta Cape Town Dar es Salaam Delhi Florence Hong Kong
Istanbul Karachi Kuala Lumpur Madras Madrid Melbourne
Mexico City Nairobi Paris Singapore Taipei Tokyo Toronto Warsaw

and associated companies in
Berlin   Ibadan

Copyright © 1998 by Albert Gelpi

Published by Oxford University Press, Inc.
198 Madison Avenue, New York, New York 10016

Oxford is a registered trademark of Oxford University Press

All rights reserved. No part of this publication may be reproduced,
stored in a retrieval system, or transmitted, in any form or by any means,
electronic, mechanical, photocopying, recording or otherwise,
without the prior permission of Oxford University Press.

Library of Congress Cataloging-in-Publication Data
Gelpi, Albert.
    Living in time : the poetry of C. Day Lewis /
  by Albert Gelpi.
      p. cm.
    Includes bibliographical references and index.
    ISBN 0-19-509863-3
    1. Day Lewis, C. (Cecil), 1904-1972—Criticism
and interpretation.
I. Title.
PR6007.A95Z68   1997
821'.912—dc21   96-45410

9 8 7 6 5 4 3 2 1

Printed in the United States of America
on acid-free paper

This book is, as ever, for Barbara;

and this time also for Edward,

dear friend and comrade of Meriden Court

ACKNOWLEDGMENTS

THE GENESIS OF THIS book goes all the way back to the academic year 1964–65 at Harvard, when I met C. Day Lewis. He had come as the Charles Eliot Norton Professor to deliver, in the fall and spring, the series of lectures later published as *The Lyric Impulse*; I was an assistant professor with a brand-new Ph.D. But the differences in age and culture and experience somehow worked to kindle the regard and friendship we instantly felt for each other and found in each other. I was beginning to study the American poetic tradition, and it was daunting and thrilling that he came to my lectures on American poets whenever he could. I was deeply moved when he told me that if I were ever to write about his poetry, he would be very pleased. I knew even at the time that I had to gain the knowledge and perspective and critical distance necessary for such a task, and today, three decades later, I date these words of acknowledgment in completion of the first critical assessment of the whole body of his work in verse.

From the outset Jill Balcon, the poet's widow, has been encouraging and unfailingly helpful, giving me access to the papers, manuscripts, and books in her possession, even making copies of unpublished lectures and letters for me. I worked many hours, out of time, in the panelled study at Crooms Hill, under the pencil sketch of Thomas Hardy, where Day Lewis had worked for the last decades of his life, and later in the snug, book-lined study at Vine Cottage, looking out at the gently declining vista of Jill's beautiful garden.

Acknowledgments

•

VIII

I am grateful to the National Endowment for the Humanities for a summer stipend that allowed me to do some archival research in the British Library and in Rosamond Lehmann's papers at King's College, Cambridge. A number of friends and colleagues have given this book the benefit of their comments and insights, and I want to thank particularly Marjorie Perloff, Edward Socola, Thomas and Joyce Moser, and Clark and Jane Emery. Peter Mallios's discerning and accurate eye was very helpful in the final checking of the book manuscript; he asked questions and made connections that made me clarify and extend my argument in a number of places, and he cared for this book as though it were his own.

Sean Day Lewis, Day Lewis's first child, born the same year as I and only a month later, generously made available to me all the unpublished papers and manuscripts in his possession as well as the files of correspondence he had compiled in writing his father's biography. He said he regarded himself as the biographer and me as the critic. Though the two roles cannot be kept completely separate, I have tried to live up to my critical responsibility here. In the process I have come to know and honor both the poet and the poetry more deeply and truly.

As always, I owe more to Barbara Charlesworth Gelpi than even she can know. She is my first critic and my sole anima. With and through her I have come to whatever I have learned about living in time, and to those graced occasions when the desire going forth does meet the desire returning.

The photograph on the jacket and for chapter 2 (page 79) appears by courtesy of the Mary Evans Picture Gallery. The photographs for chapters 1 (page 13) and 3 (page 145) appear by courtesy of the National Portrait Gallery, London. The photograph on the title page is by Pat Prezioso.

Stanford, California   A. G.
August 1996

CONTENTS

LIVING IN TIME

. . . for certain temperaments the only Paradise
is Paradise lost.

The Buried Day, 234

INTRODUCTION

• I

WHEN W. H. AUDEN SAT down in 1968 to write an epistolary introduction
to a bibliography of his old Oxford chum C. Day Lewis, recently appointed
poet laureate, he took the nostalgic occasion to confront and lay finally to
rest the poetic "chimaera" that Roy Campbell had dubbed "MacSpaunday"
in an otherwise forgotten and forgettable satire called "Talking Bronco."

This derisive caricature reduced the poets associated one way and
another with Auden during the thirties—Day Lewis, Stephen Spender,
Louis MacNeice—to a grotesque synthesis of the left-wing poets of the
decade, with the Auden phoneme "au" in the middle surrounded by elements of MacNeice, Spender, and Day Lewis. In the crude Popean couplets
of Campbell's right-wing doggerel, this compound poetic monster, viewed
from the perspective of 1946, had irresponsibly spouted phony and fash-
ionable revolution for publicity and profit:

> While joint MacSpaunday shuns the very strife
> He barked for loudest, when mere words were rife,
> When to proclaim proletarian loyalties
> Paid well, was safe, raked in heavy royalties,
> And made the Mealy Mouth and Bulging Purse
> The hallmark of Contemporary verse.
> The joint MacSpaunday, with quadruple bun
> Commercially collectivised in one,

> A Cerberus-Hydra, could not cease
> His fierce Belligerence (in time of peace!)
> But plagiarised from Blimp, ten years before,
> The most vociferous arguments for war.
>
> (*Talking Bronco*, 79)

Campbell's parting shot came years after the "group" had disintegrated because of the poets' separate inclinations and because of the collapse of the political idealism of the thirties under the contradictory forces that exploded into the Second World War. However, even after the war Campbell's envy was still unappeased because the "MacSpaunday" poets had dominated the literary scene through the thirties and in his view fouled it with their "bolshy" propaganda. At the time Spender and Day Lewis wrote back and forth about responding to Campbell's venom and in the end decided not to credit it with a reply. By 1968 Auden, like the others long since weary of literary chat about that mythical beast, observed yet once more in his "Letter" to Day Lewis that while "four poets of more or less the same age, confronted by the same historical events, will exhibit certain responses in common," nonetheless "what we happened to have in common was the least interesting thing about us"; on the contrary, "what there may be of value in what we have written is peculiar to each of us" (Handley-Taylor and Smith, v).

Campbell's spite was fueled by literary jealousy and his own reactionary hostility to the leftist leanings of the group, but in fact the poets themselves had been complicit during the thirties in accepting and promoting their association as the movement of the future in British and Irish poetry. After all, twentieth-century poetry in English had been dominated by a remarkable generation of Americans; despite the magnificent individual achievements of W. B. Yeats and Thomas Hardy in their old age, there was nothing in Britain comparable in generative energy and ambition to the Imagist experimentation of Ezra Pound and H. D. and William Carlos Williams, or the radical language games of Gertrude Stein, or the aestheticist symbolisme of T. S. Eliot and Wallace Stevens. Wilfred Owen, Rupert Brooke, and Edward Thomas were dead in the war; Robert Graves and D. H. Lawrence were exotic anomalies, the one drawn to the classical Mediterranean, the other to Walt Whitman and the New World. In any case, none of the British poets, including Hardy and Yeats, were committed Modernists, and most, including Lawrence and Graves, were committed anti-Modernists. Modernism, the ruling aesthetic and cultural ideology of the first half of the century, passed British poetry by almost completely, or rather with few exceptions British poets chose, on aesthetic principle, not to join in the seemingly dangerous iconoclasm of Modernist experimentation.

"MacSpaunday" represented the most visible and organized response and challenge to American poetic Modernism, the first effort to inject into the enervated Georgian poetry of postwar Britain a self-conscious identity and collective purpose in order to reclaim the laurel wreath from the energetic Americans. What is more, their campaign to fill the void in British poetry met with immediate success; by the mid-thirties the poets later lampooned as "MacSpaunday" were talked about on both sides of the Atlantic as the avant-garde of British poetry. Allen Tate signaled the quickening American interest when he allowed that while "for the last twenty years the best verse in the English language has been written" by Americans, recent volumes like Spender's *Poems* indicated a new and important development in British poetry (*New Verse*, No. 3, May 1933, 21).

In the long run, however, Auden was fundamentally right about the group: what was most interesting and valuable about their work comes from what is "peculiar to each of us." The labels that serve historians and reviewers and poets themselves to plot out movements and new directions prove short-sighted and short-lived as the shared program and values that identify a movement and provide the impetus for launching a poetic career give way to the need to define, by trial and error, a distinctive poetic stance and the individual voice to articulate it. The time is long overdue for readers and critics of modern poetry to undertake the kind of discriminating reassessment that Auden's remarks implicitly call for. Just as from the outset Auden got (and expected) the limelight, he has been widely written about since his death, and his poems and plays are available in authoritative editions, including an *English Auden* to restore the poems of the thirties that he had revised or suppressed. The *Collected Poems* that appeared after MacNeice's death in the early sixties initiated the process of his critical evaluation, and the publication of Day Lewis's *Complete Poems* in 1992, twenty years after his death, provided the occasion for this book to trace the distinctive and distinguished trajectory of his poetic career. Spender's death in 1995 should open the way for a proper edition of his poetry and a fresh look at his career.

In the last year of his life Day Lewis commented about "MacSpaunday": "I don't think we were the same kind of poets, except when we were at Oxford insofar as Auden was the predominating influence upon us" ("On a Tilting Deck," 5). Even at the time Spender declared that "although Auden's, Day Lewis's and my name have been linked together ever since the publication of *New Signatures* [in 1932], I had never met Day Lewis or read any of his work until some time after my own *Poems* were published [in 1933]: so that if there is a common factor in Day Lewis and me, it must be the influence of Auden" ("Oxford to Communism," 9). The effect of Auden's influence was relatively brief and was in any case very different on the two poets and, a little later and to a lesser extent, on MacNeice. Unfortunately, however, Auden's voluble domination of the group in that brief early period and of critical opinion since then has made it difficult to hear Day Lewis and MacNeice and Spender on their own terms and in their own distinct voices. Samuel Hynes's excellent *Auden Generation* is typical in treating the other three poets of "MacSpaunday" almost as ancillary consequences of Auden's career and consequently exhibiting Day Lewis as a failed

Auden rather than as the very different poet that he is. But in fact the mis-reading and misjudgment of Day Lewis via Auden began in the thirties and reached its most virulent and even pathological expression in Geoffrey Grigson's turning against Day Lewis in 1934 and in his subsequent use of his powerful position as editor and reviewer for an unrelenting vendetta against Day Lewis. The intention of this book is to undertake a reassessment on a clean slate.

In some ways Day Lewis played into the underestimation of his poetry, almost as if to anticipate it. He seemed to go out of his way to call himself a derivative, even an "unoriginal" poet (see, for example, "On a Tilting Deck," 3), but originality has never functioned in the British tradition as it has in the American. The hallmarks of the American poet in the lineage (not "tradition" in the British sense) of R. W. Emerson and Whitman have always been originality, individuality, even eccentricity. A number of commentators have noted that the ruptured continuity of American poetry comes from the imperative to move on, start over, begin again, make one's self. American poets who were in some sense derivative, like Pound or Robert Duncan, almost instinctively strove to be original as well, making what was derived experimentally new. Eccentric British poets, like William Blake or Christopher Smart or Lawrence, seem sports in a way that Whitman and Emily Dickinson, Pound and Duncan do not. British poets, trained to tradition, are quite expectedly derivative, even, in a sense, un-original. The challenge to them is to define their own place within the tradition and thereby enrich and extend it. Eliot's mediating position between American and British poetry is summarized in the very title of his essay "Tradition and the Individual Talent."

As a result, reading and hearing British poetry require an ear finely tuned for different, less obvious, in some ways subtler qualities and more modu-lated effects. Like Auden, Day Lewis played off and against the lines and voices of other poets—most noticeably, at different stages of Day Lewis's career, off and against John Donne and George Herbert, Auden and Gerard Manley Hopkins and Yeats, Hardy and Matthew Arnold and Robert Frost. However, when Day Lewis echoes Frost or Auden or some other poet, that correlation sets the terms of distinction as well as connection within the community of poets; that is how tradition works. So Day Lewis regu-larly undercut his self-deprecating defensiveness by insisting, rightly, that to the finely tuned ear and mind the subtle interplay of voices serves to discriminate difference within consonance, and thus finally to define differ-ence over consonance.

• 2

If the Auden "group" represented the British avant-garde of the thirties, it was an avant-garde consciously different from that of Pound and even Eliot. Day Lewis is, then, a modern but not a Modernist poet, and that defining distinction suggests the profound difference not only between his work and that of his American peers but, more generally, between British and American poetry in the twentieth century. It is for that reason that Pound, for instance, felt closer to prose writers like Henry James and James Joyce and Ford Madox Ford than to the poets he met in literary London. It is true that Frost and Stevens rejected Modernist formal experimentation, and it is no coincidence that Day Lewis shares more with them than he does with Pound or Williams or Stein, Hart Crane or H. D. or Marianne Moore. Day Lewis and many of his fellow poets in Britain remained suspicious of the experimentation of *The Waste Land* yet could gingerly accept Eliot, because they recognized that Eliot was, in fundamental and prevailing intention, a traditionalist.

Stevens made the useful differentiation between poets, like himself and Frost, who were modern in content, and those, like his Modernist contemporaries, who were modern in form as well as content. The skirmish between the modern and the Modernist will run through the chapters that follow, and the opposing sides began to sort themselves out in the decisive decade of the teens. At the time that the little magazines were displaying early experiments in Modernist American poetry, the various anthologies of *Georgian Poetry* were simultaneously seeking to demonstrate that "English poetry is now once again putting on a new strength and beauty" (M[arsh], "Prefatory Note," *Georgian Poetry 1911–1912*) by extending metered pastoralism into the new century.

Indeed, the strategic projection of a Georgian renewal precisely coincides with and counters Pound's proclamation of Imagism and the advent of Modernism in American poetry. The "Prefatory Note," announcing "another 'Georgian period'" in poetry, was signed by the editor, "E. M." (Edward Marsh), and dated "Oct. 1912"—the year in which Pound formulated the three axioms of Imagism. Admittedly he did so in London not just with fellow-American H. D. but also with Richard Aldington, an Englishman. However, this manifesto for a Modernist poetry appeared in Harriet Monroe's *Poetry* (Chicago) because there was no British magazine to publish it, and while Imagism temporarily attracted Lawrence and Ford Madox Ford and aroused often hostile arguments in London literary circles, it made no serious inroads into British poetic practice. Even Aldington's presence at the famous tearoom near the British Museum had more to do with his personal interest in H. D. than his poetic interest in Pound, and his subsequent career reverted to a vocal opposition to Pound and poetic Modernism in general.

Thus the divergence between British and American poetry in this century is already predicated in the fact that publication of the five *Georgian Poetry* anthologies (1912, 1915, 1917, 1919, 1922) began in the year of the Imagist manifesto, continued through the years in which *Des Imagistes* (1914) and the several collections of *Some Imagist Poets* (1915, 1916, 1917) appeared, and concluded in the year of *The Waste Land*'s publication, as Pound was revising his first *Cantos*. It is true that Pound was invited to contribute to the first collection of *Georgian Poetry* (but, significantly, did not) and that the Imagist anthologies included, amidst the Americans, several poems by Aldington and Joyce and Lawrence. Nonetheless, the lines were quite clearly drawn by the time the second collection of *Georgian Poetry* was published in 1915. An advertisement on the same page of that volume offered both *Georgian Poetry 1911–1912* for three shillings and six pence and, separately below it, *Des Imagistes* for two shillings and six pence. The reader had a choice, and the British readers' choice was clear; *Georgian Poetry 1911–1912* was touted as running through its "Thirteenth Edition," with sales over 15,000 copies, numbers that *Des Imagistes* could not come close to matching.

What is more, even after Modernist experimentation had become a matter of note in the popular press as well as in the little magazines, the lines separating British and American verse continued to be quite strictly drawn and maintained. *A New Anthology of Modern Verse 1920–1940*, edited by Day Lewis with his friend L. A. G. Strong and published in 1941, gives a clear picture of how "modern verse" was constituted from the British perspective. To begin with, the opening date of 1920 excludes from notice—to name just a few defining books in the emergence of Modernism—Eliot's *Prufrock* and *Poems 1920*, Pound's *Cathay* and *Hugh Selwyn Mauberley*, Stein's *Tender Buttons*, Williams's *Sour Grapes*. Indeed, Eliot is the only one of those writers who is mentioned at all in the Introduction. Not a word about Pound, Stein, or Williams, and Eliot is cited with the observation that he did not really begin to influence British poetry "till about 1930" (xx)—that is to say, after the experimental period of *The Waste Land* and *The Hollow Men*.

The Introduction is presented as a chummy dialogue between the two editors, and their discussion complains of the difficulty and obscurity of modern verse, caused by the enormously increased complexity of the twentieth century and the decline of "tradition" and a "common ground of belief" which could serve to comprehend and configure the new and contradictory sensations and experiences of contemporary existence. Strong took primary responsibility for the initial choice of poets from the twenties and Day Lewis for poets from the thirties, but they agreed that because the Georgians dominated the twenties, a really modern British poetry must be dated only from 1930. Strong even put off the American influence on modern poetry to "the emergence of Hart Crane in 1927" (xx), thus erasing the emergence of Stevens and Marianne Moore, H. D. and E. E. Cummings and Carl Sandburg, not to mention the previously mentioned triumvirate of Williams, Pound, and Stein.

This virtual suppression of developments in American poetry is reflected in the selections that represent "modern verse" of the thirties and forties. The only Americans included are Eliot (who by then had become a British subject) and Laura Riding (who is allowed two poems through her anti-Modernist alliance with Graves). Eliot is allotted the largest number of pages—nine; but the selections are "Gerontion," "Journey of the Magi," two sections of *Ash Wednesday*, and one passage of *Murder in the Cathedral*, with nothing from *The Waste Land* and only one section from *The Hollow Men*. On the other hand, the space allocated to other poets gives a reasonably accurate cross section of British modern verse from the perspective of the late thirties; besides Eliot's nine pages, there are eight pages each for Auden and MacNeice, seven and a half pages each for Yeats and Edith Sitwell, six each for Hardy, Day Lewis, and Laurence Binyon, and five and a half for Spender. In the same vein, when Day Lewis wrote in 1947 *Enjoying Poetry: A Reader's Guide*, the modern poets he listed as most difficult and radical were Eliot, Sitwell, Auden, and Dylan Thomas; and the only Americans in his list of recommended poets were Eliot and Frost. Indeed, none of the influential contemporary critics of poetry— J. Middleton Murry, C. M. Bowra, Edmund Wilson, I. A. Richards—go beyond Eliot, Yeats, and the Symbolistes to deal with the truly radical formal experimentation of Pound and the other Americans.

At the same time, Day Lewis's resistance to the "Georgian" label sometimes attached to his own work indicates his determination to find a more vital and effective way to be a modern poet within the tradition than the Georgians managed to achieve. In the Introduction to the anthology he summed up their failure:

> [H]owever considerable their poetic merits, they seemed to lack the impetus and authority which some common religious or social belief would have given them. Like so much of the verse of the Georgians, these poems struck me as having been written at random, as being the fag-ends, often glowing with a not inconsiderable light, of a poetry and tradition that are now exhausted.
>
> (xix)

Day Lewis's objection is not formal and metrical but substantive: the Georgians seemed to him to lack the spiritual and ethical vision—"some common religious or social belief"—which could reenergize the traditional forms and meters with a new voice, new rhythms, new images.

Yet, in Day Lewis's view, formalist experimentation was even more fundamentally and irretrievably wrongheaded because the new voices it was generating seemed narcissistically elitist and solipsistic and because the new forms bespoke the disintegration rather than the reinspiration and reconstruction of society. If modern scepticism made a religious vision and hope for heaven hard to achieve, except in individual instances like Eliot, we still had to learn to live in time, and the challenge and responsibility of the modern poet was to forge some other common ground in order to clarify, for himself and his fellow seekers, how to live in time meaningfully and responsively. Rejecting the Modernists, on the one hand, and the Georgians, on the other, Day Lewis dated modern poetry in Britain from 1930 because he found in his generation the beginnings of such a possible secular vision, "much more politically minded: more speciWcally concerned with social problems" (xx). His essay *A Hope for Poetry* served as a manifesto for the era because it called for a poetry that would reformulate the tradition by addressing the private and public crisis that threatened personal and social existence in the twentieth century.

This revisionary study of Day Lewis's poetry seeks to distinguish his voice within "MacSpaunday" during the thirties and then follow its development in the remaining thirty years of his career, and it seeks to accomplish this large task with something still of the coherence and integrity of a long essay. A close reading will show that, striking as Day Lewis's work from the thirties remains, much of his best work came later, especially during and after the war in the forties, and in his last years. As often happens, since his death in 1972 Day Lewis's poetry has largely fallen from notice or discussion, and a combination of factors—the vocal opposition of enemies he made during the thirties and after, the aura of faded respectability that the laureateship rightly or wrongly brings with it, the snooty ideological opposition of contemporary Poststructuralists to structured form and the lyric speaker in poetry—has contributed to the recent neglect of his work. However, the publication of *The Complete Poems*, edited by Jill Balcon, the poet's widow, in Britain and the United States in 1992 has provided the occasion and impetus for me to undertake a reassessment that will confirm his place as one of the major British poets of this century.

I have always taken it that the critic's task is to serve as clarifying explicator of the poem rather than as theorist or dissecting pathologist. So I was delighted to find a lucid statement of that function in the first chapter of Day Lewis's *Poetic Image*. His words can stand as a summary of my own assumptions and aims in writing this book:

> A critic is going on record now, and what is to be recorded is not poetic experience so much as a series of abstractions from it. To be of any value whatsoever, these abstractions must in some way illuminate their source; they will fail to illuminate it unless the critic has brooded over the poem, surrendered himself to it absolutely, strained his ears to catch its remotest undertones, with the same absorption that the poet gave to the experience from which it was shaped. A critic who imposes his own abstractions upon poetry may be writing good history, good sociology, good psychology, but he will never be writing literary criticism.
>
> To put it quite simply, the critic has one pre-eminent task—that of easing or widening or deepening our response to poetry.
>
> (*The Poetic Image*, 16)

In this spirit I have done my best to brood over and surrender to the poems, to listen for their undertones and overtones with as much as I could manage of "the same absorption that the poet gave" in writing them. I assume with Keats that we each and all write our allegory in our individual lives, and that the poet's task—and particularly perhaps the task of the lyric poet in society—is to write the allegory of his or her life with more expressive skill and sense of calling than most of us have. What Keats said, in one of those long, reflective letters to his younger brother and sister-in-law in America, was: "A Man's life of any worth is a continual allegory— and very few eyes can see the Mystery of his life—a life like the scriptures, figurative— . . . Shakespeare led a life of allegory; his works are the com- ments on it—" (*Letters*, 2:67). Keats's allegory, then, does not inscribe a didactic lesson, an abstract principle that the life illustrates and the works record, but, on the contrary, inscribes the individual's effort at meaning and signification. As it evolves, this distinctive "figurative" design traces out, first for the scribe and then for the reader, what he or she managed to piece out of the "Mystery" in the engagement with self and world in lan- guage. In Day Lewis's words from the Postscript to his autobiography,

> [A]lthough everyone, through the inner monologue that is his reflec- tive commentary on experience, selects and subtly distorts the facts so as to make him more interesting or more tolerable to himself, in doing so he creates a personal mythology which, because it modifies him, does become representative truth.
>
> (*The Buried Day*, 243)

In this view the function of the poet is to write autobiography as repre- sentative truth into which readers can enter.

The three chapters of this book, therefore, examine Day Lewis's poetry informed by biographical information, literary history, and cultural con- text. Demarcating what might be called the early, middle, and late phases of Day Lewis's career, the progression of the chapters coincides with the ruptures that precipitated and determined those transitions, and corresponds roughly with the years of the poet's deepest involvement with each of the three women whose presence shaped the course of his adult life: Mary King, Rosamond Lehmann, and Jill Balcon. Moreover, the subtitles of the chap- ters point to the ongoing and underlying areas of concern and difficulty— politics and social responsibility, love and sexuality, faith and death—that impelled the poet's lifelong search for a vision that would confirm his sense of identity and reconcile him to the mortal round. The chapters indicate shifting emphases among these abiding and interconnected concerns in different periods. However, the continuity running through the turns and dislocations of Day Lewis's life and work, through his shifting engage- ment with politics and eros and thanatos, is the never-satisfied need of the "Churchy agnostic" ("On a Tilting Deck," 13) to reach bedrock, to press toward realizing (in the double sense of comprehending and fulfilling) human limits and human possibilities.

A note on the poet's Anglo-Irish name(s). His grandfather Frederick Day was born in England but of Irish stock that could (the poet learned late in life) trace the name Day back to Celtic origins in County Clare. The two elements of his name came into hyphenated combination when Frederick Day entered the Dublin soap business of his adopted father Fred

Lewis. His own father was the Rev. Frank Day-Lewis, but the poet dropped the hyphen early in his literary career: He was Cecil Day-Lewis in *Ten Singers* (1925) and *Beechen Vigil* (1925), Cecil Day Lewis in *Country Comets* (1928), and C. Day Lewis in *Transitional Poem* (1929) and in all subsequent volumes. Sometimes in his last years he considered restoring the hyphen, in large part to avoid confusion about his last name (not, as he was often called, Mr. Lewis) and so about how he should be alphabetized in lists and libraries and catalogues. Even the venerable ledger books that constitute the catalogue of the British Library, with entries pasted in as new books appear, still mistakenly locate his work in the Ls rather than Ds. Perhaps in the end he concluded that reinserting the hyphen might only compound the confusion; in any case after *Transitional Poem* C. Day Lewis remained his literary name for the rest of his career.

ONE • "IN ME

TWO

WORLDS

AT WAR"

Poetry and
Politics
1925–1940

• I

AFTER THE THIRTIES, when the "MacSpaunday" poets had gone their separate ways, Day Lewis was as eager as Auden and the others to play down the notion that they had come together in a concerted and self-conscious movement: "Though Auden, Spender, MacNeice and I have all known each other personally since the mid-Thirties, each of us had not even met all three others till after the publication of *New Signatures* in 1932, while it was only in 1947 that Auden, Spender and I found ourselves together for the first time in one room" (*The Buried Day*, 216–17). Nevertheless, Day Lewis did see the four of them, in their association during the thirties and in their divergence later, as sharing a common background of social class and educational privilege at a particular critical point in British history, and so as sharing certain moral and cultural assumptions. In an unpublished lecture on "The Thirties in Retrospect," the last in the series of lectures he gave while occupying the Chair of Poetry at Oxford in the mid-1950s, Day Lewis summed up their common ground :

> Of the four poets who were at Oxford between 1923 and 1930, two [MacNeice and himself] were sons of clergymen [both of tne Church of Ireland], one [Auden] had a strongly Anglo-Catholic mother, the fourth [Spender] grew up in a milieu of high-minded Liberalism. None, at that time, held any religious faith. We had all been at public schools: we were schoolboys during the first World War, suffering, though re-

motely, its stresses. We were all, I think, emotionally immature for our years, unsophisticated, vaguely dissatisfied, sure of almost nothing but the vocation we felt for writing poetry. We were too young to share either the hopes, the cynicism or the hectic gaiety of the war-survivors and the immediate post-war generation. Life at Oxford felt, to me at least, like living in the trough after a great wave—a swirling, bewildering, uneasy existence, affected by eddies and cross-currents from the disoriented world outside. We did not have to read *The Waste Land* to know that this world had been fragmented. We obscurely felt the need to do more with the fragments than shoring them against our ruin. The magic word, the cant word, of the time was 'synthesis'.

("The Thirties in Retrospect," 5)

This succinct passage could stand as an epigraph for this book; the chapters will explore its ramifications and consequences as they determined the course of Day Lewis's life and poetic career.

Cecil Day Lewis was the only child of Reverend Frank Cecil Day-Lewis, an ordained priest of the Church of Ireland, and Kathleen Blake Squires, born on April 27, 1904, in Ballintubbert, County Laois. Instinctively Day-Lewis continued to think of himself as Irish in his roots, and he returned to the homeland for summer vacations in his later years. His father's pastoral assignments took the family to England in 1905 and to London in 1908; there Kathleen Day-Lewis died when her son was four years old. Her elder, unmarried sister, Agnes, lovingly known to her nephew as Knos, moved into the household and became the surrogate mother. She was saintly in her unstinting and self-sacrificing love, while the father's fierce love for the boy made muted demands through his reserved demeanor. Day Lewis went to Wilkie's Prep School in London and to Sherborne School in Dorset, with its Gothic chapel, old stone buildings, and enclosed courtyard, before going up to Oxford as a student at Wadham College in 1923.

He had begun to write poetry even before leaving Sherborne. The earliest surviving efforts are contained in a notebook, with the title and author variously identified: on the cover, *Poems, 1st Series* by Cecil Day-Lewis 1921–1922; on the spine, *Early Poems* by C. Day-Lewis; and on the title page, *Clivus ad Parnassum / Early Poems First Series // C. D. L. 1921,* with an epigraph: "'Dream then, for this is also sooth.' W. B. Yeats." The first poem in the notebook is accompanied by a sweetly effusive statement of dedication to the "imagination & mystery":

> They say that one of the greatest factors in poetry is imagination; the power to conjure up visions before readers' eyes. Imagination & mystery go hand-in-hand; & so, though I am no poet—yet would be one— & because, though I have small power to translate them into verse, yet would I attempt to express the feelings of imagination & mystery in me, do I launch my poor verses into the sea of poetry.

The young man's poetic craft almost immediately proved seaworthy and found port in the school's literary magazine. The printed text of one poem is pasted into the notebook with the following proud comment as landmark:

"Note: this poem was published in the Shirburnian [sic] under the title of 'Reverie.' July 25, 1921." The citation from Yeats and the cultivation of visionary reverie indicates the Celtic and Georgian late-Romanticism from which the thirties poet would emerge with a modified sense of vocation.

Day Lewis's first hardcover appearance came at Oxford in the anthology *Ten Singers*, published in October 1924, though the verso of the title page is dated 1925. That year saw his first (and privately printed) collection, *Beechen Vigil* (August 1925), and his first meeting with the slightly younger Auden, then in his first year at Christ Church. The poems in *Ten Singers*, *Beechen Vigil*, and his second collection, *Country Comets* (1928), echo the Yeatsian and Georgian legacy from the first decades of the century. Though the Georgian poets had coexisted in the English literary scene of the teens with the group around Pound, they sought to exorcize fin de siècle decadence not through Modernism (particularly since its iconoclasm was championed by the expatriate Americans) but through the invocation of the native English pastoral tradition. Not Pound but Frost was the American expatriate the English found congenial, and Frost's friendship with Edward Thomas seemed to confirm his affinity with the English pastoral mentality. But Georgian pastoralism was itself too much a vestige of the now collapsed Romantic mystique to generate a new poetry; and by the time it was echoed by Day Lewis and his contemporaries, their balladlike songs of country reverie wrung from an aching heart sounded too thin and tired to rouse an enthusiastic response.

It is instructive to read Day Lewis's early efforts (all included in *Beechen Vigil*) in their Georgian context among the other nine contributors to *Ten Singers*. The titles of these dreamy poems announce their connection with natural setting and seasonal cycle, but the texts long for a timeless security, a lost or projected golden age, or, since such release from fret is beyond the grasp of mortal consciousness, for oblivious dissolution back into natural process. The two opening poems by Edgar Bishop set the pattern. Lulled by the contentment of "A Summer Afternoon," the speaker aspires to permanence: "If I could only stay / And laze and dream all time away, / How pleasant it would be to pass / Eternity in summer grass." But the next lyric, "At Last," transforms "Eternity in summer grass" into a wish not for transcendence but for annihilation into "Sunshine, and trees' dim laughter, / And the gentle splash of rain."

Day Lewis's verses in *Ten Singers* deal with the same themes, distinguished only intermittently by flashes of more vivid sensory perception, by fresher phrasing, and by tighter control of the verbal melody. But it is worth noting that already he was in fact showing something of the skilled inventiveness with formal patterns and syllabic texture that would characterize his later work. The opening stanza of "Sanctuary," for example, is woven together with alliteration, assonance, and rhyme and enlivened by the synesthesia of sight and sound in the last three lines. (Unless otherwise indicated page references to Day Lewis's poems throughout this book come from his *Complete Poems*.)

Swung in this hammock between hills
we have dreamed a nobler quietude
than the breathless after-hush when bells
tire of their silver tumbling.
Our mood
is crystal, bright as primrose laughter
rippling beneath the bracken, clear
as rain's metallic plash from a rafter.   (19)

"Sanctuary" aspires to a holy, arcane, and Yeatsian moment of erotic consummation "nobler" than time allows: an aspiration idealized as Irish myth
(here the kiss of Deirdre and Naisi) and reiterated as dream ("to witch
Time's eyelids into dream"). The poignance in the phrase "Once Time
rested" is picked up again in the classical title of "Once in Arcady," in
which the beauty of nature personified as woman inspires "songs for which
all poets have wept, / Waking to find them dream." The title of another
poem calls the poet "Dream-Maker." It is clear that Day Lewis, like his
contemporaries, was steeped in the Yeats of the Celtic Twilight.

These early poems Day Lewis regarded as forgivable but forgettable
juvenilia, and he included no poems from his first two books in the several *Selected Poems* and the *Collected Poems* he put together during his lifetime. On the other hand, the juvenilia established the point of departure
for the work to come—or rather the point of reversal. One of Day Lewis's
chief reasons for rejecting the Georgian label sometimes pinned on him is
that by the end of the twenties he had set his work in deliberate resistance
to the seductive death wish to "laze and dream all time away" and had
already determined, by the time he left Oxford, to focus the limited resources of consciousness, through the lens of language, on bringing mortal
existence to as clear and full realization as he might manage. As he declared of "The Thirties in Retrospect," "We obscurely felt the need to do
more with the fragments than shoring them against our ruin. The magic
word, the cant word, of the time was 'synthesis.'" Instead of seeking to
escape time like Yeats or to transcend time like Eliot, he would risk living
in time and accept the consequences.

It was the Romantic gamble without the Romantic's idealization of
self and cosmos, indeed with only the fearful postwar prospect, in Oswald
Spengler's phrase, of "the decline of the west." On the one hand, the
nostalgic resort of the Georgians to native ground seemed to many besides
Day Lewis a retreat from the challenge of the modern crisis, but, on the
other hand, the Modernist experimentation of *The Waste Land* and *The
Cantos* seemed only an anatomy of disgust and disillusionment. The old
way and the new presented a Janus face, one way or the other, of contemporary defeat and impotence. What drew Day Lewis to Auden and Spender,
and thus created the energy and force of what Campbell sought to dismiss
through the derisive term "MacSpaunday," was the effort to revitalize
British poetry by avoiding the Scylla and Charybdis of Georgianism and
Modernism.

Before leaving Oxford in the summer of 1927, Day Lewis jointly edited the anthology *Oxford Poetry 1927* with Auden. Their Preface, written by both of them in alternating paragraphs, provided the first planks for the new platform by proposing poetry as a way through and past the dilemma of the modern individual confronting the schisms within and without. Poetry, Auden and Day Lewis declared with a deliberate sense of purpose, initiates a "progression toward a new synthesis"—Day Lewis's "magic word"—out of "the chaos of values" that has resulted from the failure of any "universalized system—political, religious, or metaphysical." Poetry functions, therefore, as the ordering act of the "self-consciousness" that has characterized modernity "since the Reformation," using language as the medium to form "private spheres out of a public chaos." Thus far the Preface has not pushed past the Modernist impasse: Eliot's private, last-ditch maneuver of shoring his fragments against his ruins, and Stevens's uneasy resignation that the ordering of art merely made him, in the title of a poem written in the thirties, a "Connoisseur of Chaos." But Day Lewis and Auden begin to search out a more public and collective function for poetry in the three sets of interlocking polarities that, they say, the poetic act should reconcile: (1) "the psychological conflict" within the divided consciousness "between self as subject and self as object"; (2) "the ethical conflict" between the autotelic, Modernist art object ("Pure Art . . . isolated from everything but its own laws of operation") and social and cultural "conditions" from which the artwork arises; and (3) "the logical conflict" within the linguistic medium itself between the "classic" and "ascetic" tendency toward denotation and the "romantic" and hedonistic countertendency toward connotative suggestibility. (The text of the Preface is reprinted as an appendix to Samuel Hynes's *The Auden Generation*, 397–98.)

The "psychological conflict" is a result of the split in post-Cartesian epistemology between mind and body, and so between subject and object, which first Romanticism and then its Modernist aftermath sought to transcend at the aesthetic level. The poem became Keats's Grecian urn and Stevens's round jar in the Tennessee wilderness. However, as poets felt with growing panic that preserving the integrity and impenetrability of the art object required insulation from the violence of public chaos, aestheticism after the Enlightenment hardened between Keats's urn and Stevens's jar, became opaque between Coleridge's translucent crystal and the bedazzling bricolage of Pound's *Cantos*. As for the "ethical" dimension, how could poetry be politically responsive and socially responsible? Pound was trying to reconcile his poetics with his economics, but the totalitarian tendencies of his rightwing politics (and of the politics of Yeats, Wyndham Lewis, and both T. E. and D. H. Lawrence) seemed repellently consonant with the elitism of Modernist aesthetics. Nevertheless, already in the 1927 Preface, written the year after the General Strike had paralyzed the country's transit and polarized the political views of Oxford students into leftist sympathy and rightist antipathy for the striking workers, Day Lewis and Auden acknowledged the need to implicate the artwork in actual social "conditions," however violent, even at the risk of the poem's urnlike, jarlike integrity, because "Pure Art," were such possible, would constitute an unethical and irresponsible aestheticism. And finally, on the "logical" or linguistic level, they saw that a socially engaged poetry had to move beyond Romantic-Modernist hemeticism, ellipsis, "multiplicity of associations" in the direction of statement, synthesis, argumentation, even didactic comment that they designated by contrast as "classic." The "classic" goal of the Preface reverses Archibald MacLeish's Modernist axiom that "A poem should not mean but be" and insists that the effective and responsible poem must have meaning, including social significance, beyond its being.

However, the implications of the brief Preface remain largely latent and inchoate, to be drawn out as the poets will try actually to open their sensibilities and language to politics. It is true that this Preface still conceives of politics principally in individualist terms, and so does the verse sequence that Day Lewis had begun even before the publication of *Country Comets* early in 1928. Nevertheless, Auden's enthusiastic response to this new work confirmed his own sense that it took a significant step forward politically as well as poetically. And indeed the publication of *Transitional Poem* in October 1929 by Virginia and Leonard Woolf's Hogarth Press launched Day Lewis's career and placed him at the center of the effort to write a modern poetry that avoided the hermeticism of Modernist experimentation and the private nostalgia of the Georgians.

Day Lewis had earlier referred to the new work as "Transitional Poems," but the title's switch to the singular indicated his hope that the poems' exploration of divisions cohered at least as an aesthetic whole. It is worth noting that in the Preface to *Oxford Poetry* Day Lewis wrote the paragraph which declares that if the poet's mind can "bear the brunt of the conflict," he "may be the first to realize the new harmony" (Hynes, 379). Day Lewis's note to *Transitional Poem* makes the same point, and over the years he reiterated the drive to synthesis as the continuity underlying the dislocations of his life recorded in his poems. "The central mind," conflicted in its allegiances and purposes, was always "in the pursuit of [a] singlemindedness" that could reconcile or subsume those divisions into a "realized self." In his autobiography, he would designate "self-knowledge" as "the only kind of power . . . I have ever valued" (*The Buried Day*, 150).

Emerson had phrased the Romantic's dilemma as "the problem of the one and the two"—the need to negotiate duality into unity. But without genuine Christian conviction or Emerson's transcendentalist faith the Romantic problem had become a modern conundrum. Day Lewis was the only child of an Anglo-Irish clergyman whose firm but unexamined religious views were characterized, at least in the son's recollections, by "distaste for enthusiasm" and a "lofty attitude toward dissent" (*The Buried Day*, 52). Reared in that unquestioning yet unimpassioned religious atmosphere, the boy and later the man found himself torn between "the agnosticism into which I lapsed during my youth" and a persistent longing for the sustaining certitude of faith. Like Hardy, he remained to the end "a Churchy agnostic" ("On a Tilting Deck," 13).

Day Lewis would recall a childhood nightmare in which eternity appeared as a forbidding and annihilating glacier. The eight- or nine-year-old boy awoke crying, "again and again, 'I don't want to live forever,'" and the grown man still understood the boy's fright: "[E]ven today, although I know that eternity, if it has any meaning, means a state outside time, not an infinite extension of time, the thought of eternal life can fill me with horror, revolt, repudiation" (*The Buried Day*, 53). *Transitional Poem*, a forty-page sequence of thirty-four poems organized in four parts, begins to test whether he can discover the terms for living *in* time. The concluding note, expanding on the categories of the Preface to *Oxford Poetry 1927*, associates the four parts of the sequence with four interconnected and troubled aspects of "the central mind" in pursuit of wholeness: the metaphysical, the ethical, the psychological, and the aesthetic. The parts of the sequence do not proceed successively and discursively through the four aspects, as the note seems to suggest, but move associatively and lyrically around and among them, seeking to stitch together a central identity. By the end of these circulations the reader feels not so much that a resolution has been reached as that the field of contention has been laid out and surveyed, illumined by momentary flares of an intuited harmony with nature or the beloved—those Wordsworthian "spots of time" that transfix mortality with timelessness.

Taking off from a Latin epigram from Maximian whose final line might be translated as saying that "in the end only the single mind lasts," the first poem in the sequence initiates the transition with verses whose intellectual and metrical nimbleness radiate the cocky high spirits of the young man fresh out of college, facing out existential angst:

Now I have come to reason
And cast my schoolboy clout,
Disorder I see is without,
And the mind must sweat a poison
Keener than Thessaly's brew;
A pus that, discharged not thence,
Gangrenes the vital sense
And makes disorder true.
It is certain we shall attain
No life till we stamp on all
Life the tetragonal
Pure symmetry of brain.

I felt, in my scorning
Of common poet's talk,
As arrogant as the hawk
When he mounts above the morning.
'Behold man's droll appearance,
Faith wriggling upon his hooks,
Chin-deep in Eternal Flux
Angling for reassurance!'
I care not if he retorts—
'Of all that labour and wive
And worship, who would give
A fiddlestick for these thoughts
That sluggishly yaw and bend,
Fat strings of barges drawn
By a tug they have never seen
And never will comprehend?'

I sit in a wood and stare
Up at untroubled branches
Locked together and staunch as
Though girders of the air:
And think, the first wind rising
Will crack that intricate crown
And let the daylight down.
But there is naught surprising
Can explode the single mind:—
Let figs from thistles fall
Or stars from their pedestal,
This architecture will stand.   (59–60)

Though the new sequence was undertaken during the poet's closest
association with Auden (was indeed begun on a country jaunt with Auden),
Day Lewis heard middle Yeats more strongly in the verse than Auden ("On
a Tilting Deck," 3). But it is here middle Yeats in a particularly metaphysical mode, bristling with something of the wit and brio of the young
Donne. The verbal pyrotechnics are strategies to admit but not succumb
to anxiety in the declension from Romantic idealism through Victorian
doubt to modern neurosis. The rhyming of "reason" against "poison"
shows the mind sickened by nature's "Eternal Flux," yet the poem can go
on to postulate that only the "single mind," cleansed of its disabling gan-
grene, can impress its "pure symmetry" and "architecture" on the "disorder without." (Poem 8 describes Auden as "the tow-haired poet" whose
"single mind copes with split intelligence" [67].) The initiating supposition, to be turned this way and that in the remainder of the sequence, is
(in a trope that recurs throughout Day Lewis's early poetry) that the resil-
ient mind can rise like a hawk into its own "pure" dimension and survive
amidst the stormy flux through the exertion of mental control.

And, since the poet thinks and feels metrically, metrical structure formulates inchoate thought and feeling: "This architecture will stand." The architectural symmetry of the three-four construction of the poem plays the volatility of three against the stability of four: three stanzas of three-beat lines organized in "tetragonal" groups of four lines rhyming a-b-b-a, three quatrains in the first and third stanza and four quatrains in the middle stanza. The tension between congruence and incongruence is played out to the very end, even in the disparity between the shape of the argument and the shape of the verse form; that is to say, the argument moves in zig-zag uncertainty to an affirmation of the mind's durable "tetragonal symmetry" in the last lines, while, contrastingly, the prosodic structure reaches its "tetragonal symmetry" in the middle stanza only to lapse or collapse again into triadic imbalance in the last.

No less purposefully than the Modernist experimenters did Day Lewis and Auden seek a resolution of conflicts at the aesthetic level, but theirs was a deliberately different kind of formalism. They sought to be modern without having to be Modernist. Modernist poets—in the English-speaking world, all Americans—were more revolutionary in this respect than their British contemporaries. They stood for a radical break with old forms, beginning with the word, the grammar of the sentence, the meter of the line, in order, in Eliot's phrase, to fracture language into new meanings. In one of the late cantos, Pound would recall exultantly: "To break the pentameter, that was the first heave." Hugh Underhill, in his study of twentieth-century British poetry, makes a point about Frost's friend Edward Thomas that is equally applicable to the British poets of this century almost without exception: "Modernism . . . longs to take poetry out of the realm of linguistic signification altogether, to disrupt and transform it, whereas Thomas [read Day Lewis or Auden] is content with speech as it is practised" (Underhill, 118). The British poet, in other words, "repossesses rather than making it new" à la Pound (Underhill, 48). Mina Loy left England and went to New York to pursue her Modernist inclinations. The only British disciples of Pound were Basil Bunting and David Jones, and for his part Pound shed contemporary British poetry when he left for the continent in 1920. With characteristic decisiveness Pound instructed his American disciple Louis Zukofsky in 1930 that the special issue of *Poetry* that Zukofsky had been invited to edit could be made into a catalyst comparable to Pound's own Imagist anthology of 1914 only through "emphasis on the progress made since 1912"; and such emphasis meant: "make it a murkn number; excluding the so different English"; "I don't think you need the English" (*Pound/Zukofsky*, 46, 47, 51).

Thus the ingenuity and variety of prosodic forms exhibited in the early poems of Auden and Day Lewis are meant to offer, as an alternative to the Modernist deconstruction of old forms, the reinvention of old forms. Their poetic program proceeded from the assumption that the infusion of contemporary diction and rhythms and images shared by speaker and audi-

ence articulates the modern sensibility more effectively than the fracturing of prosody and grammar into an esoteric and hybrid language. Dis-
ruption of poetic and linguistic forms, from this perspective, might con-
sider itself revolutionary, but this kind of revolution was elitist and
dismissive of any possible community of readers; by contrast, an evolu-
tionary development within the tradition maintains the integrity and com-
municability of the medium as well as the mutual bond of expectation and
respect between poet and popular audience. For the social function of the
traditional poet depended on the means of communication—referential
words, coherent syntax, synthesizing metaphor, formal ordering devices—
where Modernists' doubts and anxieties about signification led them to
deconstruct the medium at the risk of alienating its audience.

British poets continued to have the sense of predecessors and peers and
audience that American poets have never enjoyed. So instead of violating
grammatical and metrical coherence as Pound and Stein and Williams
seemed to be doing, they set out—as Day Lewis does in this first section
of *Transitional Poem*—to charge sentences with fresh diction and charge
meters with fresh rhythms. They were able to do so because, in contrast
to the Modernists and even more sharply to contemporary Postmodernists,
they never seriously questioned the efficacy of the linguistic medium. What
is more, their deepening commitment to the political left only served to
reinforce their commitment to traditional forms. Indeed, the logic of the
thirties required conventional forms for revolutionary effectiveness, as the
Soviet experience seemed to confirm. The efforts of Russian avant-garde
artists to employ their revolutionary aesthetic in the service of the new
Communist regime quickly met official opposition—indeed, brutal suppression and bitter exile—in the very name of the workers' revolution.

The twin issues in the "argument" of *Transitional Poem* are epistemo-
logical and erotic: the poet as nature's philosopher and as would-be lover;
for natural process and human sexuality are functions of the same irratio-
nal "Flux" that needs the mind's comprehension and control:

> Above, below, the Flux tight-packed
> Stages its sexual act—
> An ignominious scuffling in the dark
> Where brute encounters brute baresark.   (87)

Nature as whelming flood: the epigraph to Part 3 shows Melville's Ishmael
as an observing consciousness high in the crow's nest above the wash of
the Atlantic. In Poem 14 "the closet of the brain" becomes an "ark" like
Noah's, sending out dovelike searches for "a Messiah sprig of certitude"
(73). At other times the mind, more hawklike than dovelike (Poem 8, 66,
hails Day Lewis's Oxford comrade Rex Warner as "the hawk-faced man"),
rises to catch "an ideal tone that stills" the noisy welter, or dives down to
find the "promise of ground below the sprawling flood" (73). Intimations
of a final and finalizing reality above or below nature's "Eternal Flux"

would, the passage says, "inform the seer and uniform the seen"—that is to say, would bring mind and nature, subject and object to coherent form and so to correspondence with each other. Yet at other times, for example in Poem 18, the lofty, self-inflated hero, faced with failure, seems solipsistically adolescent ("boy Achilles"), even bogus and falsifying ("counterfeit Achilles," 78). For when he descends to the material reality beyond his mental perch, he finds, if not a flood, then "a rubbish heap": "Hero, you're safe, in the purlieus / Of God's infernal acre, king and thrall" (78–79). Such a modern mock-hero, bound to the worthless world over which he presides, recalls Stevens's "Man on the Dump" or his "Man Whose Pharynx Was Bad," musing "the malady of the quotidian."

In the turns and counterturns of the sequence, therefore, the poet comes time and again to question as vanity the heroics he at other times aspires to: vain doubly in the emptiness of the pride that impels ego-"ambition." Poem 17 asks "Why must I then unleash my brain / To sweat after some revelation," and instead turns to the quotidian for whatever nourishment and sensual satisfaction it can avail:

> Charabancs shout along the lane
> And summer gales bay in the wood
> No less superbly because I can't explain
> What I have understood.

> Let logic analyse the hive,
> Wisdom's content to have the honey:
> So I'll bite the crust of things and thrive
> While hedgerows still are sunny.   (77)

Between the idiot's "disgust" with mutability (Poem 9, 68) and the seafaring "ambition" of Ulysses and Columbus and "the hard-headed [clear-minded? or just stubborn?] Phoenicians" (Poem 10, 68), a middle ground offers the invitation for a positive and active commitment to mortality, an acceptance of natural process that releases and subdues the ego into the vagaries of human love. Epistemology yields to sexuality; mind's quest succumbs to body's; frustrated philosopher contents himself in love's springtime.

In Poem 11 the metaphysical wit, the elision of run-on lines, the lapsing of rhyme into half-rhyme suggest the playful ease of carpe diem when the vaunting ego surrenders its self-conscious drive to the seasons' rhythms so that heart and imagination can live in the given:

> If I bricked up ambition and gave no air
> To the ancestral curse that gabbles there,
>   I could leave wonder on the latch
>   And with a whole heart watch
> The calm declension of an English year.

I would be pædagogue—hear poplar, lime
And oak recite the seasons' paradigm.
　　Each year a dynasty would fall
　　Within my orchard wall—
I'd be their Tacitus, and they my time.

Among these pippin princes I could ease
A heart long sick for some Hesperides:
　　Plainsong of thrushes in the soul
　　Would drown that rigamarole
Of Eldorados, Auks, and Perilous Seas.

(The God they cannot see sages define
In a slow motion. If I discipline
　　My flux into a background still
　　And sure as a waterfall
Will not a rainbow come of that routine?)

So circumscribe the vampire and he'll die soon—
Lunacy and anæmia take their own.
　　Grounded in temperate soil I'll stay,
　　An orchard god, and say
My glow-worms hold a candle to the moon.　(69–70)

From a fallen world (here dynasties, seasons, apples, and water all "fall")
the sickened consciousness seeks escape to a hesperidean but unattainable
paradise across Keatsian (or Yeatsian or Stevensian) "Perilous Seas." But
such an "ambition" becomes the self-engendered "vampire" (or Franken-
stein monster) that turns against its progenitor, and rather than perish in
that doomed Romantic venture, the speaker gives himself over "with a
whole heart" to "the temperate soil" of his allotted time. This kind of
"paedagogue" to nature's round was the ideal not just of classicists like
Tacitus but even of moderns like Frost or Hardy. At this point Day Lewis
had not come to Hardy or Frost but would in time find them the modern
poets closest to his perspective.

Thomas Carlyle had instructed the self-doomed Romantics: "Close thy
Byron, open thy Goethe." In a similar spirit this speaker turns from Keats
to Horace, from "sages" like Spinoza (thrice cited in the notes) to the
historian Tacitus, the chronicler of the times. His ground is material, not
metaphysical: the orchard ripening toward fall. However, "to live deliberately"—that is, with conscious will, as Thoreau said of his sojourn at
Walden Pond—might allow him to become something like a genius loci—
not the God of the "sages" but a god (with a small "g") of his own orchard plot. "Not as a god, but as a god might be," as Stevens wrote in
"Sunday Morning." Of course, human consciousness does not ever surrender its mortality to nature's round totally. The "pædagogue" learns
nature's lesson in order to teach it and make it his own, and in the "disci-

pline" of formulating it to himself and others lies the saving remnant of control that raises the "pædagogue" to "god"-like status and allows him to live in nature's round and live it out.

For a modern like Day Lewis, the "discipline" that can kill the vampire of false idealism and at the same time can comprehend and thus "still" nature's runaway waterfall—or make it for the moment in the human imagination seem still—does not derive from divinized nature, as the Romantics postulated, but, in Stevens's phrase, from the human mortal's "rage for order." For the poet, the "discipline" is verbal: the "circumscription" (or "writing around") of his rhymed stanzas and enjambed verses. The "routine" of skilled and ordered speech summons not God's rainbowed covenant after the flood (remember the "ark" of Poem 14) but the shine and shimmer of the speaker's (and hearer's) own locale. Still beneath that radiant arc the "orchard god" can "say / My glow-worms hold a candle to the moon." The line sounds Stevensian long before Day Lewis knew Stevens's poetry. The play on "hold a candle" inverts the slang put-down "doesn't hold a candle to" into an affirmation and turns the ephemeral glowworms into votive lights to the celestial moon. And the rhyming of "stay" and "say" underscores the point that the very saying provides the staying power to survive in life's "calm declension." The texture of echoes and allusions emphasizes Day Lewis's dense implication in poetic tradition but also underscores the point he liked to make about such implication: namely, that echoes serve to differentiate as well as connect. This poem could not have been written by any of the poets alluded to here in passing; it is entirely Day Lewis's.

Erotic love offers nature's way out of the solipsistic mind's fixation on the antinomy between matter and spirit. In Poem 4 the male poet presents the "twin poles energic" (63) of the feminine archetype: body and soul, earth and air. But Poem 5 depicts love as finally not so much a tower in air as a ground or base solid as earth. So by Poem 21 acceptance of love's seasonal round comes in lines that absorb the Donne-like conceit of the lovers as "hemispheres" into something like the stoic naturalism of "Sunday Morning" (which, again, Day Lewis would not at this point have read):

> For they [the woods' wildflowers], whose virtue lies
> In a brief act of beauty, summarize
> Earth's annual passion and leave the naked earth
> Still dearer by their death than by their birth.
> So we, who are love's hemispheres hiding
> Beneath the coloured ordeal of our spring,
> Shall be disclosed, and I shall see your face
> An autumn evening certain of its peace.   (82–3)

Poem 23, near the end of the sequence, seeks to balance the feminization of the poet-lover by casting him, with self-conscious melodrama, as a hero:

But look within my heart, see there
The tough stoic ghost of a pride was too severe
To risk an armistice
With lesser powers than death: but rather died
Welcoming that iron in the soul
Which keeps the spirit whole. . . .

. . . .

In you alone
I met the naked light, by you became
Veteran of a flame
That burns away all but the warrior bone.   (84–85)

The mixture of epic battle with amatory pastoral signals Day Lewis's need
to reconcile Keats and Tacitus, the Romantic's private satisfaction and the
classical hero's active quest. Nevertheless, the overall transition of the sequence tracks the shift from the doomed quest for fixed absolutes toward
a realization of possibilities within the circle of life. Here is the conclusion
to Poem 22:

I'd live like grass and trees,
Familiar of the earth,
Proving its basalt peace
Till I was unperturbed

By synod of the suns
Or a moon's insolence
As the ant when he runs
Beneath sky-scraping grass.   (83)

Not, here, the hawk's heroic view from aloft, but instead the ant's view
from ground level. Thus, too, in Poem 29, the poet chooses as his totem
not, as before, the high-flying hawk gazing "in plain bewilderment" at
the "Himalayas of the mind" and the waves breaking against "the Absolute Cliffs" but instead ("Better by far") "the household cock / Scratch-
ing the common yard for corn" and the shorebird "[p]eering for barnacles
and weeds" among the rocks (91–92). Similarly, in Poem 34, the final one
in the sequence, "The hawk comes down from the air"; and in turn, "the
little lark / Who veins the sky with song, / Asking from dawn to dark /
No revenues of spring" accepts day's term and "with the night descends /
Into his chosen tree," accepting "peace" in "anonymity" (97–98).

Through the "circumscription" of the sequence, therefore, the poet
comes to realize that the round encloses but does not resolve contrarities
and so to feel "Resigned now but not reconciled" (Poem 31, 94) to living
within local limits. The philosopher yields to the lover; the hero is not the
adventurer but the homebody. The soul finds itself "now quite satisfied"
not to embark on train rides "towards an Ultima Thule" but instead to
"travel a loop-line" (Poem 20, 81) around known territory. Poem 28 opens

with the initial verses of St. John's Gospel, proclaiming in italics the divine
Word "before the Fall" (90), but then slips from the italics into dissonant,
postlapsarian language. Still, Day Lewis cannot rest in impotence and
despair. So a note to the poem insists that through the dissonance of human
speech "the individual poetic impulse" can still somehow become at times
"a part of the Logos in the theologian's sense of mind expressing God in
the world'" (100). And herein lies the poet's validation—vocation, if you
wish: the central but divided mind, casting the circumference of the poem,
can sometimes circumscribe oppositions and hold them at least in generative tension.

The epigraph to Part 2 presents lines from the conclusion of Whitman's
"Song of Myself": "Do I contradict myself? / Very well then, I contradict
myself; / I am large, I contain multitudes." Thinking of *Transitional Poem*
as Day Lewis's "Song of Myself" underscores the poets' differences far more
than their similarities, yet Day Lewis seems to imagine himself as sharing
with Whitman the modern dilemma. Consequently, even when he finds
it harder to assume Whitman's Romantic confidence about containing
contradictions, he can still manage a similar, if more chastened, declaration in Poem 25: "For individual truth must lie / Within diversity" (87).
And the next poem goes on to claim that at moments of "highest power"—
"only" then, but then nonetheless—oppositions can "become / Their
equilibrium." Then "the single mind" can write "the star-solved equation / Of life with life's negation," and, moving "[t]o earth's influence,
but proves / Itself the more intact" (88).

The concluding poems of the sequence move away from this seemingly climactic passage in Poem 26, as if in demonstration of how momentary and fragile such a sense of equilibrium is. Certainly the speaker in *From
Feathers to Iron* (1931), another transitional poem published like its predecessor in the series Hogarth Living Poets, remains divided between the
claims of subject and object, mind and material flux. Day Lewis had known
Mary King, the lovely and reserved daughter of his old master at Sherborne,
for a number of years; after a long courtship they were married late in 1928,
the year in which he was writing *Transitional Poem*, and settled into domesticity. *From Feathers to Iron* follows out the homing instincts that emerged
in *Transitional Poem*. The sequence looks to wife and family for the experience of connectedness (Poems 23, 24), hoping that their expected offspring might "resolve the factions" within him (Poem 15, 117), even hoping
that this birth may spring him into a new sense of identity ("Myself may
out," Poem 16, 117).

The sequence of twenty-nine lyrics, dedicated "To the Mother," records
the period of Mary Day Lewis's first pregnancy, from conception in the
dead of winter through spring burgeoning to late-summer fruition (Sean
Francis, born August 3, 1931, was in fact several weeks overdue). Though
From Feathers to Iron ends in a paean of celebration, it is principally concerned with the anxious time of waiting, the stresses and tensions "between winter and summer, / Conception and fruition" (Poem 16, 116).

Indeed, the sequence, like its predecessor a virtuosic display of prosodic ingenuity, has a clearer plot line and a more emphatic denouement than *Transitional Poem* that can be blocked out as follows: the separation opened between the spouses by the mother's preoccupation with pregnancy (Poems 5, 13, 19); obliquely, the husband's attraction to another woman (the radiant "white tree-rose" in Poem 6, 109, might seem to be Mary but actually is Alison Morris, a married friend of the Day Lewises [Sean Day Lewis, 68]); anticipation of the pain of birth (Poem 13); the expectant mother's diminished beauty and "veering moods" (Poem 20, 120); the prospective father's anxiety about bringing a child into a corrupt and tragic world (Poems 21, 22); the father's renunciation of other loves for "constancy" to the mother that "outlasts the fabric of desire" (Poem 24, 123–24); the anxiety of waiting and fear for the mother's life (Poems 27, 28); in the final poems, the paean to new life and new commitment heralded by the son's birth.

Along the way Day Lewis pointedly and consistently introduces industrial imagery into his pastoral poem—not to contrast sexual nature unfavorably with the machine, as Romantic or Victorian poems characteristically did, but to correlate them as analogous sources of power. The shock effect of modernizing and industrializing the pastoral is epitomized in lines like: "Look there, gasometer rises, / And here bough swells to bud" (Poem 14, 115), though the attempt at metaphysical wit—disparate things yoked by violence together—comes across here more as bathos. A more successful example is the description of the train in Poem 4, which becomes a conceit for the moment of orgasm and conception:

> Tightens the darkness, the rails thrum
> For night express is due.
> Glory of steam and steel strikes dumb;
> Sense sucked away swirls in the vacuum.
> So passion passes through.
>
> Here is love's junction, no terminus.
> He arrives at girl or boy.
> Signal a clear line and let us
> Give him the run of life: we shall get thus
> A record of our joy.   (108–9)

And later Poem 12 completes the elaboration of the train conceit in anticipating the baby's birth:

> As a train that travels underground track
> Feels current flashed from far-off dynamos,
> Our wheels whirling with impetus elsewhere
> Generated we run, are ruled by rails.
> Train shall spring from tunnel to terminus,
> Out on to plain shall the pioneer plunge,
> Earth reveal what veins fed, what hill covered.
> Lovely the leap, explosion into light.   (114)

Dated and naive as such lines strike many readers now, they sounded new and exciting at the time. Futurist poetry and painting, not to mention the newsreels and photographs and film documentaries, show the effort to naturalize the machine, often portrayed as the polished and immaculate symbol of a utopian Machine Age purportedly consonant with the pastoral myths of the preindustrial past. Even Soviet art displayed an industrialism purged of capitalist abuses, and Auden, Day Lewis, and Spender would all use mechanical imagery for the rusting decay of capitalism, on the one hand, and, on the other, for the shining prospect of a new political order in the years just ahead.

From Feathers to Iron confirmed Day Lewis's place in the poetic vanguard. In *Poetry Review* Michael Roberts's hyperbolic language indicates how urgently he and others felt the need for a poetic revolution when he hailed *From Feathers to Iron* as "a landmark, in the sense in which *Leaves of Grass, A Shropshire Lad, Des Imagistes,* and *The Waste Land* were landmarks" and went on to claim that it represented the "full solution" of the metaphorical innovations initiated by Auden (Hynes, 73–74). Industrial imagery is a device that Auden and Day Lewis began to use at the same time during the period of their close interaction after 1927, and Spender would soon follow. In fact, references to trains and airplanes, factories and mines, dynamos and pylons became such a "group" signature that they were sometimes lampooned as the "pylon poets."

Samuel Hynes repeats the consensus view of later commentators when he dismisses *From Feathers to Iron* as just an imitation of Auden, and for corroboration he points to Day Lewis's framing of the sequence with an introductory epigram from Auden and, as epilogue, a verse epistle addressed to Auden (Hynes, 73). In point of fact, however, the resemblances in imagery and phrasing are occasional and superficial. This sequence about the complexities of married love and childbearing is, obviously in theme but also in tone and style, unlike anything that Auden ever would undertake. Much of Auden's poetry from these same years consists of contorted and encoded laments about the pangs and failures of his various homosexual infatuations. Almost as if to emphasize the difference between himself and Auden, Day Lewis takes occasion in the epistolary epilogue to twit his friend about his homosexuality, and Auden took the point sufficiently to register in a letter a mock-complaint about having "my little weaknesses . . . exposed in dedicatory verses" (Sean Day Lewis, 55).

In *A Hope for Poetry* Day Lewis would profess bemusement that critics imposed a "political allegory" on the "personal meaning" of *From Feathers to Iron,* but in fact, as we have seen, he had already begun to feel compelled to make connections between sexuality and politics, between the realm of "romantic" feeling and the arena of "classical" or "heroic" action (38). Inchoate and, one might say, embryonic as these connections are in this sequence, Day Lewis later admitted that he welcomed and was heartened by a political reading: "[T]he poem had overtones of which I was only half aware when writing it: personal meaning reached out toward public meaning, and received help from it, at those passages where the expectation, the agony, the joy of a child's birth are related to the struggle and joy in which our new world should be born" ("The Thirties in Retrospect," 16). If, as he had hoped in *Transitional Poem*, the hero was a lover and the lover could still be a hero, then perhaps the father might also be the archetypal sire of the new generation's revolution. The penultimate section of *Transitional Poem* presented an industrial waste land of rusted ironworks and abandoned mines and sounded an ambiguous call for revolution with the refrain, lifted from Sophie Tucker's blues, "There are going to be some changes made to-day" (97).

But what kind of revolution, and what sorts of changes? The explicitly political poem that Day Lewis had begun immediately after *Transitional Poem* in order to answer these questions had been interrupted to write *From Feathers to Iron*, but he returned to it as soon as he could and published it in 1933 as *The Magnetic Mountain*. And by the time *The Magnetic Mountain* appeared to push Day Lewis into the front rank of the new political poetry, the "MacSpaunday" poets had been consolidated as a "group" with a literary and social platform through the impact of two anthologies edited by Michael Roberts for the Hogarth Press: *New Signatures* (1932) and *New Country* (1933).

• 3

Michael Roberts, born in 1902, two years older than Day Lewis and five years older than Auden, was teaching mathematics at a school in Holborn, when his interest in poetry, and specifically in the direction of contemporary poetry, brought him into contact with John Lehmann, recently down from Cambridge and now working at the Woolfs' Hogarth Press. That association led to the Hogarth Press's publication of Roberts's two anthologies, which brought together young Cambridge writers like Lehmann, Edward Upward, and Christopher Isherwood with young Oxford writers like Rex Warner and the "MacSpaunday" poets minus MacNeice (though Auden and Day Lewis had included poems by MacNeice in their *Oxford Poetry 1927* and MacNeice had gone on to edit *Oxford Poetry 1929* with Spender). Roberts's prefaces to *New Signatures*, a slim anthology of nine poets, and *New Country*, a hefty anthology of poetry, criticism, and fiction, constitute a self-conscious attempt to identify a new literary nexus and write the manifesto for a socially engaged, politically left writing in counterdistinction to the aesthetic of Modernism.

The leftist inclination of these writers, particularly in the early thirties, was intellectual and theoretical rather than practical. It grew out of a condemnation of an economic system based on oppression of the deprived working class (epitomized by the brutal breaking of the General Strike in 1926) and out of a somewhat snobbish disaffection with the Labour Party, which, when given a chance to form a government, seemed unable or unwilling to press for real reform. In 1931 the move of Labour Prime Minister Ramsay MacDonald to dissolve his own government and head a National government with Tories and Liberals served to demoralize the members of the Labour Party and alienate many younger writers and intellectuals, recently out of Oxford and Cambridge. Their readings in Marx and Lenin, at the university and after, made them look past the British labor movement to the Soviet Union, now in its second decade, as a radical model for the overthrow of capitalism and the creation of a new social and economic order. The left wing of the British intelligentsia would, by mid-decade, find expression and confirmation in such vehicles as *The Left Review* (published between 1934 and 1938 under a series of editors); Victor Gollancz's Left Book Club (starting in 1936, with its *Left Book Club News*, later abbreviated to *Left News*); polemical collections like *The Mind in Chains* (edited by Day Lewis in 1937) and *In Letters of Red* (edited by E. A. Osborne in 1938); theoretical analyses like John Strachey's *The Coming Struggle for Power* (1932), Edgell Rickword's *War and Culture* (1936), and Christopher Caudwell's *Illusion and Reality* (1937) and *Studies in a Dying Culture* (1938); as well as in the British Communist Party's official organ, *The Daily Worker*. Most of the leftist writers and intellectuals of the time were not card-carrying members of the Party; some never were (Auden for example), and most of those who became members (Day Lewis among them) would remain so for a relatively brief time (but Day Lewis longer than Spender). Nonetheless, the political orientation of most of this generation was clear enough and Red enough to produce vitriolic responses from right-wingers like Roy Campbell and Wyndham Lewis.

When Roberts was putting together his anthologies at the beginning of the decade, all that lay in the future. However, his introductions are important in any literary account of the period because they record an initial engagement with the issue that would obsess and finally consume the work of the thirties—namely, the connection and contention between aesthetic intentions and political commitments. There could be no question, Roberts declared in 1932, that the "new knowledge and new circumstances" that define the modern dilemma have forced poetry "to think and feel in ways not expressible in the old language at all" and demanded a new "technique sufficiently flexible to express precisely those subtleties of thought and feeling" (*New Signatures*, 7, 8). Though Roberts did not mention the great generation of Modernist poets by name, he shared the general Modernist assumption that the imagination was the only human faculty or agency left (now that "generalising logic or philosophic truth" had lost their credibility for many intellectuals) to confront and contend with the psychological and political ills of modern society. Echoing the position taken by Auden and Day Lewis in *Oxford Poetry 1927*, Roberts challenged art to forge at the formal and aesthetic level "an imaginative solution" to these problems, "a new harmonisation such as that which may be brought about by a work of art . . . without recourse to any external system of religious belief" (10,13).

Roberts spoke for his generation, however, when he insisted that the "new technique" required for that purpose was not the radical experimentation of the Modernist poets, whom he decried as obscurantist, elitist, "aloof from ordinary affairs," "abrupt, discordant, intellectual," "too analytical, too conscious." Their posture as "detached and pessimistic observer[s]" made such alienated poets into impotent aesthetes, "contemptuous of the society around them and yet having no firm belief" and so "no basis for satire," incapable of effective leadership and capable only of "esoteric work which was frivolously decorative [like, say, that of Stevens or, in Britain, Edith Sitwell] or elaborately erudite [like that of Eliot or Pound]" (8, 9, 11). Instead, the new technique Roberts found in the verse he advocated required only an updating of old forms: "imagery taken from contemporary life" and variations on the meters that derived from "the normal movement of English speech" and have served as "one of the technical delights of English verse" (15–16). In particular, "the work of W. H. Auden, Cecil Day Lewis, and Stephen Spender" deliberately mounts "a clear reaction against esoteric [that is, Modernist] poetry" in order "to remove difficulties which have stood between the poet and the writing of popular poetry" (14, 12).

These polemics presented what we have come to call Modernist poetry in purposefully simplified, sometimes even caricaturish terms, but at genuine issue here is a decisive difference about the way in which language functions politically to become an agent of transformation and revolution. The Modernists, whether of the political right or left, assumed that accepted semantic and prosodic forms were inextricably implicated in the status quo they wanted to subvert, and so the dismantling of the old grammar and the old metrics was a primary requirement to destroy the old social and cultural structures in the search for new aesthetic and social forms. Language served as the sign and instrument of the avant-garde's alienation from the dominant culture and from the uneducated masses, and thus language had to be made to serve as the radical instrument of decreation and recreation. But for Roberts's generation language remained the shared medium of communication between the avant-garde and the people, and it worked for conformity or revolution depending on the terms and purposes of its meaning, the character and consequences of its imagery and rhythms. The semantic and metrical forms were what made communication and so revolution possible; modern imagery and rhythms for a revolutionary message could breed revolution while the Modernists dissipated their energy in experimentation. The politics in "the work of W. H. Auden, Cecil Day Lewis, and Stephen Spender" required them to reach out to and reclaim the audience that the esoteric sophistication of Modernist poetry had forsaken, in order to forge an effective force against the status quo and for the new social order.

Day Lewis would soon follow up Roberts's Preface with his own group manifesto, *A Hope for Poetry* (1934). The hope was, not surprisingly, based on the poetic "boom . . . connected in certain quarters with the names of

Auden, Spender, and myself" (25). However, he begins, tellingly, not with the revolutionary future but with the need for "ancestors," the search for "father" figures and "heroes" as "the only possible patriotism, the one necessary link with the past, and the meaning of tradition" (1, 3, 4). It is typical of the myopia of Day Lewis's generation in Britain that they assumed that revolution need not mean a break with the historical and cultural traditions that they still revered. The literary ancestors he lists and discusses in separate chapters are Gerard Manley Hopkins, Wilfred Owen, and T. S. Eliot. There are nodding mentions of French Symbolisme, of Dada and Surrealism, of Yeats and Walter de la Mare and A. E. Housman, but none at all of vers libre or Imagism or any of the American Modernists except the Anglified Eliot. Hopkins's sprung rhythm is the boldest innovation in metrical form mentioned in the essay, and it represented something of a reversion to Anglo-Saxon accentual verse. Even with Eliot, Day Lewis took "Prufrock" as his best poem, not the Modernist collage of *The Waste Land*, which "does not to my mind contain his best poetry" and "seems to me chiefly important as a social document" (22–23).

The fusion of conservative formalism and radical politics in the new British poetry, which was the antithesis of the initial alignment of Russian Modernist formalism with the Bolshevik cause, saw no necessary inconsistency, in Roberts's words, between "a respect for eighteenth-century ideals" and "a revolutionary attitude" (*New Signatures*, 18). The "impersonality" of the poet who was an active "leader" did not bespeak "extreme detachment," as with impersonal Modernists like Eliot, Pound, and Stein, but rather constituted "the essence of the communist attitude": namely, the commitment "to sacrifice one's own welfare that others may benefit" (10, 19). Such poetry may resort to propaganda, "but," Roberts says, "it is a propaganda for a theory of life which may release the poet's energies" in the long run (19).

With *New Country* the next year, Roberts tried to substantiate the conclusion of the previous Preface by imagining a homegrown communism consonant with, even expressive of values and customs that were the foundation of the English middle class. In Roberts's utopia, which Stalinists would have scoffed at, "unanimity of action" would arise from "independence of thought" and from extending throughout society the ethics of the cricket team, in which "personality and consciousness" become "part of something bigger than ourselves," "working together for some common purpose" (14, 21). He warned complacent readers, "If you want cricket, you'd better join us" (113). Not surprisingly Edmund Blunden's patriotic wartime memoir would summon and sum up the spirit of Britain in its title, *Cricket Country*. In that spirit, identifying *New Country* with *Cricket Country*, heedless of the anomalies and of the possible pitfalls in attempting to enact radical change through allegiance with the values of the bourgeois culture, Roberts called upon the "helpless" victims "in an organism that is dying" "to help us abolish the whole class system," "to renounce that [capitalist] system now and to live by fighting against it"

(10, 13, 14). In *New Signatures*, Roberts had pointed to Auden's 1930 *Poems* and *From Feathers to Iron*, with their contemporary rhythms and imagery, to exemplify the modern sensibility defining itself against the earlier Georgian mode, but now Roberts summoned his poets to direct their modern stylistics to revolutionary goals by galvanizing their poetry into direct political action and making "the revolutionary movement articulate" through its material and style.

In "Letter to a Young Revolutionary," the prose piece Day Lewis contributed to *New Country*, his denomination of the poet as not just a maker but a seer, as someone who makes poems out of the conviction of his "absolute belief," reveals just how much his sense of personal and poetic identity depended on his finding a secular, materialist faith to replace the lapsed Christian faith of his fathers, so that revolution might mean continuity with tradition. Adopting a paternal attitude toward the "young" correspondent to whom the open letter is addressed, Day Lewis designates "faith" as "The prime essential for the revolutionary": a personal "conversion" compelling a new way of living for this world rather than the next. His advice is, of course, first and foremost self-counsel, and the tone and imagery of the passage register the urgency of Day Lewis's "hope" for himself and his poetry:

> An absolute belief in revolution as a way to, and a form of, new life. This faith may come as an instantaneous flash; or a harvest; or a coral reef. . . . You must have a conversion. And you are no more likely to have it by reading Marx than to experience a religious conversion by reading theological text-books. The certainty of new life must be your starting-point. Not jealousy, not pity, not a knowledge of economics; not hate even, or love; but a certainty of new life. . . . For revolutionary works without faith are vain. (27)

The scriptural echo in the last sentence anticipates his statement of the imperative: "[O]ur generation, sick to death of Protestant democratic liberalism and the intolerable burden of the individual conscience, are turning to the old or new champions of order and authority, the Roman Catholic Church or Communism" (29).

The conclusion of *A Hope for Poetry* also combines religious with Romantic overtones to describe the poet's function: "The poet is artificer by profession, a poet by divine accident" (77). The poet is responsible as artificer for acquiring the technique that informs the "conscious process" of construction, but the inspiration comes from rare moments of epiphany beyond the poet's will: "It is the nature of the poetic vision to perceive those invisible truths which are like electrons the basis of reality; the nature of the poetic imagination to become aware of the cryptic links that bind our universe together, to find similarity in difference and to make coherence out of contradiction" (75). The analogy with electrons offers a twentieth-century scientific reference, but the conception of the imagination derives from Coleridge and Shelley. Day Lewis and his peers shared with their Modernist contemporaries, beyond the differences about the function of language and form, the modern impulse to validate the imagination as the only faculty of human cognition and coherence left after the waning of Christian belief, Enlightenment rationalism, and Romantic transcendentalism:

> This is as much as we can ever know of the nature of poetry—the angel seen at the window, the air of glory. Whence these visitors come the poet cannot say: whether out of the upper air, influences from the source of all light: or are daimons, the lords of energy, alive in all matter: or from the dark continent in his own mind where mankind's past is stored, an Atlantis lost beneath the waves of consciousness. (77)

Day Lewis's politics were the opposite of those of Stevens, yet they saw the "necessary angel" of the imagination (Stevens's epithet) in similar post-Christian, post-Romantic terms. To contemporary hard-liners like Christopher Caudwell, Day Lewis's kind of communism would seem too middle-class, too Romantic and quasi-religious. And indeed the rush and blur of metaphors in the passage above leave deliberately open the question of whether the inspiration comes from God, nature, or the archetypal unconscious, but it is a strategic vagueness that allows Day Lewis to invest his nascent political vision with something of the aura of all those sources of human wonder.

The quest for political vision is the subject of *The Magnetic Mountain*, a sequence of thirty-six lyrics (seven had appeared in *New Signatures*, four in *New Country*) organized, like *Transitional Poem*, into four sections. A quasi narrative traces the journey (by train, by boat) from a sick and corrupt land to a "new world" centered on a magnetic mountain that links sky and earth, at its heart the magnetic force and rich ore waiting to be discovered and put to productive use in the brave new technological utopia. As noted earlier, Day Lewis had begun *The Magnetic Mountain* and interrupted it to write the domestic sequence *From Feathers to Iron*. However, the significant point about this separation into two sequences is that the public and private spheres still remained separate for Day Lewis. As a result, he could not, on the one hand, develop the political theme implicit in *From Feathers to Iron*, and, on the other hand, it never occurred to him to assimilate the domestic material into the unfinished political sequence. The train trip in *From Feathers to Iron* is sexual and parturitional, in *The Magnetic Mountain* is ideological and political, and the divergence between the sequences, read back to back, illustrates the split consciousness that Day Lewis was struggling to bring into single focus.

The Magnetic Mountain does follow *From Feathers to Iron* in making the journey from winter death to spring rebirth. But the trip to utopia, laid out in ballad quatrains that aim at the "popular poetry" Roberts had called for, remains still a literary allegory, an imagined wish fulfillment. Here is Poem 3 in the sequence:

Somewhere beyond the railheads
Of reason, south or north,
Lies a magnetic mountain
Riveting sky to earth.

No line is laid so far.
Ties rusting in a stack
And sleepers—dead men's bones—
Mark a defeated track.

Kestrel who yearly changes
His tenement of space
At the last hovering
May signify that place.

Iron in the soul,
Spirit steeled in fire,
Needle trembling on truth—
These shall draw me there.

The planets keep their course,
Blindly the bee comes home,
And I shall need no sextant
To prove I'm getting warm.

Near that miraculous mountain
Compass and clock must fail,
For space stands on its head there
And time chases its tail.

There's iron for the asking
Will keep all winds at bay,
Girders to take the leaden
Strain of a sagging sky.

Oh there's a mine of metal,
Enough to make me rich
And build right over chaos
A cantilever bridge.   (136–37)

The kestrel and the hero's "iron in the soul" are familiar from earlier poems.
But, though the mountain's iron ore will replace the "rusting" ruins with
arching girders and splendid bridges, the unexpected pun on "mine/me"
in the last stanza—"a mine of metal" alliterated with "makes me rich"—
reveals how much the political allegory is a personal projection. The
mountain at the heart of the new country is invested with an aura of magical
("magnetic") and religious ("miraculous") synthesis ("Riveting sky to
earth"). But often the poems read as if the speaker is the only person in

what should be a people's republic, as if it is his own "sagging sky" that first needs to be raised, his own "chaos" that has to be bridged.

In a letter written early in the composition of the sequence, Day Lewis referred to it as a "satire" (Sean Day Lewis, 58). Auden had shown Day Lewis and Spender the literary uses of satire in undermining the establishment. So in the middle sections of the poem Four Defendants of the status quo and Four Enemies of revolution speak in turn and are answered by the speaker of the poem. The Defendants who would deter or deflect the protagonist's progress are two male types, the schoolmaster and the cleric, and two female types, the mother and the wife; the Enemies are the demanding and unmanning woman who subverts her man's action, the newspaper mogul, the scientist/social scientist who perversely expropriates religious authority to secular ends, and the solipsistic, daydreaming poet. These representatives of the deliquescent social order have obvious autobiographical pertinence, but Day Lewis temperamentally lacked Wyndham Lewis's or Evelyn Waugh's or even Auden's appetite for satire. It is noteworthy that the women are exempted from satirical treatment and handled sympathetically and that the lambasting of the men is broad and caricaturish. The coming revolution is anticipated in the sections framing and containing the resistance of the Defendants and Enemies: the emerging leader is twice hailed as the "saviour," and exclamatory directives galvanize the reader into action.

The prophetic tone is anticipated in the several epigraphs to the four sections from Rex Warner, Blake, Lawrence, and Hopkins. Hopkins provided Day Lewis (and Auden, too, for that matter) with a particularly useful model of the modern but traditional poet because he achieved his prophetic tone by deriving his sprung rhythms from native Anglo-Saxon accentual and alliterative verse. In *The Magnetic Mountain* Day Lewis adapted Hopkins's techniques to his own Marxist proclamations, as in the opening apostrophe to the kestrel (personified later in the sequence as Auden):

Now to be with you, elate, unshared,
My kestrel joy, O hoverer in wind,
Over the quarry furiously at rest
Chaired on shoulders of shouting wind.

Where's that unique one, wind and wing married,
Aloft in contact of earth and ether;
Feathery my comet, Oh too often
From heaven harried by carrion cares. (135)

Or in these hortatory imperatives to himself and the reader, which transform spring's flowering into a humming industrial landscape:

Follow the kestrel, south or north,
Strict eye, spontaneous wing can tell
A secret. Where he comes to earth

Is the heart's treasure. Mark it well.

. . . .

Stake out your claim. Go downwards. Bore
Through the tough crust. Oh learn to feel
A way in darkness to good ore.
You are the magnet and the steel.

Out of that dark a new world flowers.
There in the womb, in the rich veins
Are tools, dynamos, bridges, towers,
Your tractors and your travelling-cranes.

(Poem 28,164–65)

Or in the syncopated alliteration, assonance, and internal rhyme of the concluding apocalypse (in which the present tense "is" dramatically replaces the prospective future tenses of earlier verbs):

Beckon, O beacon, and O sun be soon!
Hollo, bells, over a melting earth!
Let man be many and his sons all sane,
Fearless with fellows, handsome by the hearth.
Break from your trance: start dancing now in town,
And, fences down, the ploughing match with mate.
This is your day: so turn, my comrades, turn
Like infants' eyes like sunflowers to the light.   (175)

Only the word "comrades" in this last passage gives any clue that the dawning pastoral utopia is to be communist. But in *The Magnetic Mountain* Day Lewis was trying to effect the same breakthrough that he saw in Auden's work from the early *Poems* through *The Orators* to *The Dance of Death*—namely, a transition from "an individualist psychological standpoint" to "a Marxian standpoint" (*A Hope for Poetry*, 49). There is a question whether Auden ever really reached a Marxist standpoint, but Spender's observation that "Auden 'arrived at' politics, by way of psychology" ("Oxford to Communism," 9) is relevant for Day Lewis and for Spender himself as well.

The Magnetic Mountain was written during the closest association between Auden and Day Lewis, and Day Lewis admitted in his autobiography that "Wystan roused to its utmost my emulative faculty" (*The Buried Day*, 178). In September of 1932, when he was bringing the poem to completion, Day Lewis wrote (all too innocently, as it turned out) to Geoffrey Grigson, poet and editor of *New Verse*: "I am stealing some of Auden's thunder for it, but I don't believe either of us will be the worse for that" (Sean Day Lewis, 72). Grigson was soon to declare himself Day Lewis's implacable and lifelong antagonist, and he used the pages of *New Verse* to lambast his verse as "fake poetry. And fake Auden" ("Two Whiffs of Lewisite," 17). Even so astute a critic of the period as Samuel Hynes cites approvingly a contemporary critic, Dilys Powell, who in 1934 felt that with this poem Day Lewis "had completely surrendered" to his charismatic and bossy friend's spell (Hynes, 118). Hynes then goes on to contrast *The Magnetic Mountain* specifically and unfavorably with *The Orators*, published the year before; in Hynes's view Auden's ironic ambiguity and intellectual and psychological subtlety make *The Orators* a parable, whereas Day Lewis's comparatively simplistic and categorical presentation of issues and oppositions makes *The Magnetic Mountain* propaganda (119).

For all that, however, Day Lewis's indebtedness to Auden, in general and in this particular poem, has been very much overstated. In fact, as Valentine Cunningham's *British Writers of the Thirties* has catalogued in voluminous and convincing detail, the motifs and devices that have been taken as characteristic of Auden's thirties' poetry and thereby of Day Lewis's and Spender's poetry—the quest narrative, the industrial landscape, the hero figure, the kestrel, the armed frontiers—are neither Auden's invention nor even the exclusive property of "MacSpaunday," but were rather shared and symptomatic features of the metaphorical iconography and topography of the period.

What is more, the comparison of *The Orators* and *The Magnetic Mountain* is utterly misplaced. Day Lewis was attempting to give *The Magnetic Mountain* something of the multiplicity of voices and broader social awareness that Auden was seeking in *The Orators*. However, Day Lewis was right in telling Grigson that neither poet was "the worse" for his borrowings, because the poems are very different efforts with very different intentions. If *The Orators* is meant as some kind of "parable," as Hynes claims, it is so murky and confused as to subvert the didactic character of parable, and so forbiddingly hermetic as to seem written for a coterie of Auden's close and initiated friends. The work lacks articulated structure and meaning; the various voices function in the babel of Auden's divided consciousness, which, as Day Lewis observed in *Transitional Poem*, sometimes breeds "a piebald strain of truth and nonsense" (67). Even Hynes has to admit that *The Orators* is "willfully obscure and private" (199), and Gareth Reeves, while devoting a whole and admiring chapter to an exegesis of *The Orators*, speaks of its "stylistic narcissism" (O'Neill and Reeves, 90). Indeed, Auden's contribution of the bombastic, bluntly satirical poem "A Communist to Others" to *New Country* in the same year as the publication of *The Orators* can be read as a more genuine attempt to articulate "a Marxian standpoint" in compensation for the narcissistic obscurantism of *The Orators*.

The Magnetic Mountain is a very different kind of poem from *The Orators*, and Clifford Dyment is correct in stating that "in spite of the Auden influence in Day Lewis's work of this period, the work is quite unmistakably Day Lewis's own" (Dyment, 26). In trying to push past "the individualist psychological standpoint" of *The Orators* to a more public stance in *The Magnetic Mountain*, Day Lewis's Marxism may still seem, as Hynes suggests, too rhetorical in its Romantic projections, too far removed from the class struggle. Nevertheless, *The Magnetic Mountain* has the virtue of being a more coherent and effective poetic statement than Auden's quirky mélange of things in *The Orators*. Perhaps *The Magnetic Mountain* is closer to propaganda than anything Auden would permit himself to write, except for odd pieces like "A Communist to Others." Even here that poem is a dramatic monologue spoken by someone other than Auden; moreover, when it appeared in a volume of his poetry, its address to "Comrades" was neutralized to "Brothers," and the poem was silently dropped altogether from his *Collected Poems*.

At the same time, it must be kept in mind that the whole question of whether poetry and art could and should be propaganda was a hotly contested issue in the journals of the period and in the critical statements of the *New Country* poets about their own intentions. In that debate Day Lewis would test out the possibility in his own poetic practice more seriously than any of his Oxford peers, would allow his poetry to risk the "impurity" of propaganda more than Auden or even Spender would allow, just as he would espouse the Communist position, both outside and (briefly) inside the Party, more wholeheartedly and for a longer period than the others in the Auden circle. The kind of "faith" he hoped to have in the Marxist cause required no less; he said in his "Letter to a Young Revolutionary": "If you must join yourself to this body, then let it be without reservations, a submission of your self entire; you'll not be there to make revised versions of the faith or minister to your private salvation" ("Letter," 29–30). Day Lewis, like his peers, found his middle-class difficulties in submitting himself entire to the cause, but from about 1933 to 1938 his own psychological and spiritual need pushed him in that political direction.

Spender had contributed poems to both *New Signatures* and *New Country*, and his *Poems* appeared in 1933, the same year as *The Magnetic Mountain*. The debate about poetry and propaganda is epitomized in the contrast between Spender's essay "Revolution and Literature" in *New Country* and Day Lewis's *Hope for Poetry* the next year. Though Spender would involve himself in leftist politics and in forming a united front against fascism, would go to Spain during the civil war and join the Party (though so briefly that he was out almost before he was in), in this essay he states the case for what seems like an absolute distinction between poetry and Marxist politics: "Philosophers, statesmen and artists have always been and always will be individualists" (*New Country*, 70). Indeed, "of human activities, writing poetry is one of the least revolutionary" because "the poet, often a potential revolutionary, is able to escape from urgent problems of social reconstruction into a world of his own making . . . only bounded by the limits of his imagination" (62, 64). Since well-made artifacts constitute "separate and complete and ideal worlds," "the writing of the poem solves the poem's problems." Thus "it is impossible to write propagandist poetry," because aesthetic solutions are autotelic and self-contained (62).

Spender's aestheticism here sounds as hermetic as Pater's or Stevens's, and runs counter to Auden's and Day Lewis's determination in *Oxford Poetry 1927* to engage "Pure Art" in its social conditions. However, in "Revolution and Literature" Spender pushes his argument so far as to suggest that the incompatibility of art and politics means that art should yield to politics. Since, on the one hand, bourgeois writing is vitiated by false values and, on the other, proletarian writing fails aesthetically, the artist with a political agenda should perhaps give up art and just "go into politics" (66). Of course Spender's actual output seems to make the opposite point. His most intense and sustained period of writing poems coincided with the years of his most intense political activity, and his poetic creativity dwindled rapidly thereafter. Nevertheless, "Revolution and Literature" is significant in the debate about art and propaganda for articulating the Modernist goal of aesthetic purity uncontaminated by politics against which the *New Country* poets were reacting but from which they could never in their minds and in their practice be wholly free.

It is true that Day Lewis began his "Letter to a Young Revolutionary" with a similar claim that the poet writes not to a political formula but "because he wants to make something" (*New Country*, 26). Moreover, while still maintaining that "poetry, in fact, whatever else it may or may not be, must be poetry" (49), *A Hope for Poetry* acknowledges that the tension between the individual crisis and the political crisis (between Freud and Marx, as Day Lewis puts it in his pamphlet *Revolution in Writing*, 14) was bound further to divide against itself the already dissociated modern sensibility. However, the thrust of *A Hope for Poetry* is to argue against Spender's position in "Revolution and Literature" and to resolve the tension between lyric impulse and didactic purpose by contending that poetry *can* be political, can even be propaganda if its political views are experienced deeply enough and felt with sufficient passion (37). In other words, if the political can be made personal, then it can be "made" into a poem: "there is no reason why poetry should not also be propaganda" unless "the didactic is achieved at the expense of the poetic" (49). Consequently, to fuse poetry and politics, Day Lewis concluded, communism had to become not just the "decoration and facade" of the poem but its very "foundation and integral framework" (53).

By the time Day Lewis added a Postscript to a reissuing of the essay in 1936, he cut a dashing figure in the literary scene as a young rebel. The Hogarth Press had brought together *Transitional Poem, From Feathers to Iron,* and *The Magnetic Mountain* as *Collected Poems* (1935), and the publication of *A Time to Dance,* also in 1935, and *Noah and the Waters* in the next year increased his visibility as an advocate for the leftist position. He used the Postscript to criticize younger poets like Dylan Thomas and George Barker for rejecting "the *New Country* school" in favor of a convoluted, self-involved surrealism, and to comment, closer to home, on Louis MacNeice's newly published volume (79). MacNeice, through his friendship with Auden, had come to know Spender and Day Lewis—but always remained aloof from them and their politicking. His phlegmatic skepticism and reserve, in addition to the fact that he was several years behind the others at Oxford, kept him quite apart from "the *New Country* school," and he appeared in neither of Roberts's anthologies. Greatly as Day Lewis admired MacNeice's *Poems* (1935), he saw it as indicating a turning, within the Auden circle itself, "in the direction of 'pure' poetry" away from the political commitment he had set for himself (80). Day Lewis was arguing with proclivities within himself as much as with MacNeice when he denounced "pure" poetry as simultaneously emphasizing "a solipsistic state of mind" and "the supremacy of 'form' over 'matter'" through cultivating the "private language" of the "self-conscious individual" (87, 90, 92). His new stance required him to operate from the premise that the poetic self is inseparable from the social being, even in a bourgeois and individualist society. Since it seemed to him true that "every conscious human activity is to some extent a social activity and in consequence must be judged partly by social criteria" (88), the notion of art cleansed of social conditions and political entanglements seemed a perversion: not a truer, uncorrupted art but an art corrupted and vitiated by its very purity.

Even before adding the Postscript to *A Hope for Poetry*, in January 1936, Day Lewis had already taken up the question of pure poetry in a lecture to the Edinburgh Poetry Club and taken a somewhat more permissive view. He admitted "the existence and value of 'pure poetry,'" but only as "something fortuitous," momentary, unplanned, and unbidden: "a sudden spontaneous illumination, which might be engendered in the course of writing a poem." At the same time, he insisted that such Romantic epiphanies cannot account for the whole of the poem nor its whole function and purpose. Since the poet draws "life—not only as a human being, but as a poet—from the community[,] there must be a reciprocity, he must give life back, and to cut himself off from that source of life was much more likely to cripple than to liberate him." Poetry is therefore "fundamentally conditioned" by the poet's "duty to, and dependence on, society, which [he hastened to add] did not mean anything like writing to order" ("Surrealists Get the Bird," 20–21). So, against the aestheticist and escapist tendencies in some Modernists—Stevens would concede his aesthetic escapism to his Marxist critics and throw it back to them as his "noble" aim—Day Lewis proposed to himself and his British peers a counterpoetry:

> To the idea of poetry as exclusive, esoteric, a-moral, the private affair of the poet, moving in a different world from prose, [I] would oppose the idea of poetry as catholic, diverse in function, moral, everyone's business (potentially, at any rate), assimilating not rejecting prose meaning, a way of synthesising and communicating reality.
>
> ("Surrealists Get the Bird," 21)

In a lecture given in September 1936 before the 15th Annual Conference of the British Institute of Adult Education at New College, Oxford, Day Lewis returned to the issue crucial to the aesthetic posture of the thirties: the integration of art and politics. Day Lewis admitted their contrary commitments and inclinations: "The poet's imagination is almost exactly the opposite of everything we mean by the will: it feeds on contemplation, when the will feeds on action; it is primarily a passive quality, a more or less trained sensitiveness, the matrix on which nature breeds art: it must be a re-agent before it can become an agent." Yet the erotic sexual meta-

Erratum

Gelpi/*Living in Time*
ISBN 0-19-509863-3

An inadvertent typographical error appears
on page 145 in the chapter subtitle. The
word "Thantos" should have appeared as
"Thanatos."

phors work to connect art and politics. For, however contemplative and "passive" the imagination may be as the source and "matrix" in the generative process of art, its empathetic latency can take form and willful purpose in the body of the poem—if it "feeds on" and is quickened by social and political experience. Then, Day Lewis assured his audience and himself, "the poetic word, imagination's child, when it is made flesh, can be one of the most powerful agents in the world—potent not only in the recreation of mood and vision, but toward moral ends" (*Imagination and Thinking*, 2).

Speaking for his generation's high hopes, Day Lewis would say: "We wished to act; and poetry was our instrument of action" ("The Thirties in Retrospect," 14). Certainly he tried to push his poetry farther in this direction than even many on the left felt comfortable with. Throughout his life his most vicious detractor was Geoffrey Grigson, who, after turning against Day Lewis in 1933, used his journal *New Verse* as a vehicle to deride Day Lewis mercilessly as a bourgeois poseur tricked out in Red fleece. Though Grigson published two poems from *The Magnetic Mountain* in the first issue of *New Verse,* his shift in allegiance was set by the second issue. There his review of *The Magnetic Mountain*, recently out as a book, ridiculed the poem and excoriated Day Lewis for not heeding Spender's warning about turning poetry into propaganda. In another of his fulminations he sneered that when Day Lewis describes literature as "potentially a revolutionary force," "a vital force, to heal the breach between the living word and the living man," he "slimes from the difficulty of the restricted response to the 'best art'" ("Two Whiffs of Lewisite," 18).

In fact, Day Lewis, like Spender and other Marxist intellectuals, was painfully aware that it was difficult, probably impossible, for those of their class and education to identify with the proletariat sufficiently to speak for them legitimately. At the same time, the working classes remained silent in part for lack of education and opportunity, in part through identification with the technological and industrial system that oppressed them. For those two reasons there could not yet be a genuinely "communist, proletarian poetry." For these reasons, in Jean-Paul Sartre's words, "the poetry of the future revolution has remained in the hands of the young well-intentioned bourgeois who draw their inspiration from their psychological contradictions, in the antinomy of their ideal and their class, in the uncertainty of old bourgeois language" (*Black Orpheus*, 14). In the political and poetic ferment of the mid-thirties Day Lewis's response to the anomalies of his situation was to try—more resolutely than either Auden or Spender—to steel himself to renounce the "escapism" open to the bourgeois poet and to prove through his own practice that poetry could aim at both "social justice and artistic integrity" (*A Hope for Poetry*, 53, 56, 90, 98). "A Time to Dance" (the long title poem of Day Lewis's next volume), *Noah and the Waters*, and the Spanish Civil War narrative "The Nabara" in *Overtures to Death* (1938) represented three major efforts to fulfill the risky commitment made to his Edinburgh audience and reiterated in the Postscript to *A Hope for Poetry*.

After leaving the university in 1927, Day Lewis, like many of his generation of writers, including Auden, Roberts, and MacNeice, supported him-
self by teaching, first at Summer Field, then at Larchfield School in
Helensburgh, Scotland. Then in 1930, he and Mary moved to Cheltenham
Junior School in Gloucestershire, which had about one hundred boys as
students. Soon after Sean's birth in 1931 they took up residence in nearby
Box Cottage, roofed in Cotswold tile and graced with a garden whose
blossoming syringa tree would appear in a number of poems over the years.
There "our second child was born, in 1932 [actually 1934], Nicholas
Charles, and we stayed on in the house till 1938, three years after I gave
up teaching" (*The Buried Day*, 199). Box Cottage is the first of the series
of residences—he hoped they would be homes—that demarcate the restless, at times turbulent course of his life.

Though Day Lewis remained on the teaching staff at Cheltenham until
1935, he had to maintain his position against the growing uneasiness
of the school authorities. There were three grounds of complaint: his purportedly "'Bohemian' tendencies," his "Bolshevism" (Sean Day Lewis, 89),
and "Smut"—that is to say, the "extremely, excessively, er, SEXUAL" quality
of his poetry (Sean Day Lewis, 66, 89; *The Buried Day*, 197). The autobiography reports his unavailing response to this last stammering rebuke
from the embarrassed but outraged headmaster: "'But they're love poems,'
I blurted out, 'addressed to my wife.'" As to his Bolshevism, he was on
less certain grounds. Though he was not yet a card-carrying Party member, it was no secret that he was regularly participating in the meetings of
the Cheltenham cell of the Party, and he was known locally to be a fierce
advocate of leftist causes. On the other hand, he recalled, with rueful
amusement at the ironies of his middle-class scruples, that "the refinement
of bourgeois individualism" in which he was trained not only made for a
"gentlemanly refusal to indoctrinate my pupils with Left-Wing ideas" but
even made him "unwilling to join the Party till I was making enough
money to be able to assure myself that I was joining from disinterested
motives, not as one of the lean and hungry who would personally profit
by revolution" (*The Buried Day*, 211). Nevertheless, he learned to accommodate himself to his situation on his own terms, though in increasing
discomfort, because his poetry, however widely known and favorably received in literary circles, did not sell enough copies (despite its supposed
"er, SEXUAL" vagaries) to support him, much less a wife and two boys.

The matter came to a head in 1935 when the school's board of governors met in what Day Lewis called "a court martial" in a high-
spirited letter to his old friend L. A. G. Strong (Sean Day Lewis, 89). The
governors took no action but compelled the accused to a closeted meeting with its chairman, Lord Lee of Fareham, for a military-style dressing
down. So indignant was Day Lewis about this confrontation that he used
it as an episode in his political novel *Starting Point* (1937) and recounted it

again two decades later in his autobiography. For evidence of misconduct Lord Lee pointed to the fact that earlier that year Day Lewis had given "a talk to the local branch of the Friends of the Soviet Union on collective farming" ("a subject," Day Lewis added, "I had mugged up from books") and fumed that such a traitor to class could not be remanded to simple military justice: "D'you realise what would have happened to you if you'd done that sort of thing in the Regiment? The Colonel would have handed you over to the subaltern's mess; and when they'd finished with you, you'd have been asked to join some other Regiment" (*The Buried Day*, 204–5). The anecdote epitomizes the bitter polarization of British politics circa 1935. Although Day Lewis escaped dismissal, soon thereafter he took the opportunity to bail out of this regiment by resigning from teaching. The financial success of his first Nigel Strangeways mystery novel, *A Question of Proof* (1935), written under the pseudonym Nicholas Blake, and a publisher's advance to write more "serious" novels allowed him to become a full-time writer and an active Party member. Now, he hoped, he could connect "the living word and the living man" and thus prove poetry and politics, theory and practice compatible.

The subtitle of "A Time to Dance"—"A Symphonic Poem in Memory of L. P. Hedges"—announces its occasion and its large intention. During those difficult years at Cheltenham Junior School, the colleague for whom Day Lewis felt a deep affection was Lionel Hedges, a robust man of boisterous good humor who was also an acclaimed cricketer and a talented actor. The shock of Hedges's sudden death in 1933 struck Day Lewis with special force because the vibrantly alive and athletic Hedges had been roughly his own age. The analogy with symphonic structure is intended to suggest a succession of separate and contrasting yet interrelated movements; but though Clifford Dyment judged the poem "one of the outstanding achievements in the literature of our time" (Dyment, 29), the mélange of heroic epic, personal elegy, and political polemic manages its modulations with transitions that sometimes seem willed and manipulated. Its upward sweep is announced at the invocation—"not a dirge" but "a theme with a happy end"; and the familiar image of "a bird's buoyancy" challenges the poet to assume "the ecstatic poise of the natural fighter" (like Hedges on the cricket field) and turn lament into a heroic "stormcock's song" (198).

The first movement presents the hero's ethos by recounting the epic flight of 1920 in which Lieutenants Parer and M'Intosh, two discharged veterans, made their odyssean journey all around the world from England back to their home in Australia in a rattletrap aircraft "of obsolete design, a condemned D. H. nine" (198). Why was Day Lewis so fascinated by these high-flyers? Their lone and steely individualism, undaunted by danger or adverse weather or mechanical failure, would hardly seem to qualify them as Marxist ideals, but Day Lewis's uncomplicated admiration for their physical and moral courage indicates again his generation's need for heroes to emulate and for leaders to set the resolute course. Conspicuous acts of heroism aroused a magnetic response across political lines that were other-wise fiercely drawn, and the communist ideologue Christopher Caudwell followed Day Lewis's account of the flight of Parer and M'Intosh with his own in his book *Great Flights* (1937).

T. E. Lawrence is the obvious case in point. Despite the fascist impli-cations of his adventures in Arabia, his larger-than-life figure struck fire in hearts Left and Right. Day Lewis felt Lawrence's charisma and was him-self a sufficiently public figure by the mid-thirties for Lawrence to return his high regard. He could not but have been surprised and thrilled by a story in the London *Evening Standard* for August 15, 1934, headlined "England's Great Man," which reported an exchange between Lawrence and Winston Churchill regarding him. Churchill's gloomy remonstrance—to Lawrence, of all people—that there were no great men to meet the chal-lenge of present-day Britain drew the extraordinary response from Lawrence that he had "discovered one great man in these islands. His name is Cecil Day Lewis" (Sean Day Lewis, 79). A letter from Lawrence to Day Lewis survives; written shortly before Lawrence's fatal motorcycle crash; it praises *A Hope for Poetry* and excitedly anticipates the appearance of *A Time to Dance* : "I shall enjoy buying your book, so please don't send it—after all, you don't write so many as all that!" (Sean Day Lewis, 85).

In that poem, which Lawrence did not live to read, Day Lewis sees Parer and M'Intosh as kestrel figures and renders their heroics with a height-ened intensity derived again from the compacted rhetoric of Hopkins's "The Wreck of the Deutschland." Phrases linked by alliteration and asso-nance are spun into long lines and extended stanzas syncopated by sprung rhythm and irregular rhyme:

> Air was all ambushes round them, was avalanche earthquake
> Quicksand, a funnel deep as doom, till climbing steep
> They crawled like a fly up the face of perpendicular night
> And levelled, finding a break
> At fourteen thousand feet. Here earth is shorn from sight:
> Deadweight a darkness hangs on their eyelids, and they bruise
> Their eyes against a void: vindictive the cold airs close
> Down like a trap of steel and numb them from head to heel;
> Yet they kept an even keel,
> For their spirit reached forward and took the controls while their
> fingers froze. (201)

Where a Modernist like Joyce ironized the epic and Pound registered the heroic in splintered fragments, Day Lewis, like Robinson Jeffers (an Ameri-can anti-Modernist whose work he did not know), strove to render the full force of the heroic in sustained narrative.

But as the narrative celebration of the pilots' survival gives way in the second movement to an elegy for Hedges, the thunderous rhetoric sud-denly drops into the personal voice of the poet learning to survive the abrupt extinction of a friend who had seemed invulnerable. The stanza of ten lines (five stresses except for three in the sixth line) with a tight rhyme scheme (a-b-c-b-c-a d-e-e-d) has something of the decorum of a truncated sonnet:

> In my heart's mourning underworld I sang
> As miners entombed singing despair to sleep—
> Their earth is stopped, their eyes are reconciled
> To night. Yet here, under the sad hill-slope
> Where I thought one spring of my life forever was sealed,
> The friend I had lost sprang
> To life again and showed me a mystery:
> For I knew, at last wholly accepting death,
> Though earth had taken his body and air his breath,
> He was not in heaven or earth: he was in me.   (210)

The elegiac "mystery" is a deepening recognition that, paradoxically, we can only accept life and commit ourselves unreservedly to living in time if we accept the inescapability of death and the uncertainty of an afterlife. Live like Hedges, using his time to the full, and die like him, his body replenishing the earth, his spirit animating mortal friends within the cyclic economy of nature, that "thrifty wife" who "conceives all, saves all, finds a use for all" (212). The poet's realization of what Yeats called "tragic joy" turns Hedges' "funeral games" into "a time to dance" (213).

This pastoral resolution—mortality reconciled to the fertile country-side in the unending erotics of the mortal round—suggests the personal equilibrium that Day Lewis's psyche had sought and would continue to seek, but the social conscience of the thirties would not allow him to end the poem merely with individual survival and renewal. In the polemical third movement (omitted except for a few sections from the Collected Poems of 1954 and even from the Complete Poems of 1992, except that several songs are published as separate poems), the collective voice of the oppressed masses summons the poet to witness to their cause: "Who is he who calls us to dance," "bids us follow the free passage of ocean flyers," "mocks" us with "flash talk" of living in time? (A Time to Dance, 51–52). The rhetorical response of the poet is to protest the oppression of the poor by adapting a number of folk and popular forms: an urban pastoral ("Come live with me and be my love" [A Time to Dance, 54; Complete Poems, 195–96]); a slum lullaby ("Oh, hush thee, my love" [A Time to Dance, 54–55; Complete Poems, 196]); jazzy radio-talk ("A coast-to-coast hitch-up" [A Time to Dance, 61–62]). And as in The Magnetic Mountain "A Time to Dance" works, once again not altogether successfully, to convert satire into epic, in order to elevate the revolutionary into contemporary hero—that is to say, in order to redeem the hero from bourgeois individualism (Parer and M'Intosh) and crypto-fascism (T. E. Lawrence) and recast him as leader of the rising masses.

To that end the third movement translates the example of the airmen and of Hedges "the natural fighter" into Marxist slogans: "Freedom is the *knowledge of necessity"* and "Into your hands history commits her spirit" (57). Significantly, the latter injunction inverts Jesus' dying words, signaling His return to the heavenly Father—"It is consummated. Into Your hands I commend My spirit"—into the secular materialist's responsibility to history and for history. However, the most notorious section of the poem, which evoked immediate protests, begins "Yes, why do we all, seeing a Red, feel small?" and goes on to depict the Red in terms of the socialist realist heroics of Soviet posters:

> There fall
> From him shadows of what he is building: bold and tall—
> For his sun has barely mastered the misted horizon—they seem.
> Indeed he casts a shadow, as among the dead will some
> Living one. It is the future walking to meet us all.
> Mark him. He is only what we are, mortal. Yet from the night
> Of history, where we lie dreaming still, he is wide awake. . . .
> He is what your sons could be, the roads these times should take.
>
> (*A Time to Dance*, 58–59)

The Red is the prophet of material existence, not of immortality, and shows us how to live in present time so as to create the utopian future: paradise regained not as pastoral Eden or Christian heaven but as a loving and classless society. Thus by the end of the symphonic poem "a time to dance" is "a time to love"; revolution requires "love in action." Dancing becomes the trope linking life-giving erotics and revolutionary politics, and the two are taken to be so interdependent as to be almost synonymous. Erotics and politics are reconciled in the image of the Red as father and in the image of history (not nature now) as "the thrifty wife" who "conceives all, saves all, finds a use for all," the mother of the pioneer "sons" of the Marxist future (*A Time to Dance*, 63, 59).

In the first issue of Grigson's *New Verse* Day Lewis's friend Naomi Mitchison had published "To Some Young Communists from an Older Socialist," admonishing the young zealots for shouldering aside the middle-aged leftists who had led the way. So when she tweaked her young friend Day Lewis in a letter about romanticizing the Red in "A Time to Dance," he bristled but held his ground: "I don't think I am romantic about communism. . . . [I]t's just that I believe dialectical materialism is much nearer the truth than any other philosophy I have come up against; and that communism appeals to my prophetic (or self-hallucinatory) faculty as being the inevitable next mode of life" (Sean Day Lewis, 91). The Red's "prophetic" vision of history offers a materialist, post-Christian sense of self-fulfillment and self-sacrifice that permits—indeed, commits—him to live in time with a saving sense of participating in an enclosing and purposive design.

Yet in this same letter Day Lewis's admitted uncertainty about achieving this integration for himself makes him respond defensively to his friend and confidante: "[P]lease don't think I'm trying to appear in the least heroic." The line "love in action is best for me" returns the sexual and political challenge to the private sphere. The unresolved question is whether a politics of love, embodied in the ideal of the Red, is truly "prophetic" or, as the anxious parenthetical interpolation above suggests, merely "self-hallucinatory." "A Time to Dance" concludes the volume, but in fact its opening poems are more convincing than the symphonic poem positioned as the volume's climax because they candidly dramatize the conflicts within Day Lewis that inhibited him from becoming that Red whose "love in action" generated the new society. With *A Time to Dance* Day Lewis moved from book-length sequences, like the previous three books, to volumes constellating clusters of shorter poems around one or two longer poems. Here these shorter poems, in leading up to the title poem, expose the poet's "own divided heart": that is to say, the tensions between domestic peace and sexual discord in the private sphere and the opposition between middle-class privilege and class warfare in his engagement with politics. Day Lewis's strategy in constructing the volume was to imply that divisions articulated in the opening poems seek and find resolution in the "Time to Dance" symphony at the close. But in fact the opening poems form a kind of suite of their own, and the divisions they lay out can be seen to work as the deconstructive countertext jeopardizing and subverting the stability of any large symphonic harmony.

Day Lewis had begun his political move toward "dialectical material-ism" at about the same time that he entered married and family life, and the two themes became entwined in his experience—in idealized conso-nance but in actual dissonance. The problem was epitomized for him in the combination of Mary's withdrawal from sexual partner to "the Mother." The opposition/connection between bourgeois domesticity and class warfare, fatherhood and revolutionary patricide, marital contentment and political commitment, the claims of individuality and the claims of the masses is introduced in the first two poems of the opening suite of *A Time to Dance*, "Learning to Talk" and "Moving In." Here is the text of "Learning to Talk":

See this small one, tiptoe on
The green foothills of the years,
Views a younger world than yours;
When you go down, he'll be the tall one.

Dawn's dew is on his tongue—
No word for what's behind the sky,
Naming all that meets the eye,
Pleased with sunlight over a lawn.

Hear his laughter. He can't contain
The exquisite moment overflowing.
Limbs leaping, woodpecker flying
Are for him and not hereafter.

Tongue trips, recovers, triumphs,
Turning all ways to express
What the forward eye can guess—
That time is his and earth young.

We are growing too like trees
To give the rising wind a voice:
Eagles shall build upon our verse,
Our winged seeds are tomorrow's sowing.

Yes, we shall learn to speak for all
Whose hearts here are not at home,
All who march to a better time
And breed the world for which they burn.

Though we fall once, though we often,
Though we fall to rise not again,
From our horizons sons begin:
When we go down, they will be the tall ones.   (181)

The private and public spheres are elided in the neat shift from the first
four quatrains, wherein Day Lewis's second son, Nicholas, enters and
assumes his world through the acquisition of language, to the last three,
wherein simultaneously the boy's father's adult generation are also
entering and assuming a new social world by acquiring a new political
tongue: "We are growing too" as "we learn to speak for all" the speech-
less oppressed who "breed the world for which they burn." Now the
oppressed "burn" not because they are passive victims of the capitalist
conflagration but because they are enflamed by a consuming passion to
torch the old system and kindle the new.

The multivalence of "burn" and the alliteration of "breed" and "burn"
at the beginning and end of the line encapsulate the erotics of politics and
assert the passionate fruitfulness of revolution, which is rendered in pastoral terms in the last (and Shelleyan) line of the previous quatrain: "Our
winged seeds are to-morrow's sowing." As in the passage about the Red,
the sons complete the revolution undertaken by the (once bourgeois) fathers
who breed the seeds and sons of revolution. The elision of pronouns mirrors the succession: for the generation of fathers, the association of the
bourgeois "we" who learn to voice the revolution with the proletarian
"they" who enact the revolution; and for the sons, the identification of
the individual "he," the boy Nicholas, with the collective "they," the rising
suns/sons of the revolutionary generation. The last stanza rephrases the
last line of the first stanza to integrate "an individualist psychological standpoint" with "a Marxian standpoint" (*A Hope for Poetry*, 49): "When you
go down, he'll be the tall one" becomes "When we go down, they will
be the tall ones."

"Moving In" was written for the occasion of the Day Lewis family's taking up residence at Box Cottage in the Cheltanham suburb of Charlton Kings near Cheltanham Junior School. However, in contrast to the previous poem the domestic and familial are here seen as a reactionary antithesis to revolutionary action. The political poet warns the bourgeois part of himself that seeks safe haven in "hope's hearth, heart's home" that "[t]hough your wife is chaste, though your children lustily throng," still "[n]o private good will let you forget" the victims of the system that permits his pastoral and domestic calm (182–83). In subsequent poems in the suite a lament for the downtrodden "Losers" is converted into "A Warning to Those Who Live in Mountains" that "the peoples of the plain" will soon rise against them in their fast havens. The fertile "winged seeds" of revolutionary speech in "Learning to Talk" are contrasted here with the mountain-dwellers' sterile "wishes like winged seeds." The poem identifies with "them" on the plains rather than "you" on high (though "Moving In" has already acknowledged the privileged class from which the poet makes his radical critique). The plains people "wait for a word," for the "plain language" the poet is "learning to talk" (187). "Johnny Head-In-Air" develops the image of masses moving across the land "to a better time" (181), and again the movement opens the passage through the "sheer, unfissured walls" of bourgeois privilege to the Marxist Canaan, "down to the rich valleys / Where each can stake his claim" (190, 188). Johnny has his head in the air like the kestrel, but by the end of the long ballad he is summoned to march with the masses.

The central poems in the suite are "The Conflict" and "In Me Two Worlds." Day Lewis's comment years later that these were "the only two political poems of any value which I wrote" (*The Buried Day*, 213) is not literally true, but he is correct in noting that the drama of these poems indicates the difficulty of resolving divided loyalties into a firm political position. A careful reading of "The Conflict" shows how much of his recent poetry is distilled into these seemingly simple balladlike quatrains.

I sang as one
Who on a tilting deck sings
To keep men's courage up, though the wave hangs
That shall cut off their sun.

As storm-cocks sing,
Flinging their natural answer in the wind's teeth,
And care not if it is a waste of breath
Or birth-carol of spring.

As ocean-flyer clings
To height, to the last drop of spirit driving on
While yet ahead is land to be won
And work for wings.

Singing I was at peace,
Above the clouds, outside the ring:
For sorrow finds a swift release in song
And pride its poise.

Yet living here,
As one between two massing powers I live
Whom neutrality cannot save
Nor occupation cheer.

None such shall be left alive:
The innocent wing is soon shot down,
And private stars fade in the blood-red dawn
Where two worlds strive.

The red advance of life
Contracts pride, calls out the common blood,
Beats song into a single blade,
Makes a depth-charge of grief.

Move then with new desires,
For where we used to build and love
Is no man's land, and only ghosts can live
Between two fires.   (183–84)

The strenuous effort to force ambivalence into balance and direction is written into the combination of volatility and symmetry in the prosody. The eight quatrains are neatly halved between the speaker as individualist poet and the speaker as political activist, with "sing/song" recurring through the first half and "live/life" running through the second. The key words and their rhymes thread each half together: in the poet's half, "sing," "sings," "hangs," "sing," "spring," "clings," "wings," "singing," "ring," "song"; in the revolutionary's half, "living," "live," "save," "alive," "strive," "life," "grief," "love," "live." The poet clues the reader in to watch for these sequences by placing the key word at the beginning of the first line of the opening quatrain of the section, repeating it at the end of the second line, and then reiterating it as the rhyme word in the first line of the second quatrain of the section: thus " I sang as one / Who on a tilting deck sings," "As storm-cocks sing"; and then "Yet living here, / As one between two massing powers I live," "None such shall be left alive."

The quatrains are internally symmetrical and balanced, rhyming a-b-b-a with the middle rhyming lines longer than the shorter rhyming lines that enclose the quatrain in an end-stopped syntactic and prosodic unit. At the same time, variation and uncertainty are built into the tight units. The enjambment of many lines hangs the statement precariously, as in "As ocean-flyer clings / To height" or "And private stars fade in the blood-red dawn / Where two worlds strive." The a-rhymes of the opening and closing lines of the quatrain are full rhymes with but one exception ("peace," "poise"), but the b-rhymes of the middle lines are without exception dissonant slant rhymes. Moreover, the short opening and closing lines have sometimes two, sometimes three, stresses, and if the first has two then the fourth always has three, and vice versa. In the same way the stresses of the middle lines alternate randomly in four-five, five-four stresses. The result to the ear and tongue, in contrast to the Yeatsian sonority or the Hopkins-like drive of some earlier poems, is an unpredictable but comprehensible pattern of variations and inversions to render rhythmically the oscillations of the poet's mind and feelings.

In "The Thirties in Retrospect," Day Lewis said that the General Strike of 1926 "presented us with a near-revolutionary situation" that for the first time inescapably demanded of him and his generation "the taking of sides, the making of a moral choice" between "capitalism, reaction, the past" and "the workers, the underdog, the embattled power of the future" (8). The General Strike provides the plot situation that catalyzes political positions in his novel *Starting Point* (1937). In the mid-thirties his head was clear about the right choice, but his heart was still torn. Reared and educated in the middle-class individualism of the fathers' system, comfortably domesticated as father with wife and family at Box Cottage, could he break away, relinquish privilege, and through his actions and words help father the new and different kind of sons he already envisioned marching in some of his poems?

The first quatrains of "The Conflict" invoke familiar images to cast the reactionary, individualist stance in an acceptably heroic mold. The singer on the tilting deck of the old *Titanic*-like ship of state, heartening his fellows till the rising wave sinks them all, is like the stormcock (recalling the kestrels of earlier poems and "the stormcock's song" of "A Time to Dance"), heedless of whether the apocalypse be an end or a new beginning. He is the "ocean-flyer" (recalling T. E. Lawrence or Parer and M'Intosh), intent only on maintaining his own flight "to the last drop of spirit." But the lines that rise sonorously to present the individualist position also undercut it with a recognition of the futility of "neutrality" and the selfishness of seeking a "private" "peace, / Above the clouds, outside the ring."

Looking back, Day Lewis could see that the counterstrain to individualism in "our home and public-school backgrounds" was "a sense of responsibility, which made difficult either the Ivory-Tower attitude or the deliberate pursuit of what used to be called 'enlightened self-interest'" ("The Thirties in Retrospect," 7). So the second half of the poem turns from the "Ivory-Tower attitude" and "self-interest" of the first half and speaks instead from a "sense of responsibility." "Living here" requires spurning the individual ego (the stormcock's "pride") and patriarchal contentment (domestic havens like Box Cottage "where we used to build and love") in order that "new desires" inseminate "[t]he red advance of life." The phrases "blood-red dawn" and "red advance of life" emphasize the correlation between the unavoidable casualties in the class war and the springing of the "common blood" of the revolutionary breed under communism's red flag.

It is surprising and not surprising, then, to find "The Ecstatic" immediately after "Johnny Head-In-Air" in the opening suite: surprising because here its bird imagery represents a switch from stormcock to skylark; not so surprising because it repeats the reversion in the last poem of *Transitional Poem* from the high-flying hawk to "the little lark / Who veins the sky with song" and descends to his nest at night (97). Reviewing *A Time to Dance* for the *Observer*, Basil de Selincourt singled out the purity of "The Ecstatic" for extended notice in contrast to the political poetry that frames it. "The Ecstatic" recalls a number of Romantic lyrics, most obviously Shelley's "To a Skylark" and Hopkins's "The Windhover," but Day Lewis here omits political and theological overtones, as if instead to distill his poem into the emotional and aesthetic transparency of Keats's "To Autumn." To that end the poem eschews end rhyme and instead suffuses the lines with several patterns of internal rhymes, some of which are indicated below by the use of underlinings, italics, boldface, and boldface italics:

> <u>Lar</u>k, sky<u>lark</u>, *spill*ing your rubbed and **round**
> Pebbles of **sound** in air's *still* <u>lake</u>,
> Whose *wide*ning circles *fill* the **noon**; yet *none*
> Is *known* so small be*side* the sun.
>
> Be <u>strong</u> your *ferv*ent soaring, your skyward **air!**
> Tremble **there**, a *nerve* of <u>song</u>!
> *Float* up **there where** voice and *wing* are one,
> A *sing*ing star, a **note** of light!
>
> Buoyed, em<u>bayed</u> in heaven's *noon*-**wide** reaches—
> For *soon* light's **tide** will turn—Oh <u>stay</u>!
> *Cease* not till <u>day</u> streams to the *west*, then down
> That *est*uary drop down to *peace*.   (193)

These markings indicate how a cross-stitching of internal rhymes links the lines into stanzas in imitation of the bird that spills down sound in rising until (after the pivotal phrase "Oh stay") its descent in the last two lines. But these governing patterns are also surrounded and embellished by all kinds of sound-play: instances of alliteration and assonance too numerous to list; repeated words ("sky," "wide," "noon," "light," "down"); near rhymes that weave through the stanzas ("rub," "peb"; "pebbles," "circles," "trembles"; "spill," "still," "small"; "fervent," "heaven"; "your," "air," "soar," "star"; "up," "drop"; "voice," "buoyed"; "in," "turn," "then," "down"; "round," "sound," "down," "down"); the many "-ing" endings of the participles and gerunds; the extension of "spill," "still," "fill" from the first stanza into "will," "till" in the last; and so on. Virtually every word of the text is sooner or later implicated in the "widening circles" of sound that circumscribe the poem into the kind of "Pure Art" criticized in the Preface to *Oxford Poetry 1927* for having no purpose other than "its own laws of operation" (Hynes, 397).

Like "the little lark" in *Transitional Poem*, the lark/lyric of "The Ecstatic" also earns the "peace" of its completion, but, as we have come to see, this release and relief seem more reactionary in a suite that calls such personal lyricism into question amidst the deepening contention between the "massing powers" of capitalist status quo and Marxist future. "In Me Two Worlds" pits the future against the past in a contention between "Heir and ancestor," and the last lines of that poem collapse the "theatre of war" within the speaker himself (186). Similarly, the call to action in "Johnny Head-In-Air" is deflated by the last two lines: "Traveller, know, I am here to show / Your own divided heart" (193). "The Ecstatic" immediately follows this admission of ambivalence, and the sequence ends anticlimactically with its last two poems: "Poem for an Anniversary" and "Sonnet." (In the *Collected Poems* of 1954 and the *Complete Poems* of 1992 the sequence of short poems includes two further poems, "Two Songs" and "A Carol"; these are, however, actually remnants from the third movement of the original text of "A Time to Dance," which is omitted from both the later compilations except for these two excerpted passages.)

On the domestic front at Box Cottage, "Poem for an Anniversary" acknowledges that the marriage has passed its "volcanic age" of passion yet urges the wife (and himself) to accept instead a "country made for peace" and fruitful cultivation (194). Indeed, a reading of "The Conflict" in terms of the erotics of politics as well as the politics of eros makes the final lines not just a political admonition but a disaster signal for the marriage at Box Cottage: "Move then with new desires, / For where we used to build and love / Is no man's land" (184). On the political front, the "Sonnet" that ends the sequence of short poems in *A Time to Dance* and thus stands just before the title poem uses the octave and sestet to undermine the image of the hero. The strong, young man who in the octave moves "hard-hearted / Mountains" with "his explosive love" and binds islands with "living cable" into a single world becomes, in the sestet, a worn and aimless "traveller," "insane / As the barking of dogs at the end of a dark lane" (194–95).

Through these ambivalences *A Time to Dance* constituted Day Lewis's first attempt to move beyond the visionary industrial pastoralism of *The Magnetic Mountain.* He hoped he was at last "Learning to Talk" the "plain language" of political poetry, so that, beyond the elite coterie of literati the "people of the plains" (and of the factories and slums) might harken to the "red advance." Then the avant-garde would not be a literary coterie but a mass movement. Though the volume as a whole shows how torn he remained, he had won fame and popularity, even notoriety, as a Red poet. "A Time to Dance" sought, albeit with mixed success, to extend the new voice from elegy and epic into political advocacy more graphic and galvanizing than the utopian generalities of *The Magnetic Mountain.* And his other big Marxist poems followed, pushing, as "Johnny Head-In-Air" pointed, further left ("I look to left, to left, comrades," 192): *Noah and the Waters* in 1936 and "The Nabara" in the 1938 collection *Overtures to Death*.

• 5

After the thirties Day Lewis consistently tried to distance himself from *Noah and the Waters*. He included only the Prologue and two choruses in his *Collected Poems* of 1954 and none of it in *Selected Poems* (1967). Even the description on the dust jacket of the Hogarth Press edition, most of it lifted from his own Author's Foreword, sounded defensive: the work, readers were almost forewarned, was written "in a mixture of poetry, doggerel and rhetoric." The rendering of the flight of Parer and M'Intosh had demonstrated Day Lewis's gift for narrative, but he retold the Noah story for the stage, following other poets of the day in seeking a larger, socially broader audience in the theater. Rupert Doone's Group Theatre in London had presented in 1933 an enthusiastically received production of Auden's *The Dance of Death*, an expressionistic piece with song, dance, and dumb show, and then in 1935 *The Dog Beneath the Skin or Where Is Francis?* Auden's first stage collaboration with Christopher Isherwood. Auden and Doone had stayed with the Day Lewises and encouraged their host to develop a libretto for a choral ballet for performance at the Group Theatre. However, the enormous popular and critical success of Eliot's *Murder in the Cathedral* intervened in 1935 and redirected Day Lewis's project along the lines of medieval drama. In fact, *Noah and the Waters* is Day Lewis's (admittedly less successful) attempt to answer Eliot's Christian morality play about the martyrdom of St. Thomas à Becket with a Marxist morality play about the rising tide of revolution. In the end, however, the attempt at theater was a mistake, and the gloomy prognosis of the Author's Foreword proved correct in judging that *Noah and the Waters* was "probably not . . . suitable as it stands for the modern stage" because he had not turned his idea into a play. Doone made no move toward producing it, and even the playwright could see that "its drama derives largely from the weight and imminence of the issue it represents, and little from any conscious dramatic construction" (217).

"This issue," the Foreword goes on to instruct, "is the choice that must be made by Noah between clinging to his old life and trusting himself to the Flood" (217). The Interlude between the acts of *Murder in the Cathedral* consists of Becket's sermon on the scriptural texts for the Christmas Mass, which made explicit the theme of the play: "Glory to God in the highest, and peace on earth, good will toward men." *Noah and the Waters* places its text up front, after the Foreword, as the superscription:

> "Finally, when the class war is about to be fought to a finish, disintegration of the ruling class and the old order of society becomes so active, so acute, that a small part of the ruling class breaks away to make

common cause with the revolutionary class, the class which holds the
future in its hands. . . ."

The Communist Manifesto

(219)

This classic Marxist text, cited again and again in radical publications
throughout the thirties, would also provide the thematic subtext for Day
Lewis's second novel, *Starting Point*, the next year, and Day Lewis had
already postulated the shift in class loyalties in the conclusion of "A Warning
to Those Who Live in the Mountains":

> Oh little longer
> Will the hand be withheld that hesitates at the wire's end,
> And your time totters like a tenement condemned.
>
> Famous that fall, or shall they tell how in the final
> Moment remaining you changed your mind? (187)

The opening "Prologue" of *Noah and the Waters* offers a lovely aerial
view of pastoral England in the patriotic mode of John of Gaunt's "scep-
tered isle" speech in *Richard II*, and anticipates Day Lewis's return to the
countryside after the debacle of the thirties in his translation of Virgil's
Georgics and in the poems written early in the war. In the *Collected Poems*
Day Lewis rightly preserved, as the best lines of *Noah and the Waters*, the
evocations of the English countryside in the Prologue and choruses, but
by the Prologue's conclusion the focus shifts to the "ugly" town of the
bourgeois status quo and centers on Noah, "the figure of your fate" (224,
225). Day Lewis rewrites the Noah story from Genesis, where the patri-
arch and his family are the only faithful people saved by God from the
worldwide destruction of the Flood, and changes him into a contemporary Everyman who faces the same choice as the speaker in "The Conflict" and "In Me Two Worlds": the capitalist establishment or the Marxist revolution, clumsily personified here in a character named Flood.

Here the Flood is not, as it was in the earlier poetry, the "Eternal Flux"
of nature but the necessity of historical determinism. It is the wave of the
future sweeping away the past, liberating for the masses but deadly to those
who resist its irreversible course. The divisions in Noah's mind and heart
are dramatized through two Voices, the "life-will" and the "death-will,"
Marxist versions of eros and thanatos. Ironically, the "death-will" portrays
its adherence to the status quo as an act of self-preservation, and the "life-
will" demands alliance with the destructive Flood. Like *Murder in the
Cathedral*, *Noah in the Waters* plays out the decisive moral choice by surrounding the protagonist with a sympathetic lyric chorus and four antagonists. The four capitalist Burgesses, modeled on Becket's Tempters, speak
in colloquial prose that is meant to sound ingratiatingly persuasive but
actually works to deconstruct their self-serving case. And, as with Eliot's
Thomas, the climax comes not through action but with a long speech in

which Noah pronounces his right choice: he commits himself and his family
to the Flood. Day Lewis's "divided mind," at least in its dramatic displacement into the character Noah, here resolves its ambivalences, acts in heroic
love, and thereby becomes the Red who should make all the reactionaries
in the town and in the audience feel small.

As the ark sails off on the flood tide, the last chorus foretells "unremitting war" in the town before Noah, like his biblical antecedent, can return,
filled with an all-embracing love, to "a land greener, more great with
growth and ease / Than dreams dared imagine" (260, 261). Thus war and
violence are elided and eclipsed in the pastoral vision of the homeland that
is prehistoric and posthistoric, before and after the historical agon that the
Marxist overthrow will bring to apocalypse. Noah's lone departure on his
chosen course of action makes him seem more like Parer and M'Intosh
than a man of the people, and the working-class Flood, whose unconvincing personification speaks occasionally in multiple voices and at one
ludicrous moment performs a little ballet, remains a conceptual abstraction. (In his vicious review of *Noah and the Waters* Grigson seized the
opportunity to snigger at the depiction of the proletariat as "an undifferentiated mass of H2O" ["Two Whiffs of Lewisite," 17].) The reversion to
pastoral is the fatal sign that Day Lewis had not been able to imagine an
industrial society of liberated workers. It is true that historically pastoral
has frequently become a vehicle for political satire; however, it has also
been fundamentally an aristocratic genre in which satire has sought the
reestablishment of a traditional order rather than revolutionary overthrow.
So in this Marxist allegory the talk about "unremitting war" ends not in
pitched battle but in the restoration of the pastoral ideal imagined in the
dreamlike masquerade of the conclusion. The failure to imagine the revolution is understandable but symptomatic.

A Marxist historian like Raymond Williams can argue that the pastoral
has served—and was intended by the ruling class to serve—the deceptive
and manipulative purpose of masking and thus facilitating the advance of
industrial capitalism. Accurate as this historical observation may be, the
pastoral as myth has also allowed Marxists—theorists as well as artists, including Marx himself—to project the utopian and unrealized society of
classless workers as consonant with nature's harmony by extending its laws
into the arena of human history, of economic laws and social organization. Consequently, however the pastoral myth served the industrialists
and their agents, it served the revolutionary movement against capitalism
by making a connection, in the present and precarious moment of transition, between a prehistorical past and a still undefined future. In a work
like *Noah and the Waters*, therefore, the resort to the pastoral signifies both
the failure and the aspiration of the Marxist imagination.

For these reasons, even after the worst has been said, Day Lewis need
not have been so defensive and apologetic about *Noah and the Waters*. Yes,
it was an experiment that largely failed and remained unproduced. "The
weight and imminence of the issue it represents" remained abstractly mental

rather than imaginatively and dramatically realized, and so his most didactic statement did not reach its intended mass audience. But in fact how could it be otherwise with a class war and a classless society that had not yet happened, that did not even seem imminent to most observers? The reasons for Day Lewis's disappointment with *Noah and the Waters* are clear enough. But what remains significant and compelling—and still moving—about this failed closet drama is the moral and aesthetic seriousness of Day Lewis's effort to achieve a political allegory for a popular audience that resolved the "psychological," "ethical," and "aesthetic" conflicts that had been besetting him and his friends from the start of their movement. It is true that none of the other "MacSpaunday" poets put themselves in the embarrassing position of writing so straightforwardly polemical a work even when dealing with politics: not Spender in *Vienna* (1934) or *Trial of a Judge* (1938), nor Auden in *The Ascent of F6* (1936) or *Spain* (1937) or *Journey to a War* (1939), and certainly not MacNeice even in *Autumn Journal* (1939). This fact has often been taken as evidence of their intellectual sophistication making for ironizing complications and hesitations. But it does not by any means redound entirely to their credit and Day Lewis's discredit that he chose to forsake the safety of ironic distance and risk failure in trying to realize the imperatives of poetry as political action. Indeed, his very failure serves honorably to distinguish his engagement with politics in the thirties from theirs.

• 6

Besides writing verse, Day Lewis was producing a lot of polemical prose during the mid-thirties. *Noah and the Waters* was preceded by *Revolution in Writing* (1935, the year of *A Time to Dance* as well as the detective novel *A Question of Proof*) and followed in 1937 by *The Mind in Chains: Socialism and the Cultural Revolution*, a collection of essays, edited and introduced by Day Lewis, on a range of cultural areas by leading members of the leftist and Communist intelligentsia, among them Anthony Blunt, Edgell Rickword, Charles Madge, and Day Lewis's good friend Rex Warner (but noticeably neither Spender nor Auden nor MacNeice). At the same time, Day Lewis was writing steadily for a number of journals, notably the *Left Review*, and was increasingly visible as organizer and speaker at public demonstrations and mass rallies.

Overtures to Death (1938) was his last volume of poetry in the thirties and his first volume, after almost ten years' association with the Hogarth Press, to appear from Jonathan Cape, the house that remained the principal publisher of his poetry for the rest of his life. In some of these poems Day Lewis is still, for all the polemical prose, seeking to jolt himself from the convoluted daydreaming of bourgeois individualism—specifically from self-regarding "contemplation" and from "womanish" self-questioning and "reflection"—into a manly and heroic "act of decision" (287, 288, 289). Poems like "In the Heart of Contemplation," "Questions," and "Self-Criticism and Answer" indicate that he continued to feel inwardly uncertain about the public acts of political declaration he was increasingly demanding of himself. It was becoming harder and harder to blink away the fact that such activities cut across the grain of his temperament and training, and took precious time from his private and poetic life.

On top of this nagging personal hesitation came disturbing news of what was happening to the Bolshevik experiment under the dictatorship of Stalin: the purges, trials, and executions of dissidents and opponents, the iron imposition of Party rule, the ruthless suppression of intellectual and artistic independence, the unprincipled shifts in policy for advantage in consolidating power. At home the British Communist Party seemed to swallow Stalinism blindly and impose on its members unquestioning loyalty to the official line. Later Day Lewis would condemn as "the basic fault in Communist practice" "its pursuit of ends regardless of the corrupting and dehumanising effect of the means employed, its opportunistic turns of policy, and the lies to which it committed one" (*The Buried Day*, 212).

At the same time, the Stalinist dictatorship of the left was matched by the fascist totalitarianism that had already gripped Italy and Germany and was threatening to take over Spain under the leadership of Generalissimo Franco. The fact that Stalin could make a nonaggression pact with Hitler even as the Nazi blitzkrieg flattened Europe would bring the totalitarian threat closer to home territory and strain political allegiances to the breaking point. Consequently, as the thirties "stumbled on towards the precipice" of world war (*The Buried Day*, 220), the anticipated class war between British workers and capitalists became overshadowed by the need to draw together a Popular Front to oppose the expansionist aggression of Hitler and Mussolini. London was already preparing against the blitz that would in fact come in another few years. Almost everyone regarded the Spanish Civil War as the rehearsal for that apocalyptic confrontation.

In *Authors Take Sides on the Spanish War*, a collection of responses to a questionnaire published in 1937 by the *Left Review*, Eliot chose to "take no part" despite his expression of sympathy; Pound fumed that the point of the questionnaire was misplaced; and a few, notably Evelyn Waugh, would not condemn Franco and back the Republic because it was too far left. Day Lewis's unequivocal statement cast the conflict with quasi-religious fervor almost as a Miltonic struggle between angelic and demonic forces:

> The struggle in Spain is part of a conflict going on now all over the world. I look upon it quite simply as a battle between light and darkness, of which only a blind man could be unaware. Both as a writer and as a member of the Communist Party I am bound to help in the fight against Fascism, which means certain destruction or living death for humanity.

Even MacNeice was drawn into public commitment, and Spender made it a matter of ingrained and patriotic English liberalism: "I support in Spain exactly such a movement of liberal and liberating nationalism as the English liberals supported in many countries still groaning under feudalism in the nineteenth century." Day Lewis's "The Volunteer" is a ringingly patriotic ballad spoken by a representative of the heroes willing to fight and die in Spain in order to defeat the fascists and save England for freedom and the coming downfall of capitalism, and the poem is situated in *Overtures to Death* to lead immediately into "The Nabara," one of the two long poems around which the volume is constructed.

For his narrative Day Lewis adapted an episode from G. L. Steer's *The Tree of Gernika* about the republican loyalty and valor of the fated Basque fishermen who pitted their four trawlers against the armored firepower of one of Franco's cruisers. In order to raise the sea fight to epic heights, Day Lewis used Greek-like hexameters, heavily stressed and alliterated like the Anglo-Saxon sagas, all laid out in a tightly rhymed (a–b–b–a–b c–d–d–c–d) stanza reminiscent of Spenser's *Faerie Queene* or Hopkins's "The Wreck of the Deutschland." The dust jacket of reprintings of *Overtures to Death* prominently displayed G. M. Young's praise of "The Nabara" in his rave review of the book in *The Listener*: "It is the voice . . . of a great poet, writing in the great tradition, not as a pupil, but as a master. . . . I should like to have it on record that in 1938 someone had the wit to foresee that in 2038 Day Lewis's *Nabara* would be numbered among the great English poems." And indeed "The Nabara" continues, for all its unfashionably drum-rolling rhetoric, to be read and enjoyed, cited and anthologized as one of the best English narrative poems of the century.

The poem apostrophizes the fisherman as folk heroes with the refrain, "Men of the Basque country, the Mar Cantabrico," and the power of the poem derives from the fact that the strong, mesmerizing rhythms present the account from the outset as heroic but also tragic. The last two stanzas stand as a coda, with a variant rhyme scheme, that contrasts the fishermen's sacrifice for country and humanity with the craven cowardice of the British politicians whose official neutrality temporizes in order to preserve their rotten life of privilege a little longer:

They bore not a charmed life. They went into battle foreseeing
Probable loss, and they lost. The tides of Biscay flow
Over the obstinate bones of many, the winds are sighing
Round prison walls where the rest are doomed like their ships
         to rust—
Men of the Basque country, the Mar Cantabrico.
Simple men who asked of their life no mythical splendor,
They loved its familiar ways so well that they preferred
In the rudeness of their heart to die rather than surrender . . .
Mortal these words, and the deed they remember, but cast
         a seed
Shall flower for an age when freedom is man's creative word.

Freedom was more than a word, more than the base coinage
Of politicians who hiding behind the skirts of peace
They had defiled, gave up that country to rack and carnage:
For whom, indelibly stamped with history's contempt,
Remains but to haunt the blackened shell of their policies.
For these I have told of, freedom was flesh and blood—a mortal
Body, the gun-breech hot to its touch: yet the battle's height
Raised it to love's meridian and held it awhile immortal;
And its light through time still flashes like a star's that has turned
                                                            to ashes,
Long after *Nabara*'s passion was quenched in the sea's heart.   (301–2)

The defiant fishermen are doomed to defeat by the mechanized might of
the fascist juggernaut, and the battle becomes a (quite conscious) foreshad-
owing of the outcome of the whole Spanish Civil War.

The fascist advance made the political left veer between grandly defiant
elegies for a defeated cause, like the passage quoted above, and frenzied
resolves not to capitulate. On the brink of the Spanish Civil War, Day
Lewis had fired off an immediate riposte to Aldous Huxley's pacifist pamphlet *What Are You Going to Do about It?* with his pamphlet *We're Not
Going to Do Nothing*, published and distributed by the *Left Review*. Now,
right at the beginning of *Overtures to Death* "February 1936," " Bombers," "A Parting Shot," and "Newsreel" voice the chilled and numbed
foreboding that it was already too late to escape catastrophe. As we shall
see, the title-sequence stands as counterpole to "The Nabara," paralleling
the political crisis with a tragic loss in the poet's emotional life. The following line catches the pervasive sense of doom that gripped Day Lewis
and his contemporaries in the late thirties: "Earth shakes beneath us: we
imagine loss" ("Bombers," 269).

Day Lewis could still turn out the propaganda poem for the occasion.
In 1938, the same year as the publication of *Overtures to Death*, he contributed "On the Twentieth Anniversary of Soviet Power" to E. A. Osborne's
anthology *In Letters of Red*, hailing Lenin as the hero, "loved by the people,"
whose mind like "an oxy-acetylene flame / Sheared through the crust of
centuries" to release "man's long-exiled love." Here "Soviet power" is still
the bulwark against fascist conquest: "wherever / Man cries against the
oppressors 'They shall not pass,' / Your frontiers stand. Be sure we shall defend
them" (*In Letters of Red*, 154–55). But the Hitler-Stalin Pact of 1939 exploded
any further illusions, and Day Lewis never reprinted this piece again. The
prosy flatness and cliched hyperbole of the language told him that his mind
and imagination could not sustain what he was saying.

A sonnet at the heart of *Overtures to Death* constructs for one last time
the image of an industrialized, electrified utopia that Day Lewis had been
daydreaming since *From Feathers to Iron* and *The Magnetic Mountain*. But
the title, "When they have Lost," reveals, perhaps unwittingly, the rising
conviction that the flood of history, far from being a Marxist revolution,
was on the verge of sweeping it all away:

Then shall the mounting stages of oppression
Like mazed and makeshift scaffolding torn down
Reveal his unexampled, best creation—
The shape of man's necessity full-grown.
Built from their bone, I see a power-house stand
To warm men's hearts again and light the land. (286–87)

"Sonnet for a Political Worker" again sounds somewhat outdated, as it uses the form that Milton and Wordsworth had sanctioned for political purposes to rally a flagging, doubt-torn conviction. The scattered and flickering expressions of hope in this book—"Our life-blood springs to liberty" (273), "Our war is life itself and shall not fail" (280)—are surrounded by omens of disintegration and loss. "Regency Houses" describes the graceful remnants of a dead social hierarchy; "Landscapes" contrasts the "private elegance" of the old landed aristocrats with the squalid rapacity of the urban nouveaux riches, but views both as landscapes of "dissolution" (273). The past is well dead, the present well dying; but these poems present no prospective future, only overtures to death.

The confrontation with death in this book is personal as well as political. The fifth of seven sections in "Overtures to Death" is an elegy for Frank Day-Lewis, who died in July 1937, shortly after a visit to Box Cottage chilled by the long since accustomed reserve that muted the love between clergyman father and agnostic son and between the son as husband and his wife as mother. Day Lewis remembered the relationship with his father as "my first and longest ordeal by love" (*The Buried Day*, 155). More than the death of his friend and contemporary Hedges, the loss of his father, so like him in ways neither could admit, aroused the anxiety about his own mortality that had beset him since childhood, beginning with the loss of his mother at the age of four. Now the lead poem in *Overtures to Death*, "Maple and Sumach," presents the poet as spokesman "for all who are to die!" (267). "Passage from Childhood," at the end of the volume, recounts as his first memory a dream of a brimming "china cup somewhere / In a green, deep wood," now irrecoverable (307), and the poem goes on to rehearse his old nightmare in which "Eternity stretched like a howl of pain," its immensity reducing him to a "pin / On a glacier's floor." Self-alienation lets the speaker describe himself in the third person:

He's one more ghost, engaged to keep
Eternity's long hours and mewed
Up in live flesh with no escape
From solitude. (308)

And in a further degree of alienation not he but, more abstractly, "[h]is life walks in a glacial sleep / For ever."

Frank Day-Lewis's death also sharpened the son's anxiety about his other familial "ordeal by love" in his marriage with Mary. From the time of their long courtship in the twenties she had been shy and reserved in the face of her suitor's sexual ardor, and she remained so after marriage. Her closest and most personal relationships were with women, and she defined her role in the marriage primarily in maternal rather than sexual terms, even with her husband. Her love provided an all-suffering, self-sacrificing security and support. She made first Box Cottage, and then after 1938 their new cottage, Brimclose, both heart and hearth for husband and two growing boys. But for Day Lewis the home-haven the son in him loved came also to seem an enclosure that, for all its comfort, became increasingly associated with sterility and impotence. He had romanticized Mary in his early poems, and he was finding domestic love calming but not stimulating or creative. *From Feathers to Iron* had been dedicated to Mary not by name but by her archetypal function: "To the Mother"; but he was finding that when the wife became mother, she did not remain lover. His reaction was deeply ambivalent: the early loss of his mother drew him to Mary's motherliness but also made him resist the stifling possessiveness that could keep men boys.

The tension between sexuality and domesticity is, as we have seen, the subtext of *From Feathers to Iron* in its account of the first pregnancy in the marriage. In *The Magnetic Mountain* women are explicitly portrayed as dominating, emasculating, severing a man from action in the larger social world. The closing lines of Poem 19 satirize the maternal threat of male infantilization:

> Lock the front door, here are your slippers,
> Get out your toys and don't make a noise;
> Don't tease the keepers, eat up your kippers,
> And you'll have a treat one day if you're good boys.   (154–55)

The mother can become the possessor, and the child, especially the son, the submissive narcissist. By the time of "Questions" in *Overtures to Death* the speaker seeks to expel from himself the introjected power of the mother, abhorring his self-involvement as "feminine," his impotent wavering as "womanish" (288). The identification of hero and lover at the end of *The Magnetic Mountain* has, then, a double significance: on the political level, the Red hero must be a lover of humankind, but on a personal and psychological level the lover had to be a hero—that is, a man and not a boy. The Day Lewises' cottage was named after the box hedge around it, but as the thirties drew on, he began to feel boxed into it. The cottage belonged to "the Mother," and the peace and warmth of home life that part of him wanted and enjoyed seemed at the same time to sap his potency and creativity. One result was that he threw himself into literary associations and political activities outside and beyond Box Cottage with all the passion he could command. Mary tolerated and entertained political or literary visitors at the cottage from time to time, but it was clear that poetry and communism were both viewed as extrinsic, perhaps inimical to the functioning of her world.

Another result was, as we shall see, that he looked beyond the cottage for the life of desire and poetry. The pattern of the gender roles he and Mary played is more typical than unusual, especially in its time, and in many ways Day Lewis accepted and acquiesced in it. He and Mary were to cling to the arrangement for a long time, but their life together became increasingly drained of passion and intimacy. As a result his life became more and more sharply divided between the cottage and the world outside, which became for him the open space of men and pubs, of political meetings and literary associations, and also, in time, of sexual encounter with women more passionate than Mary. In 1936 Day Lewis was drawn to recall and fictionalize in *The Friendly Tree* (his first novel outside of detective fiction) his infatuation five years before with Alison Morris during Mary's first pregnancy; the triangular situation supplies the basis for the climax and resolution of the novel. He had covertly acknowledged it in *From Feathers to Iron*, and Sean Day Lewis's biography reports that his father "maintained a platonic friendship with Alison for some years" after giving up the pursuit of a sexual affair and cites a previously unpublished sonnet that Day Lewis sent her to memorialize the passion they had felt (Sean Day Lewis, 69):

Remember how your cool and woodland eyes
Caught fire once from the sun and burned for me,
How at high summer stretched before the sea
Your naked breasts tore heaven by surprise.
Over the world of heather where we lay
Joy like a kestrel hovered in the wind,
He swooped, he soared, he left the wind behind
Carrying our sweet bodies worlds away.

In other poems of the period the kestrel symbolizes the individual of far-seeing vision and political will, but here those heroic associations are incarnated in the man (the kestrel is "he") of sexual passion and potency. In *From Feathers to Iron* and in *The Friendly Tree*, as in biographical fact, the episode ends with the husband's return to the wife and mother, but the return did not address, much less redress, the ongoing problem or that cherished moment of the kestrel's joyful swooping and soaring.

In *A Time to Dance* "Moving In" again touched obliquely on the problem, and "Poem for an Anniversary" skirted it by saying to the wife-mother (and of course to himself) that the more tranquil years of fruitful marital cultivation within the domestic circle compensated amply for the subsiding of the passion that generated the family. By 1938 the early poems in *Overtures to Death* sound muted complaints of sterility and impotence. "Maple and Sumach," the first poem, contrasts the erotic opulence with which nature reaches its annual climax—"You leaves drenched with the lifeblood of the year— / What flamingo dawns have wavered from the east, / What eves have crimsoned to their toppling crest"—with the hemophiliac collapse of the human climacteric: "His fall is short of pride, he bleeds within / And paler creeps to the dead end of his days" (267). In this context lines like the following from "Regency Houses" register personal as well as social anxiety: "Are we living—we too, / Living extravagant farce / In the finery of spent passions?" (272). "Sex-Crime" asks for sympathy not just for the victim of rape and murder but for the man driven (by social injustice? by psychological repression?) to such sexual violence.

The lyrics that are placed at the end of the book—"Spring Song," "Night Piece," "Song"—speak explicitly of frustrated tumescence and a longing for release. In "Song" the speaker, whose "love was shy to trespass," laments the "ten-year-long regret" that has turned his beloved into a "graceful ghost" (305). "Night Piece" dreams of a consummation in which "the impotent is made straight, / The ice-queen delighted, / And the virgin loves to moan" (303). And "Spring Song" concludes with this saucy, punning quatrain:

> Now the bee finds the pollen,
> The pale boy a cure:
> Who care if in the sequel
> Cocky shall be crestfallen?   (303)

Loss of innocence is a motif that recurs in several of these poems, and one of them, "The Three Cloud Maidens," says in self-accusation that the confusions and violences "that hurt / Innocence, all arise / Out of your shallow heart" (304). "The Escapist" describes with cool distaste the "self-vindictiveness" of a man who has shunned public recrimination for an unnamed transgression but is "already / Self-flayed and branded in his heart for ever" (306). When these poems were written, the fantasy of transgression and self-accusation transpired only in the poet's fevered imagination, but before the year in which *Overtures to Death* was published had ended, he would meet the woman with whom, as we shall see, he would have his first serious extramarital affair.

At the same time, "The Bells That Signed" sounds a different but recurrent note in Day Lewis's poetry: the agnostic materialist's persistent yearning for transcendence of unsatisfied mortality, for some realization "more heavenly" and absolute than either politics or sex. The last quatrain describes the stale and sour residue of political and sexual conquest:

> Broods the stone-lipped conqueror still
> Abject upon his iron hill,
> And lovers in the naked beds
> Cry for more than maidenheads.   (276)

"Behold the Swan" also uses the word "broods" to describe the Yeatsian swan's rejection of the "complacent" bounds of the still pond, as she breaks free and strains "toward the horizon":

Her wings bear hard
On the vibrant air: unhurried
The threat and pulse of wings, the throat
Levelled toward the horizon, see—
They are prophecy.   (305)

Yet, as characteristically happens in Day Lewis's poetry, the swan's (or kestrel's or hawk's) ascent to sublimity does not break through mortal limits but ends in descent to earth, like the lark's, and accommodation to life's passing moment and bounded space. The "prophecy" remains unfulfilled.

But what if, as he wonders in "Self-Criticism and Answer," the fact that he has never been "possessed / By divine incontinence" has made his poetry "too meticulous" and "careful," "[i]ts agonies . . . but the eager / Retching of an empty heart" (309)? Urgent passages throughout the volume seek to counter death's overtures by learning to live actively in time. Lines from the title sequence offer as the "best" of humankind those who advance "life's green standards . . . to the limit of your [that is, death's] salt unyielding zone" (284, 285). Other lines pray of death itself: "Teach us the value of our stay / Lest we insult the living clay," for "Only this clay can voice, invest, / Measure and frame our mortal best" (281). Wallace Stevens had put the naturalist's credo in much the same terms in "Sunday Morning": "Death is the mother of beauty"; and for Day Lewis, as for Stevens, the poem is an instrument for living in time.

The sequence of four verbs in those lines from "Overtures"—"voice, invest, / Measure and frame our mortal best"—is extremely significant. The poem voiced into the world is an investing of embodied self in the world of experience; and the word "invest" carries the force of all these meanings: committing something valuable for expected gain or return; endowing with authority or power; providing with a pervasive or distinctive quality; clothing and adorning. That rich investment makes the "best" of mortality because accepting its limits makes it possible to realize them more fully. Besides, the voicing of that investment entails a formal framing or structuring for the measuring (precise delineation, metrical organization) of that "mortal best." Stevens is known for the gaudy gorgeousness of his language, but in the course of "In the Heart of Contemplation" Day Lewis arrives at a similarly gorgeous, globed moment in which the speaker and his beloved recover innocence and wholeness, bound (united, but also contained and defined) within the harmony of their pastoral world:

In the act of decision only,
In the hearts cleared for action like lovers naked
For love, this shadow vanishes: there alone
There is nothing between our lives for it to thrive on.
You and I with lilac, lark and oak-leafed
Valley are bound together
As in the astounded clarity before death.
Nothing is innocent now but to act for life's sake.   (287)

It is easier, of course, for Stevens's language to be gaudy because it remains studiously folded in the convoluted contemplations of what he called "the *mundo* of the imagination" (*The Necessary Angel*, 57–58). He made no bones about choosing aestheticism over politics, and Marxists called him a reactionary hedonist for his escapist stance. But, precisely because Day Lewis was a Marxist, he could not allow himself to rest in the cocoon of contemplation. In the poem just quoted "the act of decision" is a love commitment, but he continued to hope, despite evidence to the contrary, that the individual love act that starts a family might extend itself into a loving solidarity with the masses to reconstruct the whole social structure. However, the deepening melancholia of *Overtures to Death* shows his locked and "divided heart" at such an impasse in both his personal and political life that Day Lewis wondered whether he could act decisively in either sphere:

> Do you need the horn in your ear, the hounds at your heel,
> Gadflies to sting you sore,
> The lightning's angry feint, and all
> The horizon's clouds boiling like lead, before
> You'll risk your javelin dive
> And pierce reflection's heart, and come alive?   (289)

"Self-Criticism and Answer," the last poem in the volume, is a final injunction to the hesitating Noah in himself to yield to the "flooding indignation" that "channels the dry heart deeper / And sings through the dry bone" (310). Where was the "power-house . . . [to] warm men's hearts again and light the land" (287)? Political and marital anxiety as the worlds "stumbled to the precipice" of war left hanging the question of whether he would ever come passionately alive in a world charged with revolutionary fervor. What he knew in 1938 was that both at home and abroad "[e]arth shakes beneath us: we imagine loss" (269).

• 7

In the Preface to a 1951 selection of his work, published by Penguin, Day Lewis commented that "during my so-called 'political' period, most of my poems were in fact about love or death" (10). But it would be more accurate to say that the poetry of the thirties turns on the complicated connections and tensions between politics, eros, and thanatos: the three topoi that form the interconnected but shifting emphases of the chapters of this book. In Day Lewis's own words, "D. H. Lawrence got mixed into my Marxism," so that he saw the System botching not only social relations but also "the relationship between man and woman, poisoning it with a false idealism that encouraged only the self-conscious and cerebral sides of our nature" (*The Buried Day*, 210). During the writing of *From Feathers to Iron* he found a correlation "quite spontaneously" between his and Mary's expectation of a child and the foreshadowings of a new social order, "so that I could use naturally for metaphors and metaphysical conceits the apparatus of the modern world, the machinery which, made for the benefit of all, could help this world to rebirth." "For myself as a writer," he maintained, "the most potent element . . . was an interplay and consonance between the inner and the outward life, between public meaning and private meaning" (*The Buried Day*, 218). Now, however, seven eventful years after *From Feathers to Iron*, the burgeoning promise of his political and emotional commitments had dried up, and he felt the grip of sterile paralysis. The starting point had quickly moved to the breaking point, and in 1938 Day Lewis could not see past the disaster descending fast on him and the whole of Europe.

The publication of a celebratory ode "On the Twentieth Anniversary of Soviet Power," in the same year as the apocalyptic *Overtures to Death* seemed an empty echo of another era, and in fact Day Lewis left the Party in the summer of 1938—but without a "public break," because he still "felt no antipathy yet for Communist theory, and not much for Communist practice" (*The Buried Day*, 224). He "slipped the painter" of the Cheltenham cell effectively but "noiselessly" by moving his family from Box Cottage to Brimclose, in the Devonshire town of Musbury near the Dorset border, where there was no Red cell. Beyond the reports of Stalinist repression and the heartbreaking loss of Spain to fascism, his reasons for fading out were, to a large extent, personal. He found Party rule inflexible and Party jargon abstract and inhumane. Party discipline, which he had embraced in the 1933 "Letter to a Young Revolutionary," suspected and repressed individual thought and feeling and creative expression. Even Day Lewis's admirers told him what he could no longer deny to himself. A sharply phrased review of *Noah and the Waters* by Edwin Muir, till then an enthusiastic supporter of his work, gnawed at his poetic conscience and helped, in Day Lewis's pun, in "showing me the red light"; and T. E. Lawrence, who a few years earlier had hailed him as the "one great man in these islands," wrote shortly before his death to advise Day Lewis to stick to poetry and "leave politics to the politicians" (*The Buried Day*, 222). When he became convinced that ideological thinking and public speech had begun to impoverish the quality of his language and constrict the scope of his feeling and expression, Day Lewis acted in self-preservation and quietly quit the Party, less than two years after officially joining.

In retrospect Day Lewis could tick off the failures of the literary leftists of the time:

The errors of judgment, the naiveté, the muddle-headedness are obvious enough today. In a tricky, darkening decade we were a generation which had not vision equal to desire. Such vision as we had was adul-

terated by fantasy, and little of our verse reconciled its objective, classical
ends with the romantic cast of mind we inherited from our predecessors.

(*The Buried Day*, 217)

Yet out of respect for what they had aimed for, Day Lewis did not rewrite
himself or his poems, as Auden and Spender did, correcting or silently
dropping poems from the canon they wished to preserve. He was so conflicted about omitting from the *Collected Poems* of 1954 most of *Noah and
the Waters* and of the polemical third part of *A Time to Dance* that his honesty required him to alert the reader to the deletions. He did not excul-
pate his errors, as Spender and other crusading ex-Communists did in *The
God That Failed*. Nor did he capitulate as Auden did, blaming a "low dishonest decade" (in "September 1, 1939") and protesting (in the Yeats elegy
of the next year) that "poetry makes nothing happen," as he withdrew to
the relatively safe distance of the United States.

Day Lewis just moved to Brimclose without apology or explanation, and
neither then nor later did he betray or belittle the heartfelt idealism that had
inflamed him and many of his literary contemporaries during the thirties:

> There was generosity as well as absurdity in this, for my friends and I
> did at least make some attempt to imagine the conditions we did not
> share, the unemployment and malnutrition which had been rotting the
> heart out of a million working-class families, and we were prepared to
> help destroy a system that perpetuated itself by such hideous human
> wastage, even though our own pleasant way of life would be destroyed
> in the process.
>
> (*The Buried Day*, 210)

His vision, he came to see, was not equal to his desire, but it was vision he
burned for. He had dutifully read Marx and Engels and Lenin (though his
generation did not know of contemporary Marxists like Theodor Adorno
or Walter Benjamin on the continent), had tried to profess it in cell meetings, to preach it at rallies. But his Marxist beliefs were, he knew all along,
"substitutes for a faith":

> We had all, I think, lapsed from the Christian faith, and tended to de-
> spair of Liberalism as an effective instrument for dealing with the
> problems of our day, if not to despise it as an outworn creed. Inocu-
> lated against Roman Catholicism by the religion of my youth, I dimly
> felt the need for a faith which had the authority, the logic, the cut-
> and-driedness of the Roman church—a faith that would fill the void
> left by the leaking away of traditional religion, would make sense of
> our troubled times and make real demands on me.
>
> (*The Buried Day*, 209)

In fact, he saw Marxism as a materialist extension of the ethical message of
the New Testament: "[W]e felt 'from each according to his ability, to each
according to his need' or 'freedom is the knowledge of necessity' to be
concepts as inspiring as Christ's sayings in the Sermon on the Mount" (*The
Buried Day*, 208).

Not economics but a vision of human possibilities beyond middle-class individualism drove him to direct time and energy away from family and poetry to the cause: "I cannot regret that desire to be committed, that positive sense of engagement, which our upbringing and the weather of the times combined to produce." The hope was to act "as individuals but for a common end" and specifically "as writers, to bridge the old romantic chasm between the artist and the man of action, the poet and the ordinary man" (*The Buried Day*, 218). Thereby the poet would function as Shelleyan "spokesman of society," and language could function as an "instrument of action." Aware of "the risk our poetry was running" in extending lyric poetry to didactic and even propagandistic ends, "we did at any rate prefer taking a risk to burying our talent in a napkin"—especially since "we viewed political action, and the writing of verse with a social content as *temporary* necessities" in the struggle for the new order ("The Thirties in Retrospect," 10–11, 14, 23). The dashed hopes and shattered idealism needed no exculpation: "[N]o-one who did not go through this political experience during the Thirties can quite realise how much hope there was in the air then, how radiant for some of us was the illusion that man could, under Communism, put the world to rights" (*The Buried Day*, 211). Indeed, for lack of a more substantial vision, *faute de mieux*, "poetry can thrive on illusions" ("The Thirties in Retrospect," 16).

Yet the bourgeois liberal individualism that underlay and even prompted the attraction of "the Auden generation" to Marxism left them open to criticism not only from rightists like Roy Campbell and Wyndham Lewis but also from Communist Party regulars like Christopher Caudwell. *Illusion and Reality*, published in 1937 after his death fighting Franco in the Spanish Civil War, is a study, as its subtitle said, of "the sources of poetry" from the perspective of doctrinaire Marxism. In Caudwell's schema of the rise and decline of bourgeois poetry he placed the "communist revolutionary position" (132) adopted by Auden, Day Lewis, and Spender in what he designated "The Final Capitalist Crisis, 1930—?" He summarized that historical phase as follows: "*The People's Front.*—Poetry now expresses a real revolt against bourgeois conditions by an alliance of the bourgeois ideologist or 'craftsman' with the proletariat against the bourgeoisie. France still leads: Aragon, Gide, etc. In England: [Day] Lewis, Auden and Spender."

Caudwell saw their reaction against the decadent aestheticism of the fin de siècle and its Georgian aftermath as a move in the direction of inaugurating "a complete change of the whole content of poetry" (138). However, he could see the Oxford poets only as "fellow travellers" (312), writing out of their bourgeois conventions and traditions, whereas the new society required new speech and new forms. He conceded that those revolutionary forms had to wait for the revolution and that in this "Final Capitalistic" phase "[t]he question of form now tends to take a second place until the problem of social relations has been solved poetically"(138). Yet at the same time he could not but single out the disparity between content and form in Day Lewis, Auden, and Spender as the sign and consequence of a deficiency in their revolutionary attitude. They admitted that they were, as Day Lewis's poem put it, barely "learning to talk," but for Caudwell their Marxist talk, sincere as he granted it to be, masked a lingering adhesion to bourgeois roots that kept them caught in the old ways, including the old poetic ways, and thus prevented them from imagining the forms and language commensurate with the Marxist society they hailed. Caudwell had no sympathy for the formal experiments of the Modernists, but he regretted that his English contemporaries lacked the capacity for achieving a genuinely Marxist aesthetic: "[T]hey have no constructive theory—I mean as artists: they may as economists accept the economic categories of socialism, but as artists they cannot see the new forms and contents of an art which will replace bourgeois art" (312).

As a result, their efforts to imagine revolutionary content can only express itself by veering, in Caudwell's words, between "evolving backwards" into a nostalgic pastoralism and/or vague prophecies of "forward movement and blind presage" (313). Caudwell's analysis is an accurate enough commentary and helps to explain the often calculatedly jarring conjunction of pastoral and industrial imagery in the poetry of the thirties. What is more, a confirmed Party liner like Caudwell felt that the engrained individualism of the Auden "group" kept them from the development that a totalizing commitment to Marxism might bring. From his perspective, their fuss about propaganda and artistic freedom betrayed "a typically bourgeois conception of the artist as a man whose role is to be a lone wolf, a man who realises beauty for society only because he is exempt from contemporary social restraints" (316). Any attempt "to patchwork this conception into proletarian theory" is bound, Caudwell warned, to show the patchwork.

At the same time, Caudwell could not be any more censorious of the poems of "[Day] Lewis, Auden, and Spender" than of his own efforts. Even granted that Caudwell's Marxist career was prematurely cut off—from late 1934 when he began to read Marx to his death in Spain in early 1937—his posthumous *Poems* (1939) are written in conventional forms and are still mostly concerned with the vagaries of love and art, of philosophical certitude and religious faith—precisely the personal concerns of the post-Romantic poet that Caudwell shared with Day Lewis and his group. In fact, the "Poet's Invocation" written to open *Point of Departure* (a collection he prepared for possible publication whose title echoes that of Day Lewis's political novel *Starting Point*) assumes a bourgeois individualism in which poetry speaks "of oneself" and "to one's self" (*Collected Poems*, 65). An elegy for T. E. Lawrence in *Point of Departure* expresses the kind of hero-worship of the desert fighter, despite his politics, that Day Lewis and many of his generation expressed.

No wonder, then, that from a proper revolutionary viewpoint Caudwell described his poems (in a letter written to a friend before departing for the battlefront) as belonging "to my dishonest and sentimental past" (Alan Young, Introduction, *Collected Poems*, 10). The verses contain occasional and isolated references to the "beastly bourgeois air" of the leisured class and offer brief satiric epigrams "On a Tory M. P." and "On an Employer of Native Child Labor" (*Collected Poems*, 76, 90, 91). But the only Communist poem—indeed almost the only political poem of more than a couple of lines—in the 1986 *Collected Poems* (expanded greatly from the posthumous *Poems*) is "Heil Baldwin," 642 mock-heroic lines denouncing the Nazis (with Popean portraits of Hitler, Goebbels, Goering, etc.) and the complicitous British establishment, personified in Stanley Baldwin, the prime minister who in 1935 had signed a Naval Agreement with Germany. Even in Caudwell's single Communist poem, only the final twenty-odd lines rise above the satiric derision to voice a revolutionary prophecy— but written in neoclassical couplets:

> Where God, the League [of Nations], justice, abuse and prayer
> And even kindness fails, must you despair.
> You captives, hidden from the light of day?
> You workers, free to toil, yet crushed as they?
> No! Unimpassioned as the changing sky
> Resolves the dialectic, History. . . .
> . · . · . · . · . · . · . ·
>   In those bright flames, presage of brighter day,
> The rubbish of these years will melt away
> And, like a man from nightmare glad to wake,
> This land will see the dawn, the red dawn, break,
> And over ruined Nazidom unfurled
> The second banner of the classless world.
> <div align="right">(<i>Collected Poems</i>, 114–15)</div>

By comparison, even a propagandistic piece like "Yes, why do we all, seeing a Red, feel small?" seems less blunt and jargon-ridden.

The fact is that there was no real proletarian poetry, and it fell to leftist poets like Auden's group and a few others (notably Hugh MacDiarmid in Scotland) to begin to clear the way for it. Day Lewis and his peers did not delude themselves that they shared or understood or could speak for the workers' experiences, and they honestly acknowledged their bourgeois roots. Spender's *Forward from Liberalism*, published in the same year as *Illusion and Reality*, pointed the direction for all of them. Spender even took on Caudwell's critique directly, and in offering a rebuttal reversed the hypothetical position he had tentatively postulated in "Revolution and Literature" that the bourgeois artist should give up art and devote himself to politics:

> Whilst accepting its validity as a critical attitude [that is, Caudwell's complaint that the would-be revolutionaries of the "MacSpaunday" group were still bourgeois and individualist], may we not say that the position of the writer who sees the conflict as something which is at once subjective to himself and having its external reality in the world— the position outlined in Auden's *Spain* [and, as we have seen, in Day

Lewis's poetry of the thirties]—is one of the most creative, realistic and valid positions for the artist in our time?

("Oxford to Communism," 10)

Moreover, the Oxford poets were as aware as Caudwell of the anomaly of a radical message in "reactionary form"; Day Lewis would admit: "[W]e didn't use the revolutionary techniques which Eliot had used, and which Ezra Pound had used. And they made the poetic revolution. And we didn't carry it on at all. . . . I see now we were almost reactionary. We reacted away from a kind . . . of extreme novelty" ("On a Tilting Deck," 4). The real point at issue was whether revolution required new forms and a new grammar for a new sense of things or whether revolution was advanced more effectively by making the shared grammar and the given forms the means to revolutionary ends. Was revolution a function of form or content? Were forms in themselves inescapably political? Day Lewis and his friends responded by rejecting the experimentation of the Modernists, many of whom were right wing and even inclined toward fascism, as elitist and scornful of the reading public who needed political conversion. At the same time, the search for revolutionary forms was balked on the left by the socialist realism that was imposed on Soviet art by the Party. Soviet sympathizers like Spender and Day Lewis might not admire the Modernists' aesthetic, but they could at least empathize with them as artists, especially in the face of the Stalinist repression that had purged Modernism and exiled artists from the revolution.

The rejection of esoteric Modernism, on the one hand, and crudely manipulative socialist realism, on the other, served to constrict, from both the Left and the Right, the "attempt to imagine the conditions we did not share" (*The Buried Day*, 210). In the end, therefore, the poets in the "Final Capitalist" phase were left with only the traditional bourgeois forms to handle contemporary content: a world either in its death throes or in the fight for revolutionary rebirth. Caudwell might call it a flawed and flimsy patchwork to use the old forms they were trained in for the new message, but they found that they could only work with what they had in hand. One reason that Day Lewis's career in the thirties is important is that he engages and illustrates the critical issues of form and content, art and propaganda, more fully and tellingly even than his closest contemporaries.

Within "MacSpaunday," of course, MacNeice was such an anomaly that he did not belong there except through his association with Auden in the early and middle thirties. In the 1947 snapshot that is the closest thing to a "group" portrait, MacNeice is the one missing (it is also the only photograph of the other three together). Though MacNeice shared the general sense of personal, social, and cultural crisis, his cool reserve and ironic scepticism kept him, as Day Lewis observed, "untouched by political Communism" (*The Buried Day*, 217). In "A Statement" to *New Verse* in 1938 MacNeice summed up his position:

The world no doubt needs propaganda, but propaganda . . . is not the
poet's job. . . . It is quite possible therefore that at some period his duty
as a poet may conflict with his duty as a man. In that case he can stop
writing, but he must not degrade his poetry even in the service of a
good cause; for bad poetry won't serve it much anyway.

("A Statement," 7)

Through these turbulent years MacNeice sought to maintain the reserve
of the elegiac observer of self and world, and he mischievously reported,
in his travel book *I Crossed the Minch* (1938), that he had fallen asleep on a
train trying to read Day Lewis's collection of Marxist essays, *The Mind in
Chains*. Certain passages from *Autumn Journal* (1939) come as close as
MacNeice ever did to political statements, but the poem was taken, even
at the time, as one of the epitaphs for the ruined hopes of the decade.

Looking back on the work of the thirties, Day Lewis contrasted Auden
and Spender as exemplifying the tension and divergence between Classicism and Romanticism in modern (and perhaps any) poetry that his own
work was trying to reconcile. To his mind Classicism distills the clear and
direct expression of the shared moral, religious, and social values of an in-
tegrated society, whereas Romanticism arises from the convoluted, concentrated, elliptical introspections of the alienated individual:

> Classical poetry springs from a society whose system of values is on the
> whole accepted both by the ordinary man and the poet. We did not
> accept the values of our society, and in that respect we were romantic
> rebels: but, so far as we were imagining through our poetry a society
> whose values the poet could identify himself with, we were classical
> by intention.
>
> (*The Buried Day*, 217)

By these criteria Classicism moves into declaration, argument, exposition, didacticism, allegory; Romanticism moves into indirection, association, suggestion, metaphorical symbolism. Within that broad polar-
ity Day Lewis clarified his own situation by seeing Auden's early poems
as aiming at "a classical denotatory elegance of form" and Spender's early
poems as aiming at "a romantic density of connotation" ("The Thirties
in Retrospect," 18).

Day Lewis found Auden's early homosexual love poems encoded in a
"private and cryptic" language ("The Thirties in Retrospect," 19) that even
Spender found "incomprehensible" and "impenetrable" (*The Thirties and
After*, 10). But Auden's more public poems, in Day Lewis's words, "taught
us again that it is possible to think discursively in poetry without being
prosy or prolix" ("The Thirties in Retrospect," 19). From Auden, Day
Lewis learned that poetry could look beyond poetic subjectivity and engage matters of public discourse with something of the mental edge and
wit that had been largely lacking in English verse since the eighteenth
century, and it is this inclination away from lyricism toward classical or
neoclassical discursiveness that would increasingly become the hallmark

of Auden's later work. At the same time, however, the limitation of Auden's intellectual brilliance was that in seeking "speed and a kind of deliberate superficiality" it tended to work in "flat, two-dimensional" images, in "flat, diagrammatic" figures that are allegorical "types," and in the stylizing of issues and ideas into "subjects for clinical demonstration" ("The Thirties in Retrospect," 19, 21). Both Isherwood and Spender also used the word "clinical" to describe Auden's early attitude. Isherwood spoke of Auden's decision "to regard things 'clinically,' as he called it"; and Spender said that Auden's verse "fascinated me" because it was "analytical, objective, self-consciously clinical, deliberately impersonal" ("Some Notes on Auden's Early Poetry," 7; "Oxford to Communism," 9).

By contrast, from Day Lewis's perspective, Spender was "a pure romantic" whose poetry was aimed not at rational and argumentative demonstration but at honest and sincere emotional response, at what Wordsworth had called "the spontaneous overflow of powerful feelings." In Spender's own words from the Foreword to *The Still Centre* (1939), "poetry does not state truth, it states the conditions within which something felt is true" (10). At the same time, Day Lewis could see that Spender's poems—not just the personal poems of homosexual love but even the poems about the unemployed and oppressed—fell sometimes into the narcissism to which the Romantic is liable. The result, Day Lewis concluded, is that the ostensible topic or occasion seems "used less for its own sake than as a mirror to reflect the poet's response to it." For that reason in his judgment Spender "is seen at his best, during the Thirties period, not in whole poems but in those nodal points of poems where meaning is concentrated into images of great sensibility and expressiveness" ("The Thirties in Retrospect," 24). Day Lewis summed up the contrast concisely and accurately: "Where Auden and MacNeice are discursive and objective, Spender is subjective and intense" (24). Consequently, he was deeply involved with Auden and Spender as poets, beyond personal friendship, because at the beginning of his career they represented to him the thesis and antithesis that he should try to synthesize in his own work. Precisely because Day Lewis was temperamentally much closer to Spender's Romantic nature, he was the more dazzled by and susceptible to Auden's intellectuality, and he adopted Auden as model and influence for a time precisely to balance his own Romantic intensity.

Day Lewis would have been the first to admit that he had not fully or consistently succeeded in achieving the synthesis, and various poems suffer in turn from Audenesque "Classical" didacticism or Spenderian "Romantic" sentimentality. Nevertheless, the aim of Day Lewis's poetry, and to some extent that of his contemporaries, was, he claimed, synthesis—which we heard him say was the "magic word" of the decade. The pervasive fact of fragmentation was the challenge and stimulus that gave rise to their poetry, and the effort to arrive at synthesis provided its plot and drama. He said that his generation did not need *The Waste Land* to inform them that their world and their psyches were broken and in need of a remedy that went beyond the individual to societal and structural solutions. Marx and Freud were the icons of the thirties because they symbolized the connection and tension between public and private crisis, and politically the battle line shifted during the thirties as leftists were driven to see fascist totalitarianism rather than parliamentary capitalism as the primary threat. In a number of interconnected ways, therefore, the period *entre deux guerres* pictured the landscape divided into "two massing powers," and war—the shadow of the last war, the present state of conflict, the prospect of a second world war—became the obsessive trope for the psychic and social situation of the time.

The Classical/Romantic antithesis constitutes, then, just one manifestation of the split that beset the "divided mind," but it provides an explicitly literary overlay on, or frame for, the other polarities that this chapter has dealt with: head/heart; social values/individual values; solidarity with the "common blood"/personal relations; political action/hermetic art; polemical argument/lyric honesty; "public meaning"/"private meaning." Day Lewis lived and wrote between the conviction that "poetry requires the whole man" ("The Thirties in Retrospect," 29) and the experience of internal schism and external antagonism. How to synthesize thesis and antithesis? How to make the two into one? Day Lewis hoped that Marxism would provide the faith that would provide the synthesis that his lapsed Christian faith no longer could provide, and he gave himself to trying that course with clearer, stronger resolve than his Oxford friends could muster. Neither Auden nor Spender made the ideological commitment nor the day-to-day, practical commitment nor, for that matter, the poetic commitment that Day Lewis made to politics: Auden was too intellectually self-involved and Spender too emotionally self-involved.

Day Lewis's sense of desperation within and without impelled him to risk that experiment. The stakes seemed nothing less than life-or-death, and when the experiment failed, he had reached a dead end that required a radical reconstituting of his life and his poetry. Nevertheless, his thirties' poetry has to be read as a concerted effort, with Auden and Spender as thesis and antithesis, to synthesize formal elegance and concentrated feeling in verse that is at once personal and political, lyric and didactic. Such a reading locates Day Lewis not as the dominant figure in the "group"— everyone, including Auden, agreed that Auden was the dominant figure but as the pivotal figure in the configuration of "MacSpaunday."

Historians have seen the twentieth century as wracked by contradictions and dislocations that move again and again to violent outbreak. In the thirties these contradictions were played out conspicuously in the political arena and culminated in the Second World War. The polarization played itself out also in the literary wars of the decade and in the memoirs of the decade—for example, Julian Symons's *The Thirties* on the one hand, the left one, and Malcolm Muggeridge's *The Thirties* on the right. In such a charged scene of embattled extremes it is not surprising that Day Lewis—romantically handsome, fair-haired and Red-minded, vocal in his advocacy of the left, visible in the journals and reviews, widely reviewed in the steady succession of volumes of poetry—became a controversial figure, widely and sometimes extravagantly admired and envied. Responses to him ranged from the encomiums of Roberts and T. E. Lawrence and G. M. Young, cited in the course of discussion, to the increasingly hysterical and pathological epithets of Grigson ("a bad poet, a muddled writer" ["New Verse Goes Trotskyite?" 24], "not even truth's pimple squeezer" ["Two Whiffs of Lewisite, 18], "the grease in the sink-pipe of letters" ["Day Lewis Joins Up," 24]).

Thus—quite absurdly, it seems in retrospect—it became a matter of contentious public comment, left and right, as to whether the Red-identified Day Lewis could in good faith write in so bourgeois and reactionary a genre as detective fiction (though Walter Benjamin and Ernst Bloch were, at the same time and unknown to the Britons, formulating a reading of detective fiction as in many ways a subversive and revolutionary genre), and, on another occasion, whether he could without compromise serve on the selection committee of the Book Society with its middle-brow and middle-class tastes (though the Party urged him to do so and thereby influence the choice of books). Some of the enemies he made during these years—notably the implacable Geoffrey Grigson—would remain in vigilant opposition to him, his work, and his reputation long after these local disputes. Now, fifty years since the partisan atmospherics evaporated in the blitz, we are left with the actual written record. A close reading bears out the statement that appeared on the dust jacket of *Short Is the Time* (1945): "The poetry of Cecil Day Lewis is the intimate reflection of his concern with solving the problem of the modern poet." He was indeed part of the muddle of the thirties (how could he have been other?), but in articulating and negotiating those muddled yet profoundly significant contradictions he became a very good and important poet and produced some of the decade's most compelling and finely wrought poems—including many besides the memorable ones under examination here.

TWO • DESIRE GOING

FORTH AND

RETURNING

Poetry and
Eros
1940–1950

• I

THE THIRTIES MYSTIQUE—the hope for a poetry that was not merely personal but responsive to and responsible to the social condition—buckled
under the flanking pressures of Stalinist tyranny and fascist belligerence.
The sincerity and desperation of that hope can be measured by the talent
expended to realize it and by the number of disavowals and obituaries
required to pronounce it dead: among the more famous, MacNeice's
Autumn Journal (1939); Auden's "September 1, 1939," dated just days before the outbreak of war; Malcolm Muggeridge's righteously reactionary
anatomy of what went wrong in *The Thirties* (1940); and Virginia Woolf's
cool pronouncement in "The Leaning Tower" (1940) that the idealistic
didacticism of the thirties had become tainted with "discord and bitter-
ness, . . . confusion and . . . compromise" ("The Leaning Tower," 172).
The Woolfs' Hogarth Press had published six volumes of Day Lewis's verse,
but by the end of the decade Virginia Woolf inveighed against it: "Everything is a duty—even love. Listen to Mr. Day Lewis ingeminating love.
. . . We listen to oratory, not poetry" ("The Leaning Tower," 175). The
poet's own self-questioning about the competing claims of individual
expression and collective expression became located thematically in the
poetry in the relation/opposition between love and war. The conjunction of Day Lewis's marriage and family with his political engagement led
him, in *From Feathers to Iron*, *The Magnetic Mountain*, and *A Time to Dance*,
to fuse them in a projection of revolutionary love. However, by the end

of the decade his marriage had become a private battlefield in which lines were clearly drawn but no open battle decided the outcome, and that personal angst seemed absorbed into the pervasive anxiety as Britain prepared for and awaited Armageddon headed their way with Hitler's advancing blitzkrieg. His heart was "at war with itself" (*The Buried Day*, 234) even as the nation conscripted an army and organized a militia to defend the home shores.

The most succinct and mordant epitaph for thirties poetry is Day Lewis's double quatrain "Where are the War Poets?" which fires bitterly ironic epigrams back at the old guard for suggesting that their revolutionary fervor now kept the leftist poets of his generation from patriotic support for the nation's last-ditch stand against Nazism:

> They who in folly or mere greed
> Enslaved religion, markets, laws,
> Borrow our language now and bid
> Us to speak up in freedom's cause.

> It is the logic of our times,
> No subject for immortal verse—
> That we who lived by honest dreams
> Defend the bad against the worse. (335)

"Our" honesty against "their" folly and greed: the disgust with the system is still palpable. The forced alliance against fascism had put the leftist poets in the capitalist camp for the duration, but, Day Lewis's quatrains insisted, this defense of the homeland from the Axis powers did not make them capitalists. Moreover, in contrast to those of his generation who swung from Red to Tory, Day Lewis's fidelity to the "honest dreams" of the thirties would make him an ardent supporter of the Labour Party in its postwar efforts to reform Britain into a socialist democracy.

But in 1940, when those verses were written, where could the poet, caught between capitalism and totalitarianism, stand . . . or turn? The "Dedicatory Stanzas to Stephen Spender" in Day Lewis's translation of the *Georgics* bid the thirties farewell and move uncertainly into the forties. He was drawn particularly to Spender at this point of troubled transition because Spender was the other "MacSpaunday" poet who, despite disagreements with Day Lewis over specific tactics, tried seriously to write a political poetry. The early stanzas make much the same point as "Where are the War Poets?"—but in a breezier style, as the enjambed verses mask angst with wit and run playfully through a complex ten-line rhyme scheme (a-b-b-a-c-b-c-d-d-c):

> Poets are not in much demand these days—
> We're red, it seems, or cracked, or bribed, or hearty
> And, if invited, apt to spoil the party
> With the oblique reproach of emigrés:

We cut no ice, although we're fancy skaters:
Aiming at art, we only strike the arty.
Poetry now, the kinder tell us, caters
For an elite: still, it gives us the hump
To think that we're the unacknowledged rump
Of a long parliament of legislators.

Where are the war poets? the fools inquire.
We were the prophets of a changeable morning
Who hoped for much but saw the clouds forewarning:
We were at war, while still they played with fire
And rigged the market for the ruin of man:
Spain was a death to us, Munich a mourning.
No wonder then if, like the pelican,
We have turned inward for our iron ration,
Tapping the vein and sole reserve of passion,
Drawing from poetry's capital what we can.   (*Georgics*, 9)

The strategic jauntiness makes for a disarming performance, rather like hearing Byron twit the revolutionary Shelley in himself whilst at the same time invoking Shelley to damn the power brokers and war makers. But it was a performance for his own benefit, and possibly Spender's, more than for others, for in fact by 1940 Day Lewis felt played out, defeated, and deracinated.

Should he now turn from the public arena to the private, the preserve that Mary kept always in readiness for his return? Even after Day Lewis's death and after all the injuries and disappointments of the long, lonely, intervening years, Mary still clung to the notion that he knew that at any time he could come back to Brimclose; and it was only after his death in 1972 that she could bring herself to part with the cottage, not long before her death (Sean Day Lewis, 197). Brimclose was home base since the family had moved there in 1938, and would remain nominally and officially so through the forties, after Day Lewis had taken a war job at the Ministry of Information that kept him in London through the week and often on weekends. In fact, the scattered and abbreviated times he managed at Brimclose during these years seemed more visits than residence. Some deep and essential part of him had already left, though it would be years before he knew he had departed for good. He was to recall that only "after years of helplessly, obsessively tossing back and forth, like a cork between wave and backwash off a harbour wall, of inflicting the most grievous pain and suffering the dull, trapped anguish of a heart at war within itself, I left Brimclose for ever." He cast that departure in Miltonic, Byronic terms: "Self-exiled, I left what seems in retrospect a little Paradise" (*The Buried Day*, 234).

"Self-exiled": but was separation from the domestic and familial haven at Brimclose also separation from himself? From part of himself, yes; but he knew it was not so simple. The poems of the late thirties show that the marriage had long since ceased to be a marriage, though he had once imagined it as an edenic pastoral. Honesty required him to question the image of the "little Paradise":

> Did the place and people really mean so much to me? Very likely, had I stayed amongst them, I should have got bored, dissatisfied and restless. Is it that in the light of crisis—the war and my longer war within— they stand out with a momentous clarity of things dearly valued because they are direly threatened? I had set root there, certainly: but if I had not uprooted myself, might I not have gone to seed in that soft, unexacting climate of the mind?
>
> *(The Buried Day*, 234)

However necessary the break with Mary might have seemed for his development and perhaps survival, it awaited the precipitating event, and even when it came, the actual break was excruciatingly slow and painful.

Day Lewis spoke of the years "from 1941 to 1949" in catastrophic terms as a period of sustained "stress such as I had never known." For, as it turned out, Day Lewis's alternative service in the Ministry of Information, which began in 1941 and kept him away from Brimclose at his desk in London for punishingly long hours each day, often through weekends, also propelled him into a convulsive engagement with the transforming power of eros that caused what he described as "a seismic disturbance of the whole being." Yet at the same time the conjunction of "the war and my longer war within," intensified by this new encounter, was marvelously shot through by "sweet influences that for long enabled me to bear it." The result of this agonized joy was an unforeseen metamorphosis:

> From 1941 to 1949 . . . my life seemed to grow again, flowering in wider sympathies and a sensibility less crude, while my work was enhanced by the joy and the pain which seemed to purify vision and enlarge it, to show me poetry everywhere—in the most commonplace things outside me as in the precious strata of my own past experience, unworkable till now. . . .
>
> *(The Buried Day*, 234–35)

Day Lewis's poetry of the forties tells of war and eros quite literally kindled in the blitz.

• 2

But at first the blitz seemed slow in coming. For Day Lewis at Brimclose, as for the rest of the nation, the first year of wartime was a suspended waiting, especially after the heroic but tragic evacuation of British troops from France at Dunkirk, where they had been trapped by the rapid advance of the Nazi army. Day Lewis passed the months in Musbury serving as an officer in the local company of the Home Guard, and the mockheroic camaraderie of the training was deepened by the unsettling prospect of the apparently imminent Nazi invasion of their coastline. Day Lewis relieved the tension of this lull by completing his verse translation of Virgil's *Georgics*, published by Jonathan Cape in the fall of 1940. The coincidence between his engagement with the *Georgics* and the defense of the homeland was not serendipitous; on the contrary, it was precisely the psychological and moral significance of Virgil for wartime Britain that assured the issuing and then the reissuing of *The Georgics* by the Readers Union despite severe rationing of paper. So *The Georgics* marked Day Lewis's entry into the war effort, but its patriotic sentiments seemed so much part of the broad war effort that wider distribution of the volume justified the allocation of paper.

In *T. S. Eliot: A Virgilian Poet* Gareth Reeves describes Virgil as an icon for Western culture, and in a special way for British culture, as the already shaken empire reeled through the thirties toward another world war. Reeves cites a book by the German Catholic writer Theodor Haecker (translated into English in 1934 under the title *Virgil: Father of the West*) as a very influential redaction of the "convergence of ideas about literature, religion, politics and society" for which Virgil stood as spokesman in England, oddly enough, as well as in its adversary Germany (Reeves, 97–98). At the heart of this complex of attitudes is the conviction that rootedness in the land and cultivation of the land, one's own and one's people's, are the ground and basis of civilization—that is to say, of "literature, religion, politics and society." Reeves quotes the following passage from Eliot's postwar essay "Virgil and the Christian World" to illustrate the particular centrality of *The Georgics* to this national ethic, threatened by the violent conditions of modern life:

> There is I think no precedent for the *spirit* of the *Georgics*; and the attitude toward the soil, and the labour of the soil, which is there expressed, is something that we ought to find particularly intelligible now, when urban agglomeration, the flight from the land, the pillage of the earth and the squandering of natural resources are beginning to attract attention. . . . Virgil perceived that agriculture is fundamental to civilization, and he affirmed the dignity of manual labour.
>
> (Reeves, 89)

Day Lewis the socialist would have shied away from those Christian and imperial aspects of Haecker's image of Virgil that attracted Eliot the royalist-Anglican Tory: specifically the time-honored notion that Virgil, like Simeon, premonitorily heralded the coming of Christianity, and the interpretation of Virgilian *pietas* as the ethos of an "agrarian hierarchy" linking the individual and the family organically with the region, the nation, and, finally, the empire. Consequently, Day Lewis's sense of Virgil was mediated not as much by Eliot as by the more congenially agnostic and humanistic figure of Thomas Hardy. Auden recollected with great satisfaction that it was he who in the thirties introduced Day Lewis to Hardy's poetry (*C. Day Lewis: A Bibliography*, v–vi), but Day Lewis did not immerse himself in Hardy's works till the early forties. During the "MacSpaunday" period Day Lewis's verse had borne traces of his reading of Yeats and Owen, Hopkins and Auden; but from the war years till the end of his life Hardy retained primacy in Day Lewis's pantheon. The two men never met, despite their shared devotion to the hills and vales of Dorset and Devon. However, Day Lewis kept a pencil sketch of Hardy framed in his study in totemic recognition of Hardy's brooding and inspiring presence in his imagination, and his slate tombstone stands yards away from Hardy's stone in the cemetery of St. Michael's Church, Stinsford, just outside of Dorchester.

Haecker had called Virgil the type of "Western man himself" and took Virgil's influence as a sign of the very continuity of Western civilization itself (Reeves, 100). By contrast in one of the "Dedicatory Stanzas" to his translation of *The Georgics*, Day Lewis presented Virgil as the down-to-earth prototype of Hardy:

> Virgil—a tall man, dark and countrified
> In looks, they say: retiring: no rhetorician:
> Of humble birth: a Celt, whose first ambition
> Was to be a philosopher: Dante's guide.
> But chiefly dear for his gift to understand
> Earth's intricate, ordered heart, and for a vision
> That saw beyond an imperial day the hand
> Of man no longer armed against his fellow
> But all for vine and cattle, fruit and fallow,
> Subduing with love's positive force the land.
> (The Georgics, 10)

And if Hardy is the avatar of Virgil, Virgil's veteran of the Roman wars, whom Day Lewis invoked to conclude the "Dedicatory Stanzas," is kin to the Wessex countrymen who had been Hardy's neighbors and were now Day Lewis's neighbors and fellow militiamen in the Musbury Home Guard:

> Now, when war's long midwinter seems to freeze us
> And numb our living sources once for all,
> That veteran of Virgil's I recall
> Who made a kitchen-garden by the Galaesus
> On derelict land, and got the first of spring
> From airs and buds, the first fruits in the fall,
> And lived at peace there, happy as a king.
> Naming him for good luck, I see man's native
> Stock is perennial, and our creative
> Winged seed can strike a root in anything.
> (The Georgics, 11)

The last line is Shelleyan, but the rest of the stanza translates Virgil into Hardy country.

From this same anxious time of waiting, "Watching Post" and "The Stand-To," dated, respectively, July and September 1940, memorialize very simply and touchingly the deep-down fellowship with the local yeomen that allows Day Lewis to serve as their voice: "[S]ing through me" (334). That expression of solidarity across class lines can quickly become condescending, but in times of crisis, as in Laurence Olivier's glorious wartime film of *Henry V*, it can forge a conviction of British national identity:

> I felt at home amongst those people who, though I should for long be a "foreigner" and to them an oddity, accepted me as the countryman will accept any phenomenon which does not actively disturb his own life. I learnt their reticences; I loved their weathered, calm faces, their cunning, and the flavour of the stories which they never tired of repeating. They were individuals to me—later I celebrated some of them in a poem, "The Stand-To"—not quaint "characters", and still less the "toiling masses" or the "agricultural workers" of Party slogans.
>
> (*The Buried Day*, 231–32)

The kinship with workers and farmers that remained an elusive imaginative projection in the thirties Day Lewis now found outside of Party activity (though not outside of class differences) on home ground.

So he felt a special affinity with Virgil as he labored on his translation of *The Georgics* during the first months of the war:

> I felt more and more the kind of patriotism which I imagine was Virgil's—the natural piety, the heightened sense of the genius of place, the passion to praise and protect one's roots, or to put down roots somewhere while there is still time, which it takes a seismic event such as war to reveal to most of us rootless moderns. More and more I was buoyed up by a feeling that England was speaking to me through Virgil, and that the Virgil of the *Georgics* was speaking to me through the English farmers and labourers with whom I consorted.
>
> (*On Translating Poetry*, 6)

The result was a "heightened sense of the past" and an "enhanced awareness of place, of England, and especially that south-west corner of England which, because I had been at school there twenty years before [at Sherborne School], was associated with the *Georgics* I had first read there" (*On Translating Poetry*, 6–7).

Virgil's celebration of idyllic scenes and agrarian values had arisen from—and against—the imperial wars of Rome. Day Lewis emphasizes the analogy with his own situation (including, eerily, the vulnerability of both Rome and Britain to German armies on the march) by using the following lines concluding Book 1 as the epigraph for his entire translation of Virgil's poem:

> For Right and Wrong are confused here, there's so much war in
> $\qquad\qquad$ the world,
> Evil has so many faces, the plough so little
> Honour, the labourers are taken, the fields untended,

And the curving sickle is beaten into the sword that yields not.
There the East is in arms, here Germany marches:
Neighbour cities, breaking their treaties, attack each other:
The wicked War-god runs amok through all the world.
So, when racing chariots have rushed from the starting-gate,
They gather speed on the course, and the driver tugs at the
                                                    curb-rein
—His horses runaway, car out of control, quite helpless.

(*The Georgics*, 31)

The four books after this epigraph describe in loose English hexameters the cultivation of the land, of vines and orchards, of domestic ani-
mals, and of bees. In the Marxist poetry of the thirties there was some
incongruity between the revolutionary message and the pastoral mode in
which the message was cast. The conservative proclivities of the pastoral
suited the present war crisis better, but it functioned in much the same
way. The measured attunement of human consciousness to the cultivation of natural processes looks backward and forward, moving matters
outside history and beyond imperial wars to an organic and holistic polity
of the people. He had turned to *The Georgics* in 1939 at the request of Mary's
brother, a master at Winchester, who asked his classically trained brother-
in-law for a verse translation of a passage set for the students' examination
(*The Buried Day*, 233). However, what immediately struck the translator
was the ancient poem's resonance with "all that I had come to love here—
the places and the people" (234); and what impelled him to go on to translate all four books was Virgil's "vision" of humans living—long before
politics and war and long after them—as they labor within the intricate
orderings of the seasons.

Just as we saw that the pastoral myth permitted Marxists, however prob-
lematically, to suggest a vision of a utopian society, so now it offered poets
in wartime an assuaging conviction of the transcendence of personal and
national catastrophe in the persistence of the natural round. The pastoral,
then, served as bulwark against, if not refutation of, the tragedies of the
Machine Age in the poetry of Day Lewis, as it did in the poetry of the
moderns spiritually closest to him: in Hardy's and Frost's country lyrics,
for example, or in Stevens's meditations on the seasons from "Sunday
Morning" at the time of the First World War through the volumes of the
Second World War, *Transport to Summer* and *The Auroras of Autumn*.

In the "Dedicatory Stanzas" Day Lewis remarks to Spender of his
Georgics: "taking a leaf from Virgil's laurel, / I sang in time of war the arts
of peace." Disconsolate with politics, he had "turned inward" to himself
and outward to nature in the hope of finding an ur-politics or pre-politics,
a natural "economy" such as Thoreau discovered at Walden Pond. But
did a natural economy have to be as individualist and misanthropist as
Thoreau's? (Thoreau had provided the epigraph for *Beechen Vigil*.) Thoreau
had been Marx's contemporary, but their anticapitalism moved them in

opposite directions: Thoreau to an anarchic and ecological politics, Marx to collectivist, industrial politics. Day Lewis hoped to rescue his shaken hopes of Marxist comradeship from an individualism as hermetic as Thoreau's by entering the fellowship of people with the land. Thus fortified by Virgil (and Hardy), the poet can reply in the "Dedicatory Stanzas" to the power brokers and war makers: "Yes, we shall fight. but—let them not mistake it—" not for them, but instead "for dear life alone," for "the poet's living space, the love of men," "for common suffering men" (*The Georgics*, 9, 10).

What Day Lewis finds in *The Georgics* is the serenely classical assurance of a harmony at once cosmic and social, beyond economics and politics, as in these lines near the end of Book 2:

> Oh, too lucky for words, if only he knew his luck,
> Is the countryman who far from the clash of armaments
> Lives, and rewarding earth is lavish of all he needs!
> True, no mansion tall with a swanky gate throws up
> In the morning a mob of callers to crowd him out and gape at
> Doorposts inlaid with beautiful tortoiseshell, attire
> Of gold brocade, connoisseur's bronzes.
> No foreign dyes may stain his white fleeces, nor exotic
> Spice like cinnamon spoil his olive oil for use:
> But calm security and a life that will not cheat you,
> Rich in its own rewards, are here: the broad ease of the farmlands,
> Caves, living lakes, and combes that are cool even at midsummer,
> Mooing of herds, and slumber mild in the trees' shade.
> Here are glades game-haunted,
> Lands hardened to labour, inured to simple ways,
> Reverence for God, respect for the family. When Justice
> Left earth, her latest footprints were stamped on folk like these.
> $\qquad\qquad\qquad\qquad\qquad$ (*The Georgics*, 49–50)

Not aristocratic values nor bourgeois values nor proletarian values; not class values of any kind, but country values.

But country values might be extended into the construction of a good society. Virgil seemed to offer a poetics and politics and economics of nature; classical precedent bolstered the Romantic ideal of the poet as farmer, the farmer as poet. But Day Lewis also learned from Virgil that the knowing farmer-poet must actively intervene in nature's cycles with a mastering hand to prune and trim, to select and choose, to compose natural life "into shape":

> A farmer's work proceeds in
> Cycles, as the shuttling year returns on its own track.
> And now, the time when a vineyard puts off its reluctant leaves
> And a bitter north wind has blown away the pride of the
> $\qquad\qquad\qquad\qquad\qquad\qquad$ woodland,

> Even now the countryman actively pushes on to the coming
> Year and its tasks; attacking the naked vine with a curved
> Pruning-knife, he shears and trims it into shape.
>
> (*The Georgics*, 48)

The "Dedicatory Stanzas" commend Virgil's "vision" of "subduing with love's positive force the land," and the next stanza extends the trope of the farmer's copulation with the land specifically to

> the poet's search for a right soil
> Where words may settle, marry, and conceive an
> Imagined truth, for a regimen that enhances
> Their natural grace.
>
> (*The Georgics*, 11)

Consequently, in Day Lewis's Foreword to the *Georgics* "the depth and tenacity of our roots in earth to-day" renew the prospect of raising a post-war rural-industrial landscape reminiscent of *From Feathers to Iron* and *The Magnetic Mountain* and *Noah and the Waters*:

> It may, indeed, happen that this war, together with the spread of electrical power, will result in a decentralization of industry and the establishment of a new rural-urban civilization working through smaller social units. The factory in the fields need not remain a dream of poets and planners: it has more to commend it than the allotment in the slums.
>
> (*The Georgics*, 7)

The agrarian socialism of William Morris and John Ruskin has here been updated to accommodate "the factory in the fields," but it offers the same ideal: the productive and self-sustaining society operating locally in natural harmony. Pound also operated out of Ruskin and Morris to arrive at a very different poetics and politics and economics of nature, citing Hesiod instead of Virgil and adding Confucius as his Oriental source. Pound's agrarianism, however, led to his fascism; in his mind Jefferson came to anticipate Mussolini. For him the creative man was the city builder like Sigismundo Malatesta rather than the farmer, and Malatesta was the prototype of a politician like Mussolini and a Modernist artist like Gaudier-Brzeska, who hacked out of the rough stone the form he had intuited there. In the thirties, as Pound turned further and further right, Day Lewis had deliberately taken a different course. Both had hoped, against the vested interests of capitalist business-as-usual, that the polity they imagined was not just "the dream of poets and planners." But Day Lewis had followed "Johnny Head-In-Air" left rather than right, and now in the early forties the long continuity between Virgil and Hardy enabled him to seek a politics of nature that was liberal rather than totalitarian, a poetics of nature that was modern rather than Modernist. The link with Hardy was essential; Hardy served to modulate the politics of the thirties to a humanism of radically reduced expectations and to confirm Day Lewis's adherence to

the British tradition, rooted in pastoralism, over the American rupture of
tradition that led William Carlos Williams, for example, to see the farmer-
poet as the "antagonist" of nature, in whose abstracted and inventive "head
the harvest [is] already planted" (*Collected Poems*, I, 186).

In *Thomas Hardy and British Poetry* Donald Davie addresses Hardy's
pivotal role in validating the British tradition for his twentieth-century
countrymen against what Davie sees as the inflated, almost pathological
claims of American Modernists like Pound. In Davie's words, the perverse
and fatal presumption of experimental poetry since Romanticism, most
exaggeratedly exhibited by Americans like Pound and Williams, is that
"surely the poet, if any one, has a duty to be radical, to go to the roots"
(Davie, 40). As a "revolutionary" and an "iconoclast" the radical is, in
Davie's view, "childishly irresponsible," "dangerously self-deluded or self-
intoxicated," and the vaunting goals of his "prophetic poetry"—to strike
through old forms to gnosis and to seize the new forms of that revelation—
make it "necessarily an inferior poetry" (Davie, 12, 43, 150). "The open
forms, from the time of Whitman . . . , envisage man as transcending himself
by moving outward and on." Such false and iconoclastic idealism, refusing "the responsibilities of being human," is driven to violence because
it refuses necessary natural constraints; it stands "outside culture and [is]
(really) at war with it" (Davie, 128, 150–51). Davie contrasts the American
poetic tradition—in his view, incorrigibly utopian, prophetic, and absolutist in its politcs and poetics—with the British tradition as realistic in its
acceptance of the limits of nature and human nature, and, as a result, both
pragmatic and liberal in its politics and traditional in its poetics: "Between
Hardy's precedent and Whitman's," declares Davie, "there can be no
compromise" (Davie, 186, 129). The very modesty of the British tradition is for Davie the sign of its humane sanity. Hardy's antithesis is D. H.
Lawrence, almost the only British poet of the period whose radicalism
drew him to American iconoclasm. The principal intention of Davie's
book is to propose Hardy's liberalism as an antidote to the totalitarian
inclinations of Pound and Lawrence, which he, like other commentators on literary Modernism, sees as helping to create the climate for the
Second World War.

Day Lewis might not have accepted Davie's automatic association of
political radicalism in the thirties with experimentalist open form, for his
own kind of political radicalism was antithetical to Lawrence's and Pound's
fascist affinities. He and his friends had consciously chosen conventional
forms and metrics as the more effective means to communicate their collectivist message to a popular audience. But then Davie's book ignores leftist
radicalism (though as a political and social conservative he found it repug-
nant) because the target of his polemic here is the irresponsibility of American poetry. Davie could hardly omit the figure of Auden completely from
his outline of a British pastoral/humanist tradition. However, overlook-
ing entirely the poems of the thirties, he sifts out of Auden's later work
hints of Hardy's good influence, and the single mention of Day Lewis is a

brief parenthetical remark, again without notice of the work of the thirties, that he had "moved in the 1940s into using very explicitly Hardyesque forms and styles" (Davie, 130). However, the important point for this discussion is that, beyond their political and poetic differences, Day Lewis would have agreed with Davie's principal contention about Hardy's crucial place in twentieth-century British poetry. Hardy and Whitman or Pound had very different senses about what it meant to "go to the roots," and by the advent of the Second World War Day Lewis was, as Davie rightly noted, in Hardy's camp, writing from a saddened awareness of the ravages of political and psychological strife and the need to search out the roots and grounds of human connectedness.

The political and poetic effects of Day Lewis's absorption of Virgil and Hardy at this crucial time can be heard in the profound simplicities of the poem "Watching Post," which first appeared in Day Lewis's slim *Poems in Wartime*, published in the same year as his *Georgics*, and was included later in *Word Over All*:

> A hill flank overlooking the Axe Valley.
> Among the stubble a farmer and I keep watch
> For whatever may come to injure our countryside—
> Light-signals, parachutes, bombs, or sea-invaders.
> The moon looks over the hill's shoulder, and hope
> Mans the old ramparts of an English night.
>
> In a house down there was Marlborough born. One night
> Monmouth marched to his ruin out of that valley.
> Beneath our castled hill, where Britons kept watch,
> Is a church where the Drakes, old lords of this countryside,
> Sleep under their painted effigies. No invaders
> Can dispute their legacy of toughness and hope.
>
> Two counties away, over Bristol, the searchlights hope
> To find what danger is in the air tonight.
> Presently gunfire from Portland reaches our valley
> Tapping like an ill-hung door in a draught. My watch
> Says nearly twelve. All over the countryside
> Moon-dazzled men are peering out for invaders.
>
> The farmer and I talk for a while of invaders:
> But soon we turn to crops—the annual hope,
> Making of cider, prizes for ewes. Tonight
> How many hearts along this war-mazed valley
> Dream of a day when at peace they may work and watch
> The small sufficient wonders of the countryside.
>
> Image or fact, we both in the countryside
> Have found our natural law, and until invaders
> Come will answer its need; for both of us, hope

Means a harvest from small beginnings, who this night
While the moon sorts out into shadow and shape our valley,
A farmer and a poet, are keeping watch.   (331–32)

The poem resonates with the historical associations of the topography. The village of Musbury, where the Day Lewises lived, is snugly located beneath Castle Hill, crowned by the stone-age "castle" from which ancient Britons defended the home shore. Brimclose cottage, halfway up the hill, was once a forester's or gamekeeper's lodging on the ancestral estate of the Drake family.

The intersection of past and present in this place assumes a widened perspective in the course of the poem. The first stanza lays out the Axe Valley in its perilous vulnerability to Nazi invasion; the second stanza makes the valley a condensed microcosm of British history; the third stanza connects it geographically with Bristol and Portland and, implicitly, the whole country at war: "All over the countryside / Moon-dazzled men are peering out for invaders." Then in the last two stanzas the perspective returns to the conversation of "a farmer and a poet" on night watch. As talk of the war melds into "the annual hope" for crops and cider and ewes, the two men, beyond differences in class and education and daily purpose, become, in the crisis that brings them humbled and heartened together here and now, twinned witnesses standing guard at this epicenter of history and nation. The poet looks back, as the farmer perhaps cannot, through Hardy to Morris and Wordsworth and the whole British pastoral tradition, all the way to Virgil, "Father of the West." Though in this time of peril the poet could not be sure whether he was offering the poem as security against defeat or a final "valediction" to the old ways (*The Buried Day*, 234), he knew that his special responsibility was to shape their mingled voices and shared values into a poem of communion and community.

Throughout the diction and sentence structure are direct and simple, and the run-on lines echo the flow of conversation; but these unobtrusive effects are the result of careful attention to word and syllable that heightens speech into verse. For example, the bluff naturalness of the lines "The moon looks over the hill's shoulder, and hope / Mans the old ramparts of an English night" actually involves many small felicities: the assonance of "over," "hope," "old"; the interplay of "v" and "f" in "over," "of" (which threads through the rest of the poem); the alliteration of "moon," "man" and of "hill," "hope"; the subtler sound play of "over," "shoulder" and "man," "ramparts." The texturing of sound then supports the metaphorical displacement of the actual situation—the home guard's alert against a Nazi attack—onto the emblematic landscape, as "hope / Mans" the hill's ramparts defensively against the moon's sneak approach from the rear to spy over "the hill's shoulder." As the seemingly colloquial lines gather into stanzas, the poem takes the form of an abbreviated sestina, five stanzas instead of the usual six, but each comprising six lines in which the shifting reiteration of the final words of the lines—"valley," "watch," "country-

side," "invaders," "hope," "night"—forms a mantralike refrain, rehears-
ing the night's turning wherein, under threat of extinction, "we both in
the countryside / Have found our natural law."

Day Lewis would observe that sometimes, and most especially at crucial
and transitional points in a poet's development, he "will use the work of
other poets to mediate between himself and the new material: this is the
meaning of tradition—something quite different from the verbal imitation
of another poet" (*The Poet's Task*, 9). Some of Day Lewis's most fully realized achievements are such transitional poems, and "Watching Post" is
an instance of how the transmutation he has described works. Here Virgil
and Hardy meet in a verse form employed by poets all the way from the
troubadours to Auden and MacNeice. However, so deeply has Day Lewis
absorbed the tradition into his practice that the poem speaks, with seeming
effortlessness, in his own cadences and with the impress of his particular
technical mastery.

• 3

Those suspenseful first months of the war gave Day Lewis the time he
needed to reconfigure the interdependence of politics and poetics through
a return to native sources. The invasion against which the local militia was
manning the shores did not come; but the lull would not last, and soon
enough on the homefront the blitz shattered the false calm. He would have
to confront its physical and psychological terrors in the streets of London,
but even before that, back in the Axe Valley, his own emotional and sexual
life was entering its own anxious period of blitz.

The "Dedicatory Stanzas" to *The Georgics* evoked the erotics of agri-
culture, and indeed from *Beechen Vigil* on Day Lewis's poetry had invoked
the age-old association between nature and sexuality, and so between passion and pastoral. *Overtures to Death* indicated, toward the end of the thirties, how far the spring love anticipated in the earlier poems had declined
into wintry numbness at home. Several poems late in that volume fanta-
size about a sexual awakening. In this instance art anticipated life, for in
October 1938, the same month as the publication of *Overtures to Death*
and only a couple of months after moving with Mary and the boys from
Box Cottage to Brimclose, Day Lewis met, in the local Red Lion pub,
Edna Elizabeth Currall, nicknamed Billie. On the very day of their chance
encounter at the Red Lion, she had moved with her husband John to a
farmhouse down a lane and over the hill from Brimclose (Sean Day Lewis,
114ff), and the sexual attraction between them was immediate and recip-
rocal.

"Jig" recounts the rollicking rhythms of their sexual romp:

That winter love spoke and we raised no objection, at
Easter 'twas daisies all light and affectionate,

June sent us crazy for natural selection—not
Four traction-engines could tear us apart. (346)

The trope of the traction engines, powerless before the superior force of their passion, is a final instance of the eroticizing of machines that began in *From Feathers to Iron*. In September 1940 in the course of "natural selection" Billie gave birth to Day Lewis's son. She named him William, called him Willie, made no claims of recognition or support on the biological father, and set out to raise him under her husband's roof as a Currall. The home presence of Mary, to whom that earlier sequence had been dedicated, kept him from recording this pregnancy in verse, and his only public acknowledgment of the paternity was to supply Willie a pram and on occasion push him unapologetically about Musbury.

Almost three decades later, *The Private Wound* (1968), the last of his Nicholas Blake novels and one of the best, would re-create the heedless, obsessive violence of the affair with Billie Currall in what the fictional protagonist calls "a sort of confession." John Currall had kept his silence through the years, but when *The Private Wound* was serialized in the *Daily Express*, advertised by flashy posters on the newsstands, his long-repressed anger finally found voice. Coming upon Mary working in the Brimclose garden, he accosted her with contemptuous words for the husband who had exited the lives of both Mary and Curralls years before: "He may think I don't know what his story is about, but I do, damn his eyes" (Sean Day Lewis, 282). (After school William Currall lived most of his life in the English Midlands without further contact with his father and died in 1994.)

For her part Mary chose to hold her tongue in injured silence, and just as Mary hoped, the affair with Billie had burned itself out well before Day Lewis departed for London, leaving his family in the comparative safety of the Devon countryside, to assume his war job as editor in the Publications Division of the Ministry of Information. March of 1941, however, brought Day Lewis to London in the worst of the blitz, with bombs raining down and the city in flames almost nightly. In *Under Seige* Robert Hewison describes the situation in London during what would have been Day Lewis's first months. British understatement relies on dates and dry statistics to let the horror speak for itself:

> On 16 April London had its worst raid yet, advertised by the Germans as 'the greatest raid of all time' and known simply to Londoners as 'the Wednesday'. The raid lasted eight hours, and 450 planes dropped 100,000 tons of bombs. This was followed by 'the Saturday'. More than a thousand people were killed in each raid, and 148,000 houses were destroyed or damaged. An even bigger raid on 10 May set fire to the House of Commons and the Deanery of Westminster Abbey, and there were fires right across London. 1,436 people were killed, 1,792 were injured, the highest casualties for a single raid. Fire-fighting went on afterwards for eleven days.
>
> (Hewison, 33)

Elizabeth Bowen's novel *The Heat of the Day* (1948) renders the almost unbearably heightened atmosphere of wartime London and catches the simultaneous sense of dislocation and intensification that were the psychological effects of living under the blitz:

> The night behind and the night to come met across every noon in an arch of strain. To work or think was to ache. In offices, factories, ministries, shops, kitchens the hot yellow sands of each afternoon ran out slowly; fatigue was the one reality. You dared not envisage sleep. Apathetic, the injured and dying in the hospitals watched light change on walls which might fall tonight. Those rendered homeless sat where they had been sent; or, worse, with the obstinacy of animals retraced their steps to look for what was no longer there. Most of all the dead, from mortuaries, from under the cataracts of rubble, made their anonymous presence felt through London. . . . Absent from the routine which had been life, they stamped upon that routine their absence—not knowing who the dead were, you could not know which might be the staircase somebody for the first time was not mounting this morning, or at which street corner the newsvendor missed a face, or which trains and buses in the homegoing rush were this evening lighter by at least one passenger.
>
> (99)

The Heat of the Day also renders the strange and fevered quickening of sexual passion in wartime. Bowen's fictional lovers meet during "that heady autumn of the first London air raids. Never had any season been more felt; one bought the poetic sense of it with the sense of death" (98). The lovers are drawn to feel themselves "creatures of history, whose coming together was of a nature possible in no other day" (217). Moreover, these new couplings threaten to uncouple old marital ties: "There was a diffused gallantry in the atmosphere, an unmarriedness: it came to be rumoured about the country . . . that everybody in London was in love . . ." (102).

But at least some in the country were not sufficiently aware of the erotically charged "unmarriedness" of the London atmosphere. From Brimclose Mary worried about the physical danger to her husband in the London inferno, but she did not guess the vulnerability of the anxious heart laid bare by war. During one of the spring air raids of 1941, Day Lewis encountered Rosamond Lehmann, a novelist whom he had first met in 1936 at the London flat of their mutual friend Elizabeth Bowen. At their earlier meeting he had been fascinated enough to review Lehmann's most recent novel, *The Weather in the Streets*, and to invite her to address the Cheltenham Literary Society. On that occasion the visiting celebrity had spent the night at Box Cottage with him and Mary (Sean Day Lewis, 97, 141ff). The unanticipated renewal of their acquaintance under the rain of enemy bombs became a major turning point in the lives of both and initiated a love affair that lasted nine years.

The double life in which Day Lewis was caught made for psychological and moral stress "such as I had never known" before or since (*The Buried Day*, 234). But his stress seemed part of the general distress of the war years and the immediate postwar years, and the excitement and glamour of his life with Lehmann became part of the fever and exhaustion of the time. They became a visible pair in literary London and coedited three volumes of a literary miscellany called *Orion*. He dedicated his next book of verse, *Word Over All* (1943), "To Rosamond Lehmann"; she dedicated her next and best-known novel, *The Ballad and the Source* (1945), "To C. D. L." After their final and painful separation, many knowing readers of Lehmann's next novel, *The Echoing Grove* (1953), would see in its tormented love-triangle in wartime London (here, a man loved by two sisters) a heavily fictionalized reflection of the wrenching situation in which she had been embroiled.

Rosamond Lehmann was a member of a literary family nearly as well known and talked about as the Sitwells. Her sister Beatrix was a well-known actress; her brother John was one of the *New Country* poets and had edited the influential journal *New Writing* during the thirties, extended into the war years as *Penguin New Writing*. In the forties Rosamond was a novelist at the height of her fame and beauty, and the magnetic power of her physical presence and her personality was the occasion for almost as much comment, in print and among her friends, as her novels about sensitive, articulate women, suffering from the pangs and wounds of their too-passionate hearts. Reviewing *The Weather in the Streets*, Day Lewis ranked her below Virginia Woolf and Elizabeth Bowen but singled out her "remarkable flair for dialogue" and her "vivid and decorative, neo-romantic manner." However, in the words of Marghanita Laski, reviewing *The Echoing Grove*, "no English writer has told of the pains of women in love more truly or more movingly than Rosamond Lehmann" (Sean Day Lewis, 97, 142). Her first novel, *Dusty Answer* (1927), had created a stir on its publication and been followed by several others during the ensuing decade. By the time Day Lewis met her in the blitz, she was, all the more so to the poet from Hardy country new-come to London, a glamorous and shimmering figure in the literary and social scene.

Both women in Day Lewis's life were slightly older than he (Mary by two years, Rosamond by four), but otherwise the two of them could not have been more different. Mary was the daughter of Day Lewis's clerical form master at Sherborne when he met her in 1923, and her beauty and grace were matched by her emotional reserve throughout the long courtship before their marriage in 1928. Her retiring temperament and conservative social views kept her from sharing Day Lewis's more public life and his politics. Though they loved one another and by 1934 had two children, Mary's own psychological inclinations drew her increasingly into a maternal nurturing toward her husband and boys that was both self-effacing and demanding. Yet a man motherless from age four would be especially susceptible to that nurturing and its demands; he continued to draw upon her strong, quiet presence, even after he had met Billie . . . and then Rosamond.

By contrast, Rosamond, born on the day of Queen Victoria's funeral "during a violent thunderstorm" (*The Swan in the Evening*, 9), came from a wealthy, sophisticated, arty family, and with her siblings had been educated by a private tutor in the schoolhouse her father built on the grounds of their estate. She described her precocious childhood with airy self-regard:

> I have elsewhere recorded the creative surge that overwhelmed me in my first decade, but nothing from any deep, dark, unconscious level has appeared: it was all turned to favour and to prettiness. More like a bubbling forth of ectoplasm, or perhaps, more accurately, of those flimsy, faintly irridescent [*sic*] bubbles we used to produce and fling about the nursery from mugs of soapy water through clay pipes (the prototype perhaps of those emotional soap operas I later produced, according to one distinguished biographer?)
>
> (*Rosamond Lehmann's Album*, 10)

And this is how she saw herself at the time when *Dusty Answer* roused enough scandal to bring her immediate literary fame and get her picture in the papers and magazines:

> Unhappily married, childless, separated, wishing for a divorce; and now all at once, good heavens, one of the new post-war young women writers, product of higher education (Girton College), a frank outspeaker upon unpleasant subjects, a stripper of the veils of reticence; a subject for pained head-shaking; at the same time a recipient of lyrical praise, of rapturous congratulation, of intense envy, of violent condemnation, in the contemporary world of letters: a world I had burst into unawares.
>
> (*The Swan in the Evening*, 68)

By the time she had begun the affair with Day Lewis her second marriage had ended, and the two children from that union, about the same age as the Day Lewis boys, were living in the country with her mother. The following description from Spender's autobiography conjures up the power of her beauty over men, and her own pleasure in that power is indicated by the fact that she chose to include the passage as the caption to a ravishing, Mona Lisa–like photograph of herself in *Rosamond Lehmann's Album* (a book of pictures of herself with husbands, family, and friends with commentary, assembled a few years before her death and intended as her last public presentation of herself):

> Rosamond was one of the most beautiful women of her generation. Tall, and holding herself with a sense of her presence, her warmth and vitality prevented her from seeming coldly statuesque. She had almond-shaped eyes, a firm mouth which contradicted the impression of uncontrolled spontaneity given by her cheeks, which often blushed. Her manner was warm, impulsive, and yet like her mouth it concealed

a cool self-control, and the egotism of the artist. At this age she seemed at the height of her beauty: yet when I look at photographs of her then it seems to me that her features were in fact too rounded, too girlish, and that years confirmed a sculptural quality which one felt in her presence but which later showed in her features. So that she was one of those women in whom even greying hair was a kind of triumph, a fulfilment of maturity which her youth had promised.

(*Rosamond Lehmann's Album*, 51, quoted from Stephen Spender's *World Within World*, 143)

Spender's ripe words, evoking the awesome immediacy and unattainability of a goddess, indicate the image that Rosamond Lehmann aroused in the imaginations of many men who came into her orbit. It was Rosamond in the unblushing fullness of her maturity—cool yet passionate, impulsive but in command—who took up life with Day Lewis in Kensington in 1941. He had never before encountered eros in such alluring and challenging form: not with Mary or Alison Morris nor even with Billie Currall. Most particularly, Rosamond (though she had two children) did not cast herself in the maternal role. On the contrary, she combined sexual passion with literary, political, and social sophistication, and the empathy he instantly felt for her and from her seemed, suddenly and at last, to open for him the possibility of fusing the sides of his divided heart and mind into a whole and fulfilled identity. Right away she gave him self-possession, not to mention the entree to literary London, such as he never had during his rusticated years as schoolmaster and Red poet. The newly confirmed countryman-poet, late of the Home Guard, found himself at the center of a nation at war and increasingly in demand as a lecturer and reader on the BBC.

Through the decade of the forties he stood with Rosamond in the eye of the private and public storm; their liaison lasted through the war and into the uncertain years in which Britain, emotionally and economically exhausted, strove to recoup some of its former status as a major power under the stress of the Cold War with the U.S.S.R. During these years his own inner conflict became more acute, for though Day Lewis had hoped that this engagement with a passionate, intelligent, literary woman would heal his divided psyche, it was also precisely what locked him into a false and double life that threatened to pull him apart: London against Brimclose, Rosamond against Mary. Long hours at the Ministry of Information kept him at his desk in London on most weekends, and Mary's domestic responsibilities made her London visits rare, brief, and hectic. At the same time, Rosamond and her children became something like his second family even after they moved from London to the nearby Berkshire countryside in 1943 and then to the country house at Little Wittenham outside Oxford in 1946. From this point it was Little Wittenham against Brimclose.

There are no mentions of Rosamond Lehmann in Day Lewis's autobiography, which concludes with the outbreak of war in 1939, but the final pages mention ominously and without further explanation that he would be "driven [in 1944] by overwork and the anguish of a divided love to the edge of a nervous breakdown" (*The Buried Day,* 227). Rosamond later spoke of coping with his "black-ice periods" of tormented depression, and Mary wrote tersely and bleakly in her diary in 1947: "Cecil in state bordering on insanity, can't make up his mind between Rosamond and me" (Sean Day Lewis, 143, 170). For two years Day Lewis kept his other life secret from his wife, but the publication of *Word Over All,* containing poems that left no doubt about his duplicity, forced him to act. In October of 1943, a month after the book appeared, his entrapped and now self-exposed guilt forced him to write a letter confessing to Mary his betrayal of her and the children. The letter offered to divide his time between the two households at least until the boys were grown, and the day after Mary received it, he went to Musbury for a strained and painful confrontation. Despite the hurt her response to their conversation was stoic and determined; she wrote in her diary the word "Peace," because she concluded from his behavior that he would not—or could not—break off their marriage (151). She was, for the time being at least, correct in that assessment, but she resisted facing the fact that the deferral of a break represented not so much a commitment as irresolution on his part, so that the impasse left them both—left all three—locked in a state of wracked suspension through the years ahead.

• 4

Word Over All (1943) incorporated the eleven poems from *Poems in Wartime,* published three years earlier in a slim, limited edition, with newer poems. But because the constellation of Mars with Venus presided over his life and his world in the early forties, the war poems are surrounded by and intermingled with poems recounting the poet's reencounter with eros, first with Billie and then more deeply and disturbingly with Rosamond. Indeed, the verses about the affair with Billie in *Poems in Wartime* indicate the vexed conjunction of war and passion that led—was fated to lead, he might have felt at the time—to finding Rosamond during the air raid.

The arrangement of poems in *Word Over All*—always a matter of careful consideration with Day Lewis—is telling in the way it inverts chronology in organizing, or rather reorganizing, the poems. The eleven from the *Wartime* pamphlet were assigned to either Parts Two or Three of *Word Over All* depending on the their emphasis on the war (into Part Two) or the erotic affair with Billie (into Part Three). The more recent poems about Rosamond comprised Part One and enclosed the war poems in the middle of the triptych with love lyrics on either side. The framing sections had to be read backward for autobiographical accuracy, but the reversal of the chronology of the love poems (Rosamond in Part One, Billie in Part Three) served to foreground his most recent work and thereby to give his new love pride of place. Indeed, the content of Part One, coming after the dedication of the volume "To Rosamond Lehmann," necessitated, as he must have anticipated it would necessitate, his agonized and long-delayed acknowledgment to Mary of his fateful commitment to another woman and another home.

Curiously and tellingly enough, however, what contemporary readers found most striking in these poems was not Day Lewis's hesitations but a stronger, more assured voice than that of Day Lewis in the thirties. "Word over all" is the opening phrase of Whitman's poem "Reconciliation," one of the late poems in *Drum Taps* in which Whitman seeks the healing of divisions after the Civil War. By making Whitman's hope the title of his own volume, Day Lewis overtly points toward the reconciliation of opposing factions in his war-torn heart as well as in his war-torn world. The initial responses from critics and readers alike could not have been more encouraging to the poet. *Word Over All* received more consistently enthusiastic praise than any of Day Lewis's previous collections had.

Repeatedly reviewers said that they heard in the new poems a "matured" voice with a deepened and surer sense of himself than the political poems of the thirties had shown. Here, for example, is G. W. Stonier in *The New Statesman and Nation*:

> Maturity, it seems to me, with whatever limitations, is the quality, next to vision, which one should put first among the requirements for writing poetry to-day.
>
> It is because Mr. Day Lewis has matured, while his compeers, Auden and Spender, have not, that his new volume makes a more substantial appeal. He is the tortoise in that school which has produced illustrious hares: imitative, to begin with, enthusiastic, painstaking, here he comes at his own pace and with his own victories in sight. So much is *Word Over All* his own that it is astonishing to remember the pastiche of earlier years—the industrial machinery and party flags, echoes of Auden, Hopkins and the Georgians. . . .

Richard Church, writing in *The Listener*, thought he already heard notes of reconciliation in the earlier *Poems in Wartime*; the dust jacket of *Word Over All* proudly reprinted his enthusiastic remarks:

> Each [poem] is firm, self-contained, mature and objective, but the objectiveness is not that of a mere observer. The poet feels deeply and delicately together. Throughout the poem, however, this intensity of feeling is held in hand by an austerity that is spiritual, fierce, clear-eyed. . . . Mr. Day Lewis has emerged from his entanglement of ideas and political preoccupations. He is now fully himself. It is an impressive self, and likely to make a permanent mark on the history of English poetry.

But is the defining word of *Word Over All* reconciliation . . . or unresolved conflict? The poems repeatedly unmask their own wish fulfillment. Even at the time, Stonier saw accurately in the newfound maturity, that "the central point, a point of balance at which the writer's mature sympathies and powers have come to rest" is, paradoxically, a point of tension, division, even (Day Lewis's own word for these years) "stress." Consequently, Stonier concluded, while the book as a whole "could be divided roughly into two, personal life and the war," whatever the particular theme—"childhood, classical education, love, and political idealism"—"all exercise a stress which in the best of these poems is unmistakable."

How, then, does Day Lewis respond to the stress of war? Whereas Whitman's poem "Reconciliation" had earned its strategic place near the end of *Drum Taps*, Day Lewis placed "Word Over All" at the opening of the war poems in Part Two and perhaps for that reason the poem proffers no reconciliation. In the "now" of ground zero, where war and eros cross, the first stanza contemplates the poet's ultimate failure: the loss of faith, beyond God and love and politics, in his very medium and function:

Now when drowning imagination clutches
At old loves drifting away,
Splintered highlights, hope capsized—a wrecked world's
Flotsam, what can I say
To cheer the abysmal gulfs, the crests that lift not
To any land in sight? (325)

"What can I say"? Two stanzas later, the question still hangs in the smoky air of the devastated city:

I watch when searchlights set the low cloud smoking
Like acid on metal: I start
At sirens, sweat to feel a whole town wince
And thump, a terrified heart,
Under the bomb-strokes. These, to look back on, are
A few hours' unrepose:
But the roofless old, the child beneath the debris—
How can I speak for those? (326)

To this question the poem offers an almost forced formulaic response—"Yet words there must be . . ."—but without a sense of what can be said beyond the tragedy of the moment. Near the end of the poem, the phrase "Dark over all" seems to mock the Whitmanian title, but the very next phrase—"absolving all"—shifts the direction and seems to invest language with a function in the dark time. Articulating suffering may not resolve but may absolve it, even if forgiveness is only humanly and not divinely ordained, into what Yeats had called "tragic joy":

Dark over all, absolving all, is hung
Death's vaulted patience:
Words are to set man's joy and suffering there
In constellations. (327)

The final image offers only stoic heroism: "Humankind," a "mightier presence" than the slogans of any humanitarian "Cause," proves itself mortal—but also moral—in enduring tragedy, yet only such perseverance admits the possibility of being both "flooded by dawn's pale courage, [and] rapt in eve's / Rich acquiescence."

Courage in waxing and acquiescence in waning: therein lies the riddle in the wake of war (and, as we shall see, of eros). The title of a poem later in Part Two, "Reconciliation," asks that it be read against "Word Over All," and, as in "Word Over All," "Reconciliation" offers no healing except death, as we watch a soldier (presumably in the African campaign against Field Marshal Rommel's armored corps) expire slowly beside his "shattered tank," "Like a limp creature hacked out of its shell." In Whitman's poem, as the speaker kisses his enemy's corpse, Romantic pantheism absorbs death into the ongoing flow of mortal life. Eliot's Christian faith allowed him to postulate reconciliation in transcendence and to say in "Burnt Norton": "What might have been and what has been / Point to one end, which is always present" (*Collected Poems*, 176). Day Lewis, failing either Romantic or Christian reconciliation, rewrites Eliot and Whitman to say that living in time makes the present moment a farewell kiss: "The time that was, the time that might have been / . . . kiss / Before they part eternally." On the splinter-point of time, as Stonier saw in his review, seemingly irreconcilable stresses contend; "a world without, a world within / / Wrestle like old antagonists," so that "each is / Balancing each" until the "lock gates" of death yawn, beyond the antagonisms of love and war, on the hazily Yeatsian prospect of "argent, swan-assembled reaches" (339–40).

"What can I say"? "The Image" follows "Word Over All" and seeks to turn tragic joy into a strategy for surviving overwhelming odds through the wit and wiles of language:

From far, she seemed to lie like a stone on the sick horizon:
Too soon that face, intolerably near,
Writhed like a furious ant-hill. Whoever, they say, set eyes on
Her face became a monument to fear.

But Perseus, lifting his shield, beheld as in a view-finder
A miniature monster, darkly illustrious.
Absorbed, pitying perhaps, he struck. And the sky behind her
Woke with a healthier colour, purified thus.

Now, in a day of monsters, a desert of abject stone
Whose outward terrors paralyse the will,
Look to that gleaming circle until it has revealed you

The glare of death transmuted to your own
Measure, scaled-down to a possible figure the sum of ill.
Let the shield take that image, the image shield you.   (327–28)

"The Image" is a Petrarchan sonnet. The octave sets up as the unifying trope the myth of Perseus and the Medusa. The rhyming of "horizon"/ "set eyes on" and "view-finder"/ "behind her" sets a jocular tone, but the tone is as deceptive as appearances. Thus the Medusa may look like a stone from a distance, but in fact close-up her face, writhing furiously like a disturbed anthill, turns others to stone, literally petrifying them with fear. The "monument to fear" is not (as the fourth line in isolation might seem to say) her face but the face of "whoever . . . set eyes on / Her face." The internal play with vowels and consonants underlies these reversals and adds to the serious play of the opening lines: "*From far*," "*furious*," "*face*," "*fear*"; "she *seemed* to *lie like*"; "*seemed*," "*stone*," "*sick*," "*soon*"; "*Too soon*"; "*Writhed like*," "*eyes*"; "*ant*," "monum*ent*"; "*monument*," "*mini*ature *mon*-ster"; and so on. However, as in the verse of Frost or Hardy or John Crowe Ransom, the wit here is deployed as a verbal maneuver for holding off, manipulating, and reducing to bearable human scale a perilous world deadly even to heroes. In fact, it is wit—canny intelligence deployed to uncanny effect—whose "gleaming circle" makes the dark monster "illustrious" and shields the hero from a stony death, thus making Perseus a poet and the poet a Perseus.

There is a play on eyes and seeing throughout the sonnet: the "glare of death" against the Perseus-poet's capacity for sight. Though vulnerable to the Medusa, the Perseus-poet has resourcefully survived the deadly gaze by reducing the monster to an image in his "view-finder" shield. Glossing this poem in *The Poetic Image*, Day Lewis comments that by wielding "the image as a shield" the poet "may focus reality for the sword-thrust of his imagination" (99). Twenty years later he reflected again on the image in terms of the power of the imagination over tragic reality: Perseus's "major shield," which protected him from "confronting directly the petrifying face" of a violent reality, is a trope for "the strength of the moral imagination" ("Oration for the Quatercentenary Celebration of the Birth of William Shakespeare," 6). Thereby "the sum of ill" is "scaled-down to a possible figure," and "transmuted to your own / Measure." References to "image," "figure," "measure" specify that Day Lewis's "view-finder," his device or invention for seeing and outseeing all the "outward terrors" of mortality, is the measured and figured microcosm of the poem itself, whose execution is executing the monster as the reader reads. The pun on "transmuted," in "The glare of death transmuted to your own / Measure," changes Perseus's death into the Medusa's and saves the hero from becoming dumb as a stone by muting the monster into the voice of his own poetic measure.

The outcome of the contention between Perseus and the Medusa is suspended in the syntactical ambiguity of the phrase "revealed you" in line 11, "Look to that gleaming circle until it has revealed you" (mistakenly printed "have revealed you" in the *Complete Poems*); and the ambiguity of that suspension is accentuated by the break between tercets that hangs the line on that phrase. If "you" is the direct object of the verb "revealed," then the image in the poem-shield is "you," the Perseus-poet. But the continuation of the sentence beyond the line break into the closing tercet seems to change "you" into the indirect object of the verb: now "the gleaming circle" of the shield "has revealed you // The glare of death transmuted to your own / Measure." That is to say, the poem-shield encloses and frames the Medusa's scaled-down image and shows it harmlessly to you, the Perseus-poet. The circle of shield or sonnet reveals to Perseus the image of the threatening Other, but now safely reduced to bearable human scale and contained within psychological and aesthetic bounds.

However, the double meaning is intentional and intraconnected; the syntactical ambiguity makes the image in the shield both Perseus ("you") and the death-glare of the Medusa. The battle with the Other reveals a shocking but indisputable connection with the Other. This double reflection mirrors self and Other, mirrors self in Other, Other in self. The monster *against* whom you struggle becomes the monster *with* whom you struggle: an inseparable and determining part of (not apart from) who "you" are and whom "you" may become. Yet that look of recognition need not spell damnation. Yes, the process of figuring and measuring the Other reveals the crafty craftsman/antagonist in his own image of the Other; but it does so in a way that can also protect him and makes him victor rather than victim—precisely because the image can constitute his "own / Measure" of her, not hers of him. Such is the decisive nature of the transmutation or metamorphosis accomplished in the aesthetics of image making; hence the verbal inversion of the line that seals the outcome of the sonnet: "Let the shield take that image, the image shield you."

Thus the query "What can I say" finds a complicated and extended answer in "The Image," and its validation of poetry as a defensive weapon leads to the war poems that make up the bulk of Part Two: "Watching Post," "The Stand-To," "Where Are the War Poets?" "Angel," "Airmen Broadcast," "Lidice," "Ode to Fear," "The Dead," "Reconciliation," "Will It Be So Again?" In the shield of poetry the poet confronts the war and its victims, and the compassionate identification that permitted Day Lewis in "Watching Post" and "The Stand-To" to see his Musbury neighbors as individuals rather than as the stereotyped agricultural workers of Party propaganda opens wide to encompass all countrymen and women dying under enemy fire at home and abroad. "The Dead" is a poem about the victims of the blitz. Its flat prosiness—like the images of "the roofless old, the child beneath the debris" in "Word Over All"—contrasts pointedly with the rhetorical inflation of much war poetry—notably, Dylan Thomas's blitz poem, "A Refusal to Mourn the Death, by Fire, of a Child in London"—as if for Day Lewis at this point rhetoric demeaned rather than elevated the bald, brute fact of human sacrifice.

"The Dead" is also a political poem as Thomas's is not; it insists that the victims are scapegoats "for the sins of a whole world"—not just the barbarism of the Nazis but also the greed of those at home more powerful and better educated than the victims of the home front:

Still, they have made us eat
Our knowing words, who rose and paid
The bill for the whole party with their uncounted courage.
And if they chose the dearer consolations
Of living—the bar, the dog race, the discreet
Establishment—and let Karl Marx and Freud go hang,
Now they are dead, who can dispute their choice?
Not I, nor even Fate.   (339)

In a poem like this one Day Lewis is trying—no less than in the thirties,
though now through the mediation of Hardy rather than of Marx or
Freud—for a poetry that looked beyond the personal to the common fate
of fellow countrymen and all humankind.

In fact, in *The Poetic Image*, the Clark Lectures delivered at Cambridge
in 1946, which gave Day Lewis his first opportunity to articulate a post-
thirties poetics, he again rejected, as he had in *A Hope for Poetry*, the sym-
bolist-surrealist inclination in modern poetry, "which looks inwards to find
images," and he continues to advocate a social poetry that "looks freely
outward upon the human situation" and addresses the community (*The
Poetic Image*, 153). It is true that, in contrast to *A Hope for Poetry*, the muted
political stance in the Cambridge lectures proposes endurance and survival
rather than revolution. The bitter aftertaste of the thirties made Auden
conclude in his widely cited Yeats elegy that "poetry makes nothing happen," and the Christian humanism Auden soon espoused did not change
his mind on that score. A century earlier Matthew Arnold had sought to
take the opposite position and to validate the socially redemptive power
of poetry for post-Christian modernity. He argued that poetry ought to
present a significant and clarifying action and excluded his own *Empedocles
on Etna* from *Poems* (1853) because, he said in the Preface, it presents a
drama in which "suffering finds no vent in action; in which a continuous
state of mental distress is prolonged, unrelieved by incident, hope, or resistance; in which there is everything to be endured, nothing to be done."

When Arnold could find for himself no political or religious basis on
which to propose decisive action, he increasingly withdrew from poetry
into searching out limited social and ethical objectives in prose. Day Lewis,
further along than Arnold in the modern devolution into incertitude, faced
"a much wider distance to-day between the poetic image and the human
act," and, looking back at the thirties, Day Lewis concludes ruefully that
precisely the fact that the links between poem and act had become "at-
tenuated and more subtle" made the thirties poets feel compelled to force
the connection, producing instead propagandistic "pseudo-art" (*The Poetic
Image*, 31). Like Arnold, then, the Day Lewis of the forties was ready to
settle for more limited, less absolute objectives. However, unlike Arnold,
he did not associate those lowered objectives with a conscientious withdrawal from poetry. Instead, the example of Virgil domesticated in Hardy
allowed him to propose as the chastened hope for poetry a secular,
Arnoldian humanism, for "that large dream of humanism . . . bear[s] the

mould and stamp of human need, human circumstance, human virtue"
(154). Though compassionate empathy with the human condition replaces
coercive social action, nonetheless the initiating premise is that through
such poetry "the individual is brought, however remotely, into touch with
communal experience, general truths which have eternally bound mankind together" (144).

Moreover, the paradox would seem to be that the collective resonance
of the humanist poet reaches a depth that realizes the personal more freely
and truly than the polemical poet's drive toward fixed responses and quick
action ever could. Indeed, says Day Lewis, again citing Hardy as his example, the paradox is that "the poet, not burrowing towards the roots of
his own experience, not swaddling himself in his own many-colored sensations, but looking freely outwards upon the human situation, may all
unwittingly give us a creative image of himself . . . " (*The Poetic Image*,
152–53). Indeed, he would declare in "The Lyrical Poetry of Thomas
Hardy," the Warton Lecture delivered at the British Academy in 1951, it
was Hardy's whole-hearted humanism that made for a "great personal
poetry" (173). For though "the poetic image, which is the myth of the
individual," has replaced the ancient and sustaining poetic myths "created
by a collective consciousness," still out of the individual's very need and
desire the "diminished" range of the poetic image "invokes" and "returns
to that consciousness for its sanction . . . [,] as though man, even at his
most individual, still seeks emotional reassurance from the sense of community, not community with his fellow-beings alone, but with whatever
is living in the universe, and with the dead" (*The Poetic Image*, 32–33). The
failure of thirties poetry can be seen to proceed from misconception, therefore; the "MacSpaunday" poets of the thirties "sought to illuminate" ideas
that were "Marxist or Freudian," but "the images they gave off were im-
paired by that fancifulness, that emotional thinness we associate with conceits" because those ideas "were not in fact generally accepted" (82).

Reviewers and readers of *Word Over All* commended the largeness of
heart and depth of feeling in these poems, and *Word Over All* sold five
times as many copies as any of the volumes from the thirties. These responses encouraged Day Lewis to pin his future on the hope that a deeper
grounding in the myth-making commonality of experience accounted for
the greater clarity, if not assurance, of the personal, lyric voice that many
heard in the poems.

• 5

The politics of the poetic image, however, cannot be separated from the
erotics of the poetic image—or from the poetics and even the metaphysics of the eroticized image. Day Lewis could never entirely let Marx "go
hang," and still less Freud, for the forties saw him entwined more and more
in Freudian entanglements. Georges Bataille, roughly Day Lewis's con-

temporary, derived his philosophical commentary from the disillusioned complexities of postwar, leftwing French existentialism and Freudian psychology as expounded and modified by his close friend Jacques Lacan. Bataille's study *Erotism: Death and Sensuality* begins by defining eroticism—not just in "physical" but, much more importantly, in "emotional" and "religious" terms—as the essential premise and condition of human existence: the "assenting to life up to the point of death" (15, 11). Sexual activity, from Bataille's perspective, is the physical manifestation of "a psychological quest independent of the natural goal" of sexual intercourse. And, just as sexual "reproduction and the desire for children" at once arise from and resist the fact of physical and biological death, so the psychological and spiritual dimension of eroticism both arises from and resists the mortal individual's conscious recognition of inevitable extinction. The erotic drive is, then, a compulsion—at once manic and demonic—to reject human limitations, to push them riskily to the limits (and, more riskily, beyond) in the desire to break into total and immortal existence. So eroticism is the drive to transcendence that mystics and saints describe, understandably enough, in erotic terms? Yes, says Bataille the lapsed Catholic, but finally no, says Bataille the agnostic, because transcendence of human limits requires the extinction rather than the transfiguration of the human. Since immortality is the unattainable projection of apparently hopeless desire, the drive to full life is the drive to death. Consequently, at the beginning of his book, Bataille almost immediately revises his initial definition of eroticism as "assenting to life up to the point of death" to eroticism as "assenting to life even in death" (11, 15). The line between "up to" and "in" inscribes the contested distinction between life maintained and life extinguished. H. D. had learned this lesson from Freud himself, and at the end of her life she phrased the connection and conflict between eros and thanatos by giving their names as anagrams of each other: "La Mort, L'Amour" (*Helen in Egypt*, 268, 271).

It has to be said that for Bataille there is a rigorous French fatalism about the hopelessness of desire that is more extreme in its negative assessment than would suit H. D.'s—and, much more, Day Lewis's—temperament and experience. Nevertheless, just as H. D.'s life and poetry is determined by both the elation and stress of contending with L'Amour/La Mort, Day Lewis's poems in *Word Over All* and *Poems 1943–1947* also show that the contention of eros and thanatos occasionally yielded hoped-for moments of transcendence but also brought him sometimes to the brink of despair and madness at the prospect of unrelieved conflict. Bataille's extreme position is a disillusioned response to what seems to him the impossible ideal of Christian or Romantic love, and Day Lewis's poetry of the forties veers between extremes more dangerously than he had dared before or would after, risking tragedy as he seeks to escape it, risking ecstasy as he tries to preserve himself from destruction.

On the social and political level, as we have seen, "The Image" invokes the battle between Perseus and Medusa as a trope for the poet-hero's strategy in using art to control and survive the "outward terrors" of a world at war. But we do not need Cellini's famous statue of the nude and helmeted Perseus with blade brandished in his left hand and the Medusa's decapitated head lifted in his right to recall that the story presents, at the personal and psychological level, a male myth symbolizing the lure and allure of nature and of female sexuality and the consequent drive to control it, by violence if need be, in order to avoid the castration or death that men fear through weak susceptibility or abject surrender to the woman's power over him. For Day Lewis, however, if not for Bataille, the interaction between love and death may reach resolution. "The Assertion," the poem that follows from "The Image," also postulates the symbiosis between eros and violence, but now with eros as the counterbalance to violence. The first verse paragraph of the poem catalogues episodes of war's maiming and death, but "in the face of destruction" names the antidote: "[N]ow is the time we assert / . . . that men are love" (330–31). "What can I say" to the horrors of war? Here, as in the "Dedicatory Stanzas" to *The Georgics*, love is the "positive" counterforce to conflict, rather than, as in "The Image," its underlying cause. Once again, does eros assert life "up to the point of death" . . . or "even in death" and against death?

Glossing "The Assertion" in *The Poetic Image*, Day Lewis made an extremely important statement that articulates a more optimistic and beneficent version of eroticism as the source and drive and end of vital and poetic energy:

> The poet's task . . . is to recognize pattern wherever he sees it, and to build his perceptions into a poetic form which by its urgency and coherence will persuade us of their truth [that is, the truth of his perceptions of pattern]. He is in the world . . . to bear witness to the principle of love, since love is as good a word as any for that human reaching-out of hands towards the warmth in all things, which is the source and passion of his song. Love is thus to him first: but it is more; he apprehends it as a kind of necessity by which all things are bound together and in which, could the whole pattern be seen, their contradictions would appear reconciled.
>
> (*The Poetic Image*, 36–37)

Eros is experienced personally and individually ("to him first"), but "more" than a narcissistic impulse eros is the individual lover's "reaching-out" toward the warm life subtending all things. In this finally all-inclusive extension eros becomes an almost Platonic "principle" animating all forms of life and reconciling their individual "contradictions" into a cosmological "pattern." In the linguistic endeavor metaphor is the fundamental poetic manifestation and device of that erotic principle, and for that reason "every poet's work rests on an act of faith" in the power of metaphor "to discover . . . what Shelley called 'the hitherto unapprehended relations between things'" (*The Poet's Task*, 6). Just this metaphorical/erotic "reconciliation"—that "word over all"—is what we long for and live for, and it is specifically "[t]he poet's task" to "recognize" the emerging network of relations in his particular and

GOING
FORTH AND
RETURNING

•

107

admittedly partial field of experience by constructing the "poetic form" to articulate those "perceptions" in all their "urgency and coherence."

Right after the passage from the lecture quoted above, Day Lewis observes, "I have tried to say it myself, in these lines—"; and he goes on to cite most of the second verse paragraph of "The Assertion," which occurs in the poem almost immediately after the declaration that "men are love":

> Love's the big boss at whose side for ever slouches
> The shadow of a gunman: he's mortar and dynamite;
> Antelope, drinking pool, but the tiger too that crouches.
> Therefore be wise in the dark hour to admit
> The logic of the gunman's trigger,
> Embrace the explosive element, learn the need
> Of tiger for antelope and antelope for tiger.   (331)

The lines are, of course, wildly incongruent both with the just-announced notion of the solidarity of human love as antidote to violence and with the lecture's exposition of cosmic love for which these lines are purportedly a redaction. Was Day Lewis oblivious to the incongruence, or did he intend it as an indication of the difficulty of the "poet's task" because of the slippage between the principle and its realization?

Certainly Day Lewis's own experience, whatever his Romantic-Platonic aspirations, substantiated the "contradictions" and conflicts of love more than its "pattern" of harmonious relations, and that experience was confirmed by his readings in Hardy and Freud and D. H. Lawrence (including Lawrence's *Fantasia on the Unconscious*). Theorizing the erotic drive not very many years later Bataille (whose *Erotism* appeared in France in the mid-fifties) would take it that the kind of participation in the totality of being that Day Lewis invokes in the lecture is indeed the aim and end of the erotic drive, but Bataille would also aver that the hermetic isolation of individual existence and of the consciousness that was the sign and seal of that solipsism keeps the goal constantly and feverishly sought after but ever unattained and unobtainable. Bataille would have taken Day Lewis as typically doomed by his adherence to a hopeless religious or Romantic ideal. In the drive to transcend its limits individual consciousness strains those limits to the point of rupture in order to break into and join with another and then others and finally all others and the All, seeking at the extremity of life participation in undifferentiated being. However, since such transcendent union could be consummated, hypothetically and actually, only at or through the individual's death, consciousness is caught in an excruciating tension between transgressing the limits of individuality and pulling back from the consummating extinction.

Such a view of the dynamics of the psyche, derived from Freud through Jacques Lacan, posits a theoretical model that is almost the opposite of C. G. Jung's model of individuation as a progress through successive stages of both expansion and integration toward a fully realized identity. Bataille's fatalism seems to offer no exit; "[I]n essence, the domain of eroticism is the domain of violence, of violation." In short, eroticism demands a perpetual state of war, an unceasing assault, body and soul, by inviolable individuals on the inviolability of one another. For, in Bataille's words,

> What does physical eroticism signify if not a violation of the very being of its practitioners?— . . . a violation bordering on death, bordering on murder? . . . The whole business of eroticism is to destroy the self-contained character of the practitioners as they are in their normal lives.
>
> (*Erotism*, 16–17)

If Bataille were correct in asserting that lovers experience their encounter as the violation of the other's physical and psychic being, then no wonder the lover fears and resists the preemptive and possessive advances of the beloved—and sometimes instinctively fights back.

Day Lewis did not have to have read Bataille to know the destructive potential of eros; his own experience found confirmation in his avid reading of Hardy and Lawrence. Even an early Lawrence poem like "Snap-dragon," which first appeared in *Georgian Poetry 1911–1912*, presents the Lawrentian ethos in terms at least as extreme as Bataille's "violation bordering on death, bordering on murder." In the poem's narrative the snap-dragon blossom becomes the emblem of the seductive play and counterplay between the speaker and a woman with large brown hands. The concluding lines anticipate the assault and counterassault as resistance to death's "not-to-be":

> And I do not care though the large hands of revenge
> Shall get my throat at last—shall get it soon,
> If the joy that they are lifted to avenge
> Have risen red on my night as a harvest moon,
> Which even Death can only put out for me,
> And death I know is better than not-to-be.
>
> (*Georgian Poetry 1911–1912*, 116;
> see also *Complete Poems*, I, 126)

Day Lewis's temperament and training inclined him to resist Lawrence's dark determinism and would have resisted Bataille's. Nevertheless, at times— for example, in the lines from "The Assertion" cited in his Cambridge lecture (ostensibly to illustrate love's creative "principle")—he comes dangerously close to their fatalism. Those lines present three tropes for love: the mobster boss with a hit man (the phrase "the shadow of a gunman" echoing the title of Sean O'Casey's famous play); the deadly detonation of mortar shell or dynamite; the tiger preying upon the unsuspecting, defenseless antelope. "In the face of destruction" love seems to present not a counterforce but reiterated instances of violence. However, the two lines just before the ones quoted and misleadingly omitted from the lecture begin to resolve the seeming incongruity of presentation by indicating that the violent tropes (gunman, dynamite, tiger) are meant to undercut any easy or naively sentimental clichés about love: "For love's no laughing matter, / Never was a free gift, an angel, a fixed equator."

And the concluding lines of the poem, which occur just after those in the lecture but are also omitted there, push the paradox of love's duplicity toward "correction" and reversal:

> O love, so honest of face, so unjust in action,
> Never so dangerous as when denied,
> Let your kindness tell us how false we are, your bloody
> correction,
> Our purpose and our pride.   (331)

If Eros seems a double-dealer when his openness of face and candor of approach prove "unjust in action," the falsehood and betrayal may be ours rather than his. In the myth King Pentheus of Thebes, sternly repressive in the name of public virtue, saw a serenely smiling Dionysus and his female worshipers turn bloody and violent when exiled from the city, for Eros is "never so dangerous as when denied." In instances like that of Pentheus and the Thebans, the "correction" may be "bloody" but proves to be harsh "kindness," because it comes to subvert false prohibitions and convert "our purpose and our pride" from denial to celebration.

Such is the metaphoric and metamorphic message of Dionysus and Eros, and in this poem at least Day Lewis wants to act on it, ready to risk the bloody explosions at Brimclose to break out of the "false" situation there for the chance of love's realization. That purpose and pride provide the startling and disturbing conclusion of the lines cited in the lecture:

> Therefore be wise in the dark hour to admit
> The logic of the gunman's trigger,
> Embrace the explosive element, learn the need
> Of tiger for antelope and antelope for tiger.

By a convoluted "logic" that is not fully drawn out in either the poem or the lecture, these lines do in fact offer some kind of instantiation of "the principle of love." Sometimes the tangled "contradictions" of human motivation and feeling tighten into a trap. Could it be that perhaps the kindest, most salvific move is to break open the trap, trusting love to reveal itself "as a kind of necessity by which all things are bound together and in which, could the whole pattern be seen, their contradictions would appear reconciled." Then war would issue in peace, and bloody wounds find healing. Readers were shocked by the scriptural epigraph that Flannery O'Connor would give her novel *The Violent Bear It Away*, a story of the entwining of murder and grace: "From the days of John the Baptist until now, the Kingdom of Heaven suffereth violence, and the violent bear it away." Do the shadow of the gunman and the pounce of the tiger move to a graced consummation? Many of O'Connor's stories imply that decisive opportunity, and Day Lewis seems to have wanted to see the leap of his tiger as terrifyingly beneficent, like Blake's tiger, or like Eliot's, which as "Christ the tiger" in "Gerontion" "springs in the new year" and "devours" us.

In O'Connor's fiction violence is the consequence of sinful human nature and operates graciously in the Christian agon of salvation. But what if the one broken by violence were not a sinner, or an emasculating monster like the Medusa, but a defenseless antelope, or an innocent woman, a wife and mother like Mary? Was Mary the antelope or the Medusa? Or perhaps, in Day Lewis's tormented psyche, someone more alarming in her possessive love than the antelope yet by no account deserving of the Medusa's fate? To keep from being turned to stone, did Perseus have to become more violent than the Medusa? In this poem and at this point in his life, Day Lewis took the power of eros as revealing the "logic" of his need to be Perseus, to be tiger, to break the unnatural truce of their marriage, no matter how guilty part of him felt for doing so. The justifying hope expressed in the poem is that the outcome, however "bloody," would constitute a "correction" to free him and even perhaps her into the possibility of erotic consummation. Cellini's bronze statue, like Day Lewis's "The Image," celebrates the victor's triumph. And "The Assertion" seeks to justify the "bloody" consequences in the mutual "need / Of tiger for antelope and antelope for tiger." Day Lewis's guilty sense of Mary's demanding but unquestioning love for him kept him from the decapitating blow, from the tiger's pounce. But the poem stands as an expression of his baffled and ambivalent intention to justify erotic violence in order to assert a more hopeful outcome than the tragic one that Lawrence presented poetically in "Snapdragon" or Bataille philosophically in *Erotism*.

Yet what the three of them share is the conviction that the erotic drive, even at times the violence of its manifestation, is essentially, in origin and end, religious and even mystical. *Erotism* has a chapter on "Christianity" and another on "Mysticism and Sensuality." Working out of Freudian and Lacanian speculation on the nature and function of the libido, Bataille sees the desire for transcendence of individual limits through union with another or others as driving through and beyond physical copulation and emotional empathy toward the individual's desired union with and dissolution in the divine. When Marxism had replaced Day Lewis's Christian faith, secular love became the motive of revolution and the basis of the utopian social order. Now, as the Cambridge lecture indicates, Day Lewis postulated love, shorn of a political agenda, as the quasi-Platonic "principle" that animates individual lives and in which they participate and find their common source and goal. The key passage that we have been examining therefore proposes what can only be described as a metaphysic in which love, transcendent to but immanent in temporal experience, reconciles the warring conflicts driven by unsatisfied desire.

Day Lewis could offer no proof of such a principle of love except by what Pound called "natural demonstration" in Canto 36. Day Lewis sometimes felt intimations of that principle intuitively in his pulse-beat, on his nerve-ends, through the deepest stirrings of his heart and the highest flights of his imagination. And for him, as for Pound, natural demonstration was stronger than halting reason because its authentication was personal experience. Canto 36 is Pound's translation of Cavalcanti's "Donna mi prega," and that canzone is itself a distillation of the neo-Platonist mystique of love as light. In Pound/Cavalcanti's words, love-light is "postulate not by the reason / But 'tis felt, I say." However, in time and space love manifests itself in material forms whose definitions and limitations arouse the desire for completion and thence the wars of competing desires; its light is broken into the contrasting and even clashing colors of the spectrum. Yet the love-light is the single source and substance and end of these many and contrasting manifestations; in Pound's arcane version of Cavalcanti's arcane lines, it

> Descendeth not by quality but shineth out
> Himself his own effect unendingly
> Not in delight but in the being aware
> Nor can he leave his true likeness otherwhere.
> (*The Cantos*, 177)

The association of Day Lewis with Pound in this regard, for all their antithetical positions on formal and technical matters, is perhaps tenuous but by no means gratuitous. Day Lewis was no more an unambiguously believing Platonist, as Pound was, than he was a Modernist. But, despite his rational agnosticism, his "Churchy" sensibility was drawn and tantalized by the Platonist proposition as it continued to be by Christian faith. Besides, his own experience gave him "felt" moments of "being aware" seemingly beyond the limits of human reason in the cognitions of the imagination. Indeed, against the disintegrative and deconstructive force of Enlightenment scepticism, not just the Romantics but many post-Romantics, whether Modernist or not, have experienced the imagination as the supreme cognitive faculty through which the metaphysical and erotic dimensions of desire seek and on occasion find the object of longing and desire. In the nineteenth century, the great Anglo-American theorists of the metaphysical-erotic imagination include Coleridge, Keats, Shelley, Whitman, and Emerson (who spoke, with alliterative emphasis, of "the marriage of matter and mind"); in the twentieth century, they include Pound, Williams, H. D., Frost, and Stevens. Stevens's statement "We say that God and the imagination are one" voices the transition from Romantic transcendentalism to Modernist humanism by locating our perceptions of the divine in our divinizing desires, the realization of which is a manifestation of our powers of imagining and expression. In Stevens's line from "Final Soliloquy of the Interior Paramour," "we"—the desiring poet and the imagined object of his desire, in their verbal conjunction—" say God and the imagination are one" (*Collected Poems*, 524).

The passage from *The Poetic Image* that has served as a touchstone in this chapter lacks the rhetorical flair of Coleridge's or Shelley's or even

Stevens's pronouncements. Day Lewis lacks something of their bold assurance in making claims for the imagination, yet his more modestly phrased
statement makes a similar claim. "The poet's task" is, as we have seen, to
construct a poem whose "urgency and coherence will persuade us of [the]
truth" of our erotic reaching out to "the warmth in all things"; for our
desire seeks not just fulfillment in particular objects but, through those
objects, transcendence (even at the risk of extinction) in the cosmic "principle of love" in which "contradictions would appear reconciled." The
wording "would appear" leaves open the question of whether the contradictions would actually be reconciled in the "principle of love" or only
seem so. In any case, the postulation of such an erotic and metaphysical
principle as "the source and passion of his song" gives Day Lewis a motive
that the "revolutionary love" of the thirties had in the end failed to provide: a personal and admittedly metaphysical motive, yet, in this time of
war and stress, the psychological and ethical basis for living in time.

In the ordering of the poems in *Word Over All*, "The Image," in which
the poem functions as a stratagem for reducing the threat of violence, public
and private, to formal control, is immediately followed by "The Poet," in
which the erotics and metaphysics of the imagination teach the speaker to
live in time positively and creatively:

> I have learned to count each day
> Minute by breathing minute—
>
> . . . .
>
> As lovers count for luck
> Their own heart-beats and believe
> In the forest of time they pluck
> Eternity's single leaf.   (328)

The second and third stanzas seem to present such a timeless minute, as
the imagination mirrors the "visionary light" of the full moon pouring
down on the scene to "heal" the wounds of "murder" and lunacy:

> Tonight the moon's at the full.
> Full moon's the time for murder.
> But I look to the clouds that hide her—
> The bay below me is dull,
> An unreflecting glass—
> And chafe for the clouds to pass,
> And wish she suddenly might
> Blaze down at me so I shiver
> Into a twelve-branched river
> Of visionary light.
>
> For now imagination,
> My royal, impulsive swan,
> With raking flight—I can see her—
> Comes down as it were upon

A lake in whirled snow-floss
And flurry of spray like a skier
Checking. Again I feel
The wounded waters heal.
Never before did she cross
My heart with such exaltation.   (328–29)

If "murder" recalls the destructive and violent aspect of the erotic drive that Bataille emphasized, the "visionary light" recalls the opposite and creative aspect of eros that Pound found in the tradition of Cavalcanti and sought to affirm against the violences of personal and political life in the twentieth century. The lighted landscape itself—moon, lake, clouds, river, swan, and so on—incorporates Romantic elements from Coleridge and Shelley to Yeats and Stevens, but Day Lewis assimilates these elements into a moment personalized with a surprising simile: the light descends in a "flurry of spray like a skier / Checking." The last lines turn the old rune about telling the truth under forfeiture of death ("Cross my heart and hope to die") into an affirmation: "Never before did she cross / My heart with such exaltation." Moreover, the word "again" in "Again I feel / The wounded waters heal" suggests that this is no first or unique event: "never before" is really "once more."

Like all his male predecessors, Day Lewis speaks of the lunar imagination as "she," the feminine within himself that is the agent and object of erotic and metaphysical desire. The stanzas are beautifully calibrated to constellate the lines in a sense of harmony achieved and sustained. The rhyming of "light"/"flight" bridges the stanza break as do the end-rhymes linking the two stanzas: "murder," "hide her," "shiver," "river," "see her," "skier"; "full," "dull," "feel," "heal"; "glass," "pass," "floss," "cross." The elision from "Blaze down" in one stanza to "Comes down" in the next marks the transference of light's agency from the external landscape to "My royal, impulsive" swan-imagination. The plea in the second stanza that the moon shatter and possess him with "visionary light" does empower him in the third stanza ("—I can see her—") to feel the holistic vision of intuitions swarming in the fourth stanza:

Oh, on this striding edge,
This hare-bell height of calm
Where intuitions swarm
Like nesting gulls and knowledge
Is free as the winds that blow,
A little while sustain me,
Love, till my answer is heard!
Oblivion roars below,
Death's cordon narrows: but vainly,
If I've slipped the carrier word.   (329)

Even the great Romantics, however, have recorded how precariously poised on a fragile "edge" the synthesizing moment of imaginative

"exaltation" is, how threatened from below by the contumely of war and
"Oblivion." So here, the subversive conjunctions "till" and "if" ("till my
answer is heard," "vainly, / If I've slipped the carrier word") express the
contingencies that collapse the moment in the final stanza: "All I have felt
or sung / Seems now but the moon's fitful / Sleep on a clouded bay."
Nevertheless, the very last lines go on to urge Eros to draw from the poet's
heart, by violence if need be, the poem that is the moment's "witness"
and memorial: "Love, tear the song from my breast! / Short, short is the
time" (329). The conjunction of "urgency and coherence" that the lecture posited rests on and proceeds from the recognition that the intuitive
erotic moment, when it comes, is fleeting.

The poem "One and One" recalls and memorializes a globed moment:

I remember, as if it were yesterday,
Watching that girl from the village lay
The fire in a room where sunlight poured,
And seeing, in the annexe beyond, M. play
A prelude of Bach on his harpsichord.

I can see his face now, heavy and numb
With resignation to the powers that come
At his touch meticulous, smooth as satin,
Firm as hammers. I can hear the air thrum
With notes like sun-motes in a twinkling pattern.

Her task there fetched from a girl the innate
Tingling response of glass to a note:
She fitted the moment, too, like a glove,
Who deft and submissive knelt by the grate
Bowed as if in the labour of love.

Their orbits touched not: but the pure submission
Of each gave value and definition
To a snapshot printed in the morning's sun.
From any odd corner we may start a vision
Proving that one and one make One.   (342)

The village girl, distracted from the daily routine of laying the hearth-fire,
is drawn into the music played on a harpsichord by someone identified as
M. The everyday quality of the setting is suggested by stock similes like
"smooth as satin" and "fitted . . . like a glove." But this "odd corner" of
seemingly mundane experience unexpectedly yields a "vision." The speaker
is not functioning as the performing artist; M. is his surrogate. And the
girl becomes the focus and vehicle and mediatrix of the speaker's impres-
sion of the moment and the music. She is not the performer's muse, much
less Bach's, but she functions as the poet-speaker's muse, "Bowed as if in
the labour of love." His language chastely eroticizes the configuration of
male artist and female listener, like the figures in a Vermeer painting, so

that "the pure submission / Of each" composes, in the speaker's poem, "a vision / Proving that one and one make One" (342).

The initial trinity of the poem—girl, harpsichordist, speaking "I"—reduces itself to a duality—"one and one"—with the recognition of the anonymous harpsichordist as the stand-in and alter ego of the observing and speaking "I" as artist. So the seemingly simple equation of "one and one" can be read in several ways: first the girl and the musician; but also the observer/speaker with his unitary perception of the girl and musician, and, as we read, with his whole and completed poem about the girl and the musician; and even, by extension, the reader and this integral poem he has read. The important point is that at every level the sum of "one and one" is not two, as rational computation would demand, but "One," and the initial capital "O" suggests that aesthetic arithmetic adds up to a sum that integrates discreet elements in a different, visionary, maybe metaphysical dimension of reality. The "principle of love" composes the scene through the agency of the imagination; however, for moderns like Day Lewis, or Pound and Stevens, the imagination operates less through Wordsworth's "wise passivity" than through its fictive—that is, making—powers. The natural demonstration of the equation is the artifact: the poem written and read, "Proving that one and one *make* One" (emphasis added). After an a-b rhyme scheme in the earlier stanzas (a-a-b-a-b), the single rhyme in the last stanza adds up: "submission," "definition," "sun," "vision," "One."

The main burden of *The Poetic Image* is to elaborate on the metaphysical intersection of erotics and poetics implied in this multivalent equation. The Cambridge lectures discuss poetry almost exclusively as image and define image as "a word-picture charged with emotion or passion" (20). Language engages in intercourse with the world, and image as metaphor is copulative, exercising but never satisfying "the human desire for wholeness," "the human yearning for order and completeness" (144, 35). By articulating "the similar in the dissimilar" (35), metaphor serves, in Bataille's terms, as a means of fulfilling the individual's desire to transcend differentiation and apprehend wholeness safely this side of death. Modernists (and, even more pronouncedly, contemporary Postmodernists) tend to use metonymy rather than metaphor because metonymy allows them to deconstruct experience horizontally through paratactic and horizontal juxtaposition. In deliberate contrast, however, Day Lewis insists almost exclusively on the synthesizing verticality of metaphor. For him the multivalence of language need not eventuate in the infinite deferral of meaning, as a deconstructionist like Jacques Derrida has argued, but instead provides a rich ambiguity for seeking out the connective similarities between dissimilars. In Day Lewis's view the poet should use metaphor in the faith—even if it be blind faith—that it constitutes "a partial intuition of a whole world" and could not do so "unless the world had an order to satisfy that desire, and unless poetry could penetrate to this order and could image it for us piece by piece" (29, 35). In metaphor, that is, "one and one make One."

When Day Lewis asserts that "the poetic image is the human mind claiming kinship with everything that lives and has lived, and making good that claim," when he posits "a coherent order underlying all things" (35, 75), he wants to believe that his Romantic faith has classical and humanist, if no longer Christian, justification. It is for that very reason that he continues to oppose the impressionistic subjectivity and "revolutionary techniques" of Modernist poets. The hermetic symbolisme of Stevens and the formal experiments of Pound and Stein proceed from the "fallacious" assumption that, as Archibald MacLeish's famous "Ars Poetica" put it, a poem should not mean (in the sense of interpreting a reality outside the poem) but simply be (in its autotelic integrity). Old-fashioned as it might sound, Day Lewis insisted that language "cannot in fact discard sequence, cannot discard cause and effect, cannot work to a continuous present" but "must have a beginning, a middle, and an end," "must have rhythm," "must develop its theme, or develop out of its theme" in a sequence of images that has its own emotional if not rational logic (120). In short, a poem must mean as well as be. *The Poetic Image* has to be read as Day Lewis's riposte to the metonymic Modernism of Stein and Pound and Williams.

When Day Lewis speaks of "the poet's old business" of "bringing emotional order out of material and intellectual confusion" (104), it is clear that Stevens is a more congenial Modernist than Stein or Pound. After all, Stevens emphasized metaphor rather than metonymy and composed in metrical form. Day Lewis would agree with Stevens's statement in *The Necessary Angel* that the imagination seeks to create an agreement with reality through metaphor, but at the same time he would be uncomfortable with Stevens's Modernist insistence on the inescapably fictive and subjective character of metaphorical agreement. Stevens's persona in "A High-toned Old Christian Woman" counters the presumed certitude of her theological structures with the inventiveness of aesthetic structures: "Poetry is the supreme fiction, madame" (*Collected Poems*, 59). By contrast, the terminology at the end of *The Poetic Image* seems to invoke a religious sanction for the incarnational and redemptive efficacy of the poem: "In the poem you are reborn; it is a re-creation, a resurrection of the body in which your experience is given flesh and blood and bone . . ." (155).

But how literally did Day Lewis intend such quasi theologizing? Are his religious associations themselves merely metaphorical . . . and so fictive? A number of Day Lewis's poems, as well as hints and intimations in *The Poetic Image*, indicate that he was not so sure of validating the final ontological claim for metaphor. An earlier passage in the final lecture counters the religious aura of the closing affirmation cited above by describing rebirth through poetry not in terms of Christian "resurrection" (think as well of Stevens's "Sunday Morning") but in terms of resurrection of the desired "illusion." For, as that earlier passage declared, although "man yearns for the human fulfilment which is the counterpart of perfection in art,"

> Now a poem makes us happy because, being itself a complete thing and so presenting us with 'a hollow image of fulfilled desire', it creates in us the illusion of completeness. Through our experience of the poem, we are reborn—not indeed complete, for perfection is the prerogative of art alone in this world—but, because poetry's illusion is a fertile one, a degree or two nearer the wholeness for which our selfhood strives. Perfect things, as Nietzsche said, teach hope.

> (145)

"Perfect things"; but what of our imperfect efforts and failed creations? For if even a perfect poem devises only "'a hollow image of fulfilled desire'" and thus an "illusion of completeness," then the poem does not so much achieve fulfillment as fill the void with substitutes, and desire rages on to the next perhaps illusory moment of possible fulfillment. For both Day Lewis and Stevens, however, the quasi-religious residuum of secular, humanistic faith continues to posit perfection in art as an ideal but hypothetically attainable goal and to insist that even in our imperfect efforts the erotics of metaphor can be sufficiently "fertile" to generate new forms of illusory completeness that move us "a degree or two nearer the wholeness for which our selfhood strives." "The Motive for Metaphor," as Stevens titled one of his poems, is this metapoetics of desire, which served him and Day Lewis to counter, and at times to escape, the fatalistic pessimism of Bataille and Derrida.

• 6

The metaphysical or would-be metaphysical consummation of metaphor casts the poet as lover, and, as we have noted, the volume *Word Over All* begins and ends with the poems to (and about) the women who were the subjects (and objects) of the poet's desire. Of the eleven poems from *Poems in Wartime*, now scattered through Parts Two and Three of *Word Over All*, eight deal one way and another with desire, and the last four poems in the volume look specifically back on the affair with Billie Currall. The rollicking rhythms and internal rhymes of "Jig" and "Hornpipe" (both from *Poems in Wartime*) evoke the randy abandon of country dances that matched the rhythm of the lovers' roistering. "Jig" recalls the year consumed by a passion so fierce, that "not / Four traction-engines could tear us apart" (346), but the past tense of the verbs casts a crepuscular distance over their remembered rowdiness. And "Jig"'s companion piece, "Hornpipe," views the evanescence of sexual passion with brusque, rueful acceptance:

> If I could keep you there with the berries in your hair
> And your lacy fingers fair as the may, sweet may,

I'd have no heart to do it, for to stay love is to rue it
And the harder we pursue it, the faster it's away.   (347)

On the downward course of physical desire Bataille reasons that "the *innerness* of the desire" seeks but cannot finally possess the beloved "object *outside*" the lover (29):

> We know that the possession of the object we are afire for is out of the
> question. It is one thing or another: either desire will consume us en-
> tirely, or its object will cease to fire us with longing. We can possess it
> on one condition only, that gradually the desire it arouses will fade.
>
> (*Erotism*, 142)

Since consummation brings death, since possession means surrender, it is "better for desire to die than for us to die"; on the other hand, if living is desiring, then survival only perpetuates the pursuit.

Immediately after "Jig" and "Hornpipe" the postcoital *tristesse* deepens in "The Fault" and "The Rebuke," paired poems about spent passion. "The Fault" looks back past the stale aftermath of "weariness or contrition" to the excesses of passion itself:

> But for me it is love's volcanic
> Too fertile fault, and will mark always
> The first shock of that yielding mood, where satanic
> Bryony twines and frail flowers blaze
> Through our tangled days.   (348)

The geological metaphors recapture passion's seismic eruption: "volcanic," "shock," "blaze." And the "fault" is not only physical, like a fissure in the rock, but moral, the "yielding" a "mark" of the fall. What chance do "frail flowers" have in such a volcanic "blaze"? The landscape is Byronic, and the phrase "satanic / Bryony," cusped on the turn of the lines, puns on the name of the poisonous plant to suggest a "too fertile" Byronic passion, whose excesses become "satanic," the last word of much the longest line.

Yet the companion poem, "The Rebuke," seeks some redemptive residue in the ashes of passion. What if "that pandemonium of the heart, / That sensual arrogance did impart / A kind of truth, a kindling truth" (349)? "Pandemonium" seems to point again, as in the previous poem, to the all-demonism of desire, but in fact the poem ends up delivering a rebuke not to the lovers but, on the contrary, to the deniers of desire:

> Where are the sparks at random sown,
> The spendthrift fire, the holy fire?
> Who cares a damn for truth that's grown
> Exhausted haggling for its own
> And speaks without desire?   (349)

Without denying the excesses of desire and the consequent exhaustion, there is no talk here of Satan and the fall. The reversal is accomplished in the shift from "a kind of truth" to "a kindling truth," and then in the last stanza from "the spendthrift fire" to "the holy fire."

Bataille distinguishes between the passionate dynamics of "getting married" and the habitual routine of "being married," which all too often subsides into deadening habit and routine (*Erotism*, 111). Elizabeth Bowen suggested a similar contrast in *The Heat of the Day* when she contrasted the "unmarried" intensity of love and death in wartime London with the married domesticity of the safe countryside (102). Passion too often dies into marriage, but while it lasts it is driving toward a mystical consummation:

> The total personality is involved, reeling blindly toward annihilation, and this is the decisive moment of religious feeling. . . . This fusion could in no way be limited to that attendant on the plethora of the genital organs. It is a religious effusion first and foremost; it is essentially the disorder of lost beings who oppose no further resistance to the frantic proliferation of life. That enormous unleashing of natural forces seems to be divine, so high does it raise man above the condition to which he has condemned himself of his own accord.
>
> (*Erotism*, 113–14)

Day Lewis's late-adolescent romp with Billie Currall was clearly an escape from the safe but sexless "state of being married" to Mary, and the pairs of poems just discussed come to view it, ex post facto, ruefully but not, finally, remorsefully or apologetically. All the more so, since his current engagement with Rosamond Lehmann seemed to promise a deeper revelation of eros's "kindling truth."

For in Day Lewis's mind, the commitment to Rosamond Lehmann, hurtful though he knew it was to Mary, risked transgression in the hope of transformation. As early as "Poem for an Anniversary" in the mid-thirties he had acknowledged to Mary that they had declined into a "state of being married": "Our volcanic age is over" (193). He had rediscovered "volcanic" passion with Billie, but now with Rosamond he underwent "a seismic disturbance of the whole being" at a depth and of a force that he had never experienced before. Yet under that stress his life unexpectedly began to come alive and to cohere in a new kind of consciousness, a kindled consciousness:

> [M]y life seemed to grow again, flowering in wider sympathies and a sensibility less crude, while my work was enhanced by the joy and pain which seemed to purify vision and enlarge it, to show me poetry everywhere—in the most commonplace things outside me as in the precious strata of my own past experience, unworkable till now. . . .
>
> (*The Buried Day*, 234–5)

The effort to recover and integrate his younger self began with autobiographical pieces at the end of *Overtures to Death*, but now the energized landscape described in "Windy Day in August" reflects a new and trembling openness to the present as well as the past:

> The wind roars endlessly past my ears,
> Racing my heart as in earlier years.
> Here and everywhere, then and now
> Earth moves like a wanton, breathes like a vow.   (343)

Still, Day Lewis did not break from Brimclose into that metamorphosed and metamorphic world liberating as a wanton, binding as a vow. Lawrence had made such a break in eloping with Frieda von Richthofen, but the situations of the two men were different. Unlike Lawrence, Day Lewis had marital and parental bonds, and one side of him sought stability rather than seismic dislocation. Consequently, for complicated psychological and ethical reasons the meeting with Rosamond, though unquestionably one of the convulsive events of his life, did not constitute the sort of instantaneous *coup de foudre* whose single flash changed his life once and for all, as did Lawrence's fateful meeting with Frieda or—to recall other modern poetic instances—Yeats's meeting with Maude Gonne or Robinson Jeffers's with Una Call Kuster.

Day Lewis was perhaps too needful of Mary's maternal caring and assurance to break with her, too mindful of her own loving need for him; perhaps he was, as he often accused himself, caught between cowardice and selfishness. And perhaps, too, he was mindful of the fact that sublime consummation carried the promise of annihilation. In any case, with the earthquake opening under his feet, the prospect of the "seismic" plunge kept him teetering there on, but never over, the vertiginous and crumbling edge, prolonging the double thrill of death and exaltation for nine long years without a fatal fall. For if the cruel truth was that Mary represented to him the death of eros and Rosamond the recovery of eros, did his passion for Rosamond also carry, in the cycle of desire, its own dreaded foretaste of death? In time the two women came to feel that he was playing them off against each other to his own advantage and, toward the end, even became briefly and weirdly allied against him. But in his own divided mind, torn between domestic routine and erotic annihilation, self-preservation may have seemed to require the two women for a double defense: he needed Rosamond against Mary, yes, but also, as he might not at the time have been fully aware, Mary against Rosamond.

At the time Day Lewis did not write, and under the circumstances would not have written, anything like Lawrence's *Look! We Have Come Through*, celebrating the break from his and Frieda's previous lives. The opening poems in *Word Over All* do attribute Day Lewis's change of voice and stance to his new love, but, guiltily aware of Mary and the boys at Brimclose, he expressed it in relatively discreet and tempered terms. Nevertheless, as we have seen, the publication of these poems with the volume dedicated "To Rosamond Lehmann" forced him to tell Mary of the double life he had been leading for two years. In "The Lighted House" and "The Album," the first two poems in the volume (the manuscripts of these poems reside in the Rosamond Lehmann Archive at King's College), the desire that draws the speaker and his beloved to each other is the mutual attraction of two damaged and lonely people. In fact, the words "desire," "longing," "yearning" recur so regularly in this volume that they almost displace "reconciliation" as synonyms for the actual and operative "Word Over All."

"The Lighted House" brings the lovers together in a Petrarchan sonnet:

> One night they saw the big house, some time untenanted
> But for its hand-to-mouth recluse, room after room
> Light up, as when Primavera herself has spirited
> A procession of crocuses out of their winter tomb.
>
> Revels unearthly are going forward, one did remark—
> He has conjured up a thing of air or fire for his crazed delight:
> Another said, It is only a traveller lost in the dark
> He welcomes for mercy's sake. Each, in a way, was right.
>
> You were the magic answer, the sprite fire-fingered who came
> To lighten my heart, my house, my heirlooms; you are the wax
> That melts at my touch and still supports my prodigal flame:
>
> But you were also the dead-beat traveller out of the storm
> Returned to yourself by almost obliterated tracks,
> Peeling off fear after fear, revealing love's true form.   (315)

Like Brimclose in "Poem for an Anniversary" or the Box Cottage of "Moving In," Rosamond's house is the locus for a shared life. In the first quatrain he is the "hand-to-mouth recluse" of a life darkened till she comes like Primavera or Flora to light the house and awaken spring flowers. The second quatrain offers two interpretations of who she might be: the conjured projection of his desire ("a thing of air or fire") or an actual "traveller lost in the dark" (after the breakup of her second marriage) who needs him to enter the light of her love. "Each" image, the octave concludes, was, "in a way, right," and the sestet elaborates the alternatives in its two tercets. As his fantasized "thing of air or fire," her flame "supports my prodigal flame" and lightens at her hearth not just "my heart" but, punning on "air," "my heirlooms." But also the real woman, sheltered from the batterings of her previous life, is enabled to shed her fears and emerge again as her "true" self in the nakedness of their love.

"The Album" concludes with the same shared doubleness: "one and one make One." The early stanzas present three verbal snapshots of Rosamond recognizable as images from earlier stages of her life: the precociously aware child in the sheltered garden of the Lehmann estate, followed by the narcissistic girl already questioning "the heart's desire," and then the glamorous vamp, "courted, caressed," wearing "like immortelles the lovers and friends around you." The most recent image—Rosamond in the present with him—is missing from the album, but he supplies it poetically in "The Album." They had both been winter-blasted in their earlier loves—she "a tree stripped bare," he "too . . . fruitlessly shaken" (316–17). But now, in the missing photograph, she comes as Flora restoring his lost spring:

> I see her, petalled in new-blown hours,
> Beside me—'All you love most there
> Has blossomed again,' she murmurs, 'all that you missed
>   there
> Has grown to be yours.'   (317)

Her "here" would supplant his previous wintry "there."

But Day Lewis acknowledges, even in the first flush of renewed passion, the lover's defensive aggressiveness by placing right after "The Lighted House" and "The Album" the disturbing and violent song called "The Hunter's Game." The lover apprehended once again by "[t]he shadow of the gunman," by Perseus's raised blade? Years later *Rosamond Lehmann's Album* would actually include without comment, among the snapshots of family and friends, a photograph of Day Lewis grinning broadly with a rifle in his hands. (The photograph had been taken atop Musbury Castle for an article on Nicholas Blake, Day Lewis's pseudonym as mystery writer, headlined "THE POET WITH A GUN.") The weapon in "The Hunter's Game" is the bow and arrow, and at the outset the speaker identifies himself with the weapon ("I am an arrow, I am a bow—") that belongs to "my love" and that only she can wield: "Only my love can bend the bow" and shoot the arrow; "you are the skill . . ."; "You are the wanton airs / Which shape and hold its shining arc" (317–18). Flora has become Diana, and the hunter/speaker thus seems to surrender agency to his beloved, becoming merely the instrument in the hands of "the huntress." This apparently innocent displacement serves to divert attention from the object of the arrow's "shining arc," but it does not avert the deadly aim from its mark. In the sudden reversal of the last stanza the "victim" turns out to be the beloved herself, slain by the arrow she released: instrument becomes agent, and

> Pierced by a shaft of light are you
> The huntress, white and smiling, laid—
> The victim of your arrow.   (318)

If Mary puzzled about what to make of "The Lighted House" and "The Album," what did Rosamond make of these last lines of "The Hunter's Game"?

The Waste Land describes the spring's cruelty as "mixing / Memory and desire." Day Lewis and Lehmann brought to their wartime spring significantly different memories—differences in class, gender, religious background, social and economic status. But what they both brought to their meeting was the condition of unsatisfied desire: longing suffused by painful memory that suffused longing in turn. "Cornet Solo" attributes to the early loss of the mother the child's life of alienation and endless desire, the linked consciousness of lost past and unrealized future:

> Strange they could tell a mere child how hearts may beat in
> The self-same tune for the once-possessed
> And the unpossessed.   (320)

Emily Dickinson, another American poet whose work Day Lewis admired, began one poem (Number 959 in the Johnson edition): "A loss of something ever felt I— / The first that I could recollect / Bereft I was—of what I knew not," and the sense of primordial bereavement made her, she says, a "Mourner" from childhood, and propelled her along a life's course of searching for completion in a loved object lost and hence desired, but so lost that desire is limitless and insatiable and its object undefinable and unattainable: in the phrase from "Cornet Solo," "the once-possessed / And the unpossessed."

In the ordering of poems in *Word Over All* "Cornet Solo" follows upon and stands as a kind of coda to the exploration of desire in "Departure in the Dark," one of Day Lewis's most revealing and important poems. The traveler is a familiar figure in Day Lewis's work from *Transitional Poem* and *The Magnetic Mountain* to "The Lighted House," and that traveler has come a long, troubled way—from home and back, from one way station to the next, to arrive in "Departure in the Dark" at the crucial understanding of his restlessness: "the desire / Going forth meets the desire returning" (319). The poem ponders whether the clarification it reaches is the counsel of resignation . . . or of hope:

> Nothing so sharply reminds a man that he is mortal
> As leaving a place
> In a winter morning's dark, the air on his face
> Unkind as the touch of sweating metal:
> Simple goodbyes to children or friends become
> A felon's numb
> Farewell, and love that was a warm, a meeting place—
> Love is the suicide's grave under the nettles.
>
> Gloomed and clemmed as if by an imminent ice-age
> Lies the dear world
> Of your street-strolling, field-faring. The senses, curled
> At the dead end of a shrinking passage,
> Care not if close the inveterate hunters creep,
> And memories sleep
> Like mammoths in lost caves. Drear, extinct is the world,
> And has no voice for consolation or presage.

There is always something at such times of the passover,
When the dazed heart
Beats for it knows not what, whether you part
From home or prison, acquaintance or lover—
Something wrong with the time-table, something unreal
In the scrambled meal
And the bag ready packed by the door, as though the heart
Has gone ahead, or is staying here for ever.

No doubt for the Israelites that early morning
It was hard to be sure
If home were prison or prison home: the desire
Going forth meets the desire returning.
This land, that had cut their pride down to the bone
Was now their own
By ancient deeds of sorrow. Beyond, there was nothing
                                                                    sure
But a desert of freedom to quench their fugitive yearnings.

At this blind hour the heart is informed of nature's
Ruling that man
Should be nowhere a more tenacious settler than
Among wry thorns and ruins, yet nurture
A seed of discontent in his ripest ease.
There's a kind of release
And a kind of torment in every goodbye for every man
And will be, even to the last of his dark departures.   (318–19)

As with many of Day Lewis's best poems, the form is essential to making the meaning and is also of Day Lewis's own devising. Moreover, like Thomas Hardy and Robert Frost, the American poet for whose British *Selected Poems* Day Lewis had written an admiring introduction in 1936, he characteristically uses the regularities and irregularities, the predictabilities and unpredictabilities of meter and rhyme to explore intellectual, emotional, and moral ambiguity. In "Departure in the Dark" the eight lines of Day Lewis's stanza follow a fixed pattern of stresses (5–2–5–4–5–2–6–5) and a fixed rhyme scheme (a–b–b–a–c–c–b–a); however, there is no correspondence between the simultaneous patterns of line lengths and rhyming syllables. Thus the pentameters end a–b–c–a, and the dimeters end b–c; and the lines with the b-rhyme, for example, have two beats, five beats, six beats. Each stanza is end-stopped and enclosed by the rhyming of the first two lines (a–b) with the last two but inverted (b–a), but within these enclosed units the conversational tone and the enjambment of lines make for fluid movement. The b-rhyme of the second and second-to-last lines in each stanza repeats exactly the same word, but the off-rhymes (for example, "mortal," "metal," "nettles"; "ice-age," "passage," "presage"; etc.) reenforce the syncopation of the varying line-lengths. The statement of the poem seems to meander but toward the end gathers itself into gnomic generalizations—as in the remark about desire going forth and returning and in the closing lines; yet those seemingly didactic apothegms sum up the problem without resolving it, end the poem open-endedly.

Does the departure in the dark recall leaving London to visit Mary and their children? Leaving Brimclose to return to Rosamond and her children? Which home is prison, which prison home? Or is each both? The moment and place of the departure are deliberately unspecified and kept general, for "nothing so sharply reminds a man he is mortal" as the consciousness that every moment is a venture and a farewell, an opportunity and a failure to grasp, "even to the last of his dark departures." "The once-possessed / And the unpossessed" recede beyond possession into the void between each tick of the clock, leaving "the dazed heart" beating out the time "for it knows not what." The radical discontinuity of "Something wrong with the time-table" generates and frustrates desire instant by instant, eros quickened and quenched by thanatos "in every goodbye." For in the blink of the moment the desirer wavers between desire for the once possessed and desire for the unpossessed, between clutching what is always already gone and reaching out to what is always already slipping away. The penultimate stanza adapts the biblical analogy with the exodus to historicize and mythicize the crucial insight without resolving it. The poem does not mention Moses's unwavering leadership of his people through the desert under God's command but instead empathizes with the wavering affections of the ordinary and befuddled Israelites, hesitating between their Egyptian prison and the hazy promise of rich and fertile homeland, between the hardships already known and accommodated and a paradise unknown. They were human in their wanting to go and to stay, to stay behind and yet to go home: desire crossing and recrossing desire in the barren desert.

At the end of Day Lewis's autobiography, the mingling of memory and desire over the years he had reviewed moved him to recall the insight of "Departure in the Dark":

> [T]he conflict I had all my young life been cursed with—"The desire going forth meets the desire returning": a need for what is stable, habitual, familiar; and locked in struggle with it—sometimes the one prevailing, sometimes the other—an impulse toward the new, the unknown, the migrations which so delusively promise a rebirth.
>
> (*The Buried Day*, 235)

Moreover, the Janus-face of desire "is not my conflict alone, surely, but a condition of being human: not 'the blight man was born for', but the clash of irreconcilables which makes him and unmakes him." Day Lewis quotes Hopkins's phrase in "Spring and Fall" to turn the "blight" of mortality, without Hopkins's faith, into the possibility of self-creation; and he completes the paragraph by quoting most of the ninth (and last) sonnet in the sequence "O Dreams! O Destinations!" They stand, except for a brief Postscript, as the final words of the autobiography.

"O Dreams! O Destinations!" succeeds "Departure in the Dark" and
"Cornet Solo" and closes Part One, the Rosamond section, of *Word Over
All* with a major statement. Rosamond is not mentioned or invoked, but
the sequence explores the paradoxical workings of desire to which the
relationship with her had given him access. His recollection of the genesis
of the sequence becomes a paradigm for the creative process as he often
experienced it:

> For me, many—but certainly not all—poems begin with a *donnée*, a
> phrase or line which comes to me out of the blue, and often bears no
> apparent relation with the field of experience I am involved in or medi-
> tating at the time. . . . During the last war, this line came unbidden into
> my head—"The flags, the roundabouts, the gala day." It seemed like a
> riddle, an oracle. What sort of poem was it pointing to? Contemplat-
> ing this enigmatic line, I became aware that it was charged with a kind
> of childish expectation and excitement; and out of this seed grew a son-
> net about childhood—a subject I had rarely attempted before: it was as
> though the violent happenings of the war, together with a private emo-
> tional crisis of my own, had like an earthquake thrown up strata of my
> early experience which, till then, had not been available to me as a poet.
> And out of that sonnet grew a sequence of nine sonnets expressing,
> through images only, states of mind connected with childhood, ado-
> lescence, and middle age.
>
> (The Lyric Impulse, 147)

To the end of his life Day Lewis singled out "O Dreams! O Destinations!"
as his most concentrated piece of poetry and perhaps the one most likely
to find a permanent place in the canon.

Though the sonnets present stages of psychological and moral development in general rather than personal terms, many of the details and images
are autobiographically based, and the sequence traces the course of desire
("O Dreams!") in the life cycle ("O Destinations!"). Sonnet 1 presents the
infant ignorant of time and loss. Sonnet 2 depicts the young child still
swaddled in illusions of permanence and continuity imaged in the line that
generated the sequence: "The flags, the roudabouts, the gala day." Sonnet
3, like Dickinson's "A loss of something ever felt I," recounts "the ruin-
ation / Of innocence" as the fall into consciousness:

> When in the lawless orchard of creation
> The child left this fruit for that rosier one.
> Reaching towards the far thing, we begin it;
> Looking beyond, or backward, more and more
> We grow unfaithful to the unique minute. . . . (322)

So "we begin it": the dualism that betrays the living moment ("looking
beyond, or backward"), "the ambiguous power of choice" ("this fruit" or
"that rosier one"), the vacillations of unrequited desire. In Sonnet 4, the
"alternating light and shade" in which "all's dark or dazzle" dissolves experience into illusions "that flickered on our cave": "Only your fire, which

cast them, still seems true." But is this fire casting shadows in the cave of consciousness the flame of divine love or the flickerings of human desire?

The next sonnets tease out this question. In Sonnet 5 the material world, awaiting "heaven's delegated / Angel" who never arrives, fades and glows "like a fire's heart" with "breathless inspiration" of our expectant desire until phenomena appear to be "divinely charged," "a near annunciation" of the "veiled Word" (323). However, Sonnet 6 confronts a world turned into "gross experience" when loss of faith reduces near annunciations to failed epiphanies. The octave looks back at the Marxist idealism of the thirties that compensated for his religious unbelief: "Desire bred fierce abstractions on the mind, / Then like an eagle soared beyond belief." But such flights were doomed by ignorance ("we hardly knew . . . what ached in us, asking to be born"), and the phrase "soared beyond belief" anticipates, in the sestet, the descent of such high-flying schemes into "impotence." The closing couplet sums up the wisdom Day Lewis had come to by reassessing through Virgil and Hardy the thirties' broken hopes on the brink of war: "Ah, not in dreams, but when our souls engage / With the common mesh and moil, we come of age" (323). In that chastened maturity (Sonnet 7), "the half-hearted" have to learn to settle for "half-loaves, half-truths": "We're glad to gain the limited objective, / Knowing the war we fight in has no end" (324). Still, Sonnet 8 presses beyond the paralysis of disillusionment as desire "freshly yearns" and seizes the seeming "perfection" of certain moments of mortality. Such an intimation of immortality may prove to be only a "deathless illusion"; nevertheless, it relays the "limited" and contingent "truth of flesh and spirit, sun and clay / Singing for once together all in tune!" (324).

The ninth sonnet closes the sequence (and Day Lewis's autobiography) with as much of a resolution as he could reach:

> To travel like a bird, lightly to view
> Deserts where stone gods founder in the sand,
> Ocean embraced in a white sleep with land;
> To escape time, always to start anew.
> To settle like a bird, make one devoted
> Gesture of permanence upon the spray
> Of shaken stars and autumns: in a bay
> Beyond the crestfallen surges to have floated.
> Each is our wish. Alas, the bird flies blind,
> Hooded by a dark sense of destination:
> Her weight on the glass calm leaves no impression,
> Her home is soon a basketful of wind.
> Travellers, we're fabric of the road we go;
> We settle, but like feathers on time's flow.   (325)

The landscape and figures are familiar—the windswept boundary of land and ocean, the travelers on life's road or time's river or flood, the bird in flight and descent—but they are reassembled here in a major declaration.

The octave poses the old oppositions: traveling, settling down; the risk of the unknown, the safety of the known; escape from home, return home. The sestet admits that "each is our wish" but seeks to apprehend the contrarities of desire in paradoxical symbiosis, so that their reconciliation might after all be posited as the "word over all."

Since the "unique minute" is the meeting point of desire going forth and returning, then living in "the irreconcilables" minute by minute both "makes" and "unmakes" us. It marks our passing and marks us in our passing. The paradox is enclosed in the last couplet. We become "the fabric of the road we go," the measure and substantiation of our individual passage, epitomized in the measured sequence we are finishing. We settle into our movement, "like feathers on time's flow." That closing couplet represents Day Lewis's phrasing of what Bataille meant in defining eroticism as "assenting to life up to the point of death"—each moment, all the way—and thus "assenting to life even in death."

• 7

In contrast to the previous collections, the title of *Poems 1943–1947* (1948) records the dates of composition without a thematic phrase or image offering a key, perhaps because the poems do not follow out the hesitant hopes of the most recent pieces in *Word Over All*. The theme of the volume is in fact the shadowy pall cast by the past on the present. "The Double Vision," the first poem in the volume, posits as forcefully as ever the sense of internal division against which Day Lewis was still contending. Early in the collection "Heart and Mind" says that even in the unusual instance "when heart and mind agree," as in Sonnet 8 of "O Dreams! O Destinations!" "they kiss / Over an opening grave" (370). "Sketches for a Self-Portrait" follows an erotic pursuit of "images" of a beloved generated by his own haunted desire: "Was he hunter or hunted? He cared not. / . . . Till at last they came to the verge of the sea, where hunter / And hunted face the effacing sea and are one" (362). This is the implosion of the equation in which "one and one make One": not the Oneness of transcendence but the submergence of distinctions in universal annihilation.

F. Scott Fitzgerald ends *The Great Gatsby* with his narrator elegizing the life of unfulfillable desire as the pursuit of a lost love into "the orgastic future that year by year recedes before us. . . . So we beat on, boats against the current, borne back ceaselessly into the past" (182). Day Lewis had placed the Rosamond poems as Part One of *Word Over All* to signal his sense of new forward movement in his life, but the arrangement of the book registers instead Fitzgerald's sense of simultaneously being swept back into the past, as the reader moves from the Rosamond poems through the war poems to the recollections of Billie Currall. We may be, as Day Lewis clearly wishes to believe, "fabric of the road we go," but that forward thrust can be arrested when "the desire / Going forth meets the desire returning."

So in *Poems 1943–1947* the erotic quest is stymied by the compulsion to look back. Where in *Word Over All*, dedicated to Rosamond Lehmann, Mary Day Lewis is absent, in *Poems 1943–1947* she is more vividly, if agonizingly, present than Rosamond. In "The Revenant" Orpheus's parting from Eurydice at the mouth of the underworld is presented as an allegory of the Day Lewis marriage and specifically not as his tragic loss of Eurydice but as his rebirth in separation. Escape from the place of death depends on his observing the prohibition of Thanatos himself that he not turn his gaze back at her on the way out. But the fabled power of his song "held her / To him" and "haled her / Lifeward" (375) with him. The song is the poignant distillation of all that Eros desires and promises:

> On the gist of that lay or its burden
> Legend is dumb.
> How else, though, with love-looks forbidden
> Could he say, 'Come back to me, come'—
> Could he touch the long-hidden
> Spring of a shade unfleshed, unfertilized
> Than by singing, oh, crust and crumb,
> Bark, sap, flesh, and marrow—
> Life's all, in the narrow
> Ambit of sense flowering, immortalized?   (375)

The last two lines sum up the erotic drive: to know "Life's all" in the full flowering and so immortalizing of sense. The separation occurs, however, because Eurydice is drawn back to Pluto/Thanatos rather than to life with Orpheus/Eros:

> She wept for astonishment,
> Feared she could never belong
> To life, be at home there,
> Find aught but harm there,
> Till that last step seemed less a birth than a banishment.   (376)

With "one step" she could "break from her cerement" ("like a daffodil when its stem / Feels trembling the first endearment / Of amorous bloom") and become "a golden wife again," but instead she chooses to remain "a shade unfleshed, unfertilized." When her inner "terrors" keep her from moving forward, the poet-husband consigns her to the dead past and moves on: "He felt the cord parting, / The death-wound smarting: / He turned his head but to glimpse the ghost of her." Eurydice is Mary, or rather the "Mary" who functions in his psyche as negative muse or anima.

In representing "Mary," Eurydice represents also the part of himself that is drawn by "desire returning" to die back into the mother and deny the "desire going forth" into erotic adventure. He had dedicated *From Feathers to Iron* "To the Mother" with hopeful expectations, but now as Orpheus he imagines leaving "her" at the silent mouth of death's womb in order to deliver himself as poet. A revenant is a ghost or shade, like Eurydice, but in its etymological meaning of "the one who comes back" it designates Orpheus more strongly. In Day Lewis's version of the story even the usually judgmental gods are made to view his act of abandonment "non-committally." He does not so much abandon her as she banishes herself; his desire goes forth as "hers" returns to Hades:

>   as a pebble thrown
> From a cliff face, soaring
> Swerves back, less like a stone
> Than a bird, ere it falls to the snoring
> Surf . . . (376)

Of course, neither Mary nor the "Mary" in himself could simply be left behind: "being married" meant in this case a long letting go. However disembodied a revenant the figure of his wife might be in his own emotional life, in biographical fact her actual presence reenforced the demands and responsibilities of her patient devotion, and her ignorance about Rosamond for the first two years of their liaison added deceit to betrayal. However, *Poems 1943–1947* indicates that the situation only became more openly painful after *Word Over All* exposed the triangulation of desire. In "Marriage of Two" "marital" becomes "martial" with metaphors of warfare to characterize their relationship:

> *How did the marriage end?*
> Some marriages die not.
> The government goes into exile; then
> The underground struggle is on, whose fighters fly not
> Even at the bitter end.

> *What is the marriage of two?*
> The loss of one
> By wounds or abdication; a true
> Surrender mocked, an unwished victory won:
> Rose, desert—mirage too. (363)

The wife is the desert rather than the rose (a pun, of course, on Rosamond's name), for a desert-blooming rose is a mirage. In the rhyming of the first and last lines of this final stanza "marriage of two" withers to "mirage too." Day Lewis's visits and vacations to Brimclose from London—first from his war job at the Ministry of Information and, starting in fall 1946, from his position as senior reader, later partner, at the publishing firm of Chatto and Windus—became excruciating for husband and wife, and were made all the more excruciating by the fact that accusations and recriminations seethed "underground" beneath a "mirage" of life as usual steadfastly maintained before the boys and visitors. The speaker of "The Double Vision" ponders "how most human loves protract / Them-

selves to unreality—the fact / Drained of its virtue by the image it made"
(355).

The one or two occasions on which Day Lewis found the courage or
desperation to challenge their false composure by proposing divorce left
them both exhausted but still impotently bound together in suffering rendered more acute by the unresolved confrontation. Otherwise Mary con-
fined her thoughts and feelings to her diary, and its entries veer from terse
stoicism to equally terse hopelessness. For his part Day Lewis understood
her position more compassionately than he allowed in "The Revenant"
and gave her anguish voice in the two searing poems that follow "Marriage of Two": "Married Dialogue" and "The Woman Alone."

"Married Dialogue" has a complicated scheme of rhyming and variation that mimics the differences that turn the couple's "dialogue" into
parallel monologues, side by side but untouching. Each pair of five-line
stanzas spoken in turn by HE and SHE has its own distinctive rhyme scheme
of only two rhyming syllables. In the following passage, for example,
the first pair of stanzas rhymes: a–b–a–b–a a–c–a–c–a, and the second
pair rhymes d–e–d–d–e d–f–d–d–f. But within each pair's pattern the
triple rhyme is repeated in both stanzas (the a-rhymes in the first pair,
the d-rhymes in the second) while the double rhyme differs between the
two stanzas (the b-rhymes and c-rhymes in the first pair, the e-rhymes
and f-rhymes in the second). At the same time the number of stresses
per line varies from three to six between pairs of stanzas, but is repeated,
like the rhyme scheme, in the two stanzas paired. Thus in the stanzas
below the number of stresses in the first pair runs: 5–4–6–3–5; in the
second pair the pattern of stresses runs: 4–5–3–5–4. The form locks the
pairs of stanzas, like the couple themselves, in a pattern with shifting
dissonances.

> HE   There was a time, But time piles flake on flake
> Lapping the traveller asleep:
> And in that sleep the heart grows numb. So we awake
> To severance. Oh deep
> The drifts between, treacherous the frozen lake!

> SHE   Once I watched a young ocean laugh and shake
> With spillikens of aspen light.
> I was your sail, your keel. Nothing could overtake
> Love trimmed and stiffened aright.
> But now I drown, a white reef in your wake.

> HE   No reef I saw. If we were shoaled,
> It was the ebbing of some tide within.
> But aching I behold
> Fingers upon a gunwale blue with cold,
> And one too weak to draw you in.

SHE   Oh crooked tide, what lies it told
         So to get round me. Then, cut off, I lay
         Weeping. And then I doled
         My scraps of you, with hopes of you consoled
         Myself, like any castaway. (364–65)

"The Woman Alone," written in five-line stanzas of heavily enjambed blank verse, drops the husband's voice and viewpoint and enters candidly and empathetically the wife's hurt and outrage. Here she is not Eurydice but Ariadne, hoping that the thread she is following traces the passage out of "this sick labyrinth of grief" but finding instead that her "life line" only leads back to the glacier that holds the former lovers frozen but "will not let their forms dissolve" (367–68).

Nor is Mary Day Lewis the only revenant in these poems. "The Meeting" tries to celebrate a renewal of his friendship with Billie Currall, but it ends in conditional clauses and subjunctive verbs instead of declarations. In "On the Sea Wall" a girl glimpsed on a beach recalls Billie, "as though / You were dead and your shape had returned to haunt me / On the very same spot" where they had dallied five years before (398). "The House-Warming," dated May 5, 1946, on the manuscript, is addressed to Rosamond about the Manor House at Little Wittenham, her newly acquired Berkshire residence, which would become Day Lewis's second home for the next few years. But in the poem it is clearly her house, not his, and though he imagines himself as having warmed it with his love against her arrival, he is present there only as a house-haunting shade described in terms that echo again Fitzgerald's image of a future already lost in the past before it can ever come to be:

Not a phantom risen like spray from the past,
    But a ghost by the future made.

Love enmeshed in his own folly—
    Mischance or folly—
Expiates a deed for ever undone,
Weeps for all that it could have won
    Of living together wholly. (377)

The Rosamond Lehmann papers also contain in Day Lewis's hand this plangently gnomic nursery rhyme. It is the purest lyric in *Poems 1943–1947*:

Is it far to go?
    A step—no further.
Is it hard to go?
    Ask the melting snow,
    The eddying feather.

What can I take there?
  Not a hank, not a hair.
What shall I leave behind?
  Ask the hastening wind,
  The fainting star.

Shall I be gone long?
  For ever and a day.
To whom there belong?
  Ask the stone to say,
  Ask my song.

Who will say farewell?
  The beating bell.
Will anyone miss me?
  That I dare not tell—
  Quick, Rose, and kiss me.   (379–80)

Like many folk ballads and nursery rhymes, this one is a dialogue whose message of seizing the day stands as a counterpoint to the barrenness of the earlier "Married Dialogue." But like most seeming celebrations of carpe diem this one is first and foremost an elegy; the lover's face is a death's head. The woman's voice asks italicized questions about her seemingly imminent death, and the poet responds to his "Rose" with runes that urge a consummating "kiss" that is also the kiss of death. For Rose's elegy is also the lover-singer's own, and in fact the third stanza appears on Day Lewis's tombstone at the Stinsford church in Dorset, pointing all questions about love and death back to the poems for whatever gnomic answers they can give: "Ask my song."

"Buzzards Over Castle Hill" presents a trio of predatory birds circling above Brimclose as a configuration of tragic revenants: "earth-souls doomed in their gyres to unwind / Some tragic love-tangle wherein they had mortally pined" (392). Day Lewis was drawn during these years to George Meredith's verse sequence *Modern Love* and published an edition of the poem in 1948 with an excellent introductory essay. Rosamond Lehmann shared his empathy with Meredith; the last poem in Meredith's sequence supplied the titles both of her first novel, *Dusty Answer*, and of his autobiography, *The Buried Day*. Meredith had shocked his Victorian audience with this story, fictionalized in verse from the autobiographical situation of his own first marriage, of a poet torn between his "Lady" wife and his mistress. But Meredith's circumstances were actually different from Day Lewis's. His adultery began in retaliation for his wife's sexual dalliance, but Day Lewis could claim no such motive. On the contrary, it was Mary's sexual reticence that first opened the breach between them, just as it was his corrosive guilt before her long-suffering blamelessness (and the presence of the boys) that kept him from severing their relationship. By the spring of 1947 the strain between Brimclose and Little Wittenham had become so acute that, as we have seen, the depressive withdrawals of his recurrent "black-ice periods" deepened into what Rosamond described as "a near breakdown," and Mary's diaries corroborate that diagnosis: "Cecil in state bordering on insanity, can't make up his mind between Rosamond and me" (Sean Day Lewis, 143, 170, 173).

The most graphic evidence of his psychological and spiritual state comes from the poems themselves. "A Failure" uses the trope of a ruined grain-field and argues the necessity of simply annihilating, without further waste of empathetic explanations, a failed crop such as his life represents:

> But it's useless to argue the why and the wherefore.
>   When a crop is so thin,
> There's nothing to do but to set the teeth
>   And plough it in.   (371)

The sonnet "All Gone" uses the trope of flotsam on a beach exposed by the tide's withdrawal:

> The sea drained off, my poverty's uncovered—
> Sand, sand, a rusted anchor, broken glass,
> The listless sediment of sparkling days
> When through a paradise of weed joy wavered.   (399)

The self-destructive figure in "The Neurotic" is described as "walking a treadmill there, grinding himself / To powder, dust to greyer dust," and his self-description inverts the comforts of the biblical psalm into a demonic vision:

> 'I will not lift mine eyes unto the hills
> For there white lambs nuzzle and creep like maggots.
> I will not breathe the lilies of the valley
> For through their scent a chambered corpse exhales.
> If petals float to earth, I am oppressed.
> The grassblades twist, twist deep in my breast.'   (400)

The grass imagery here, coming after the many images of sea and sand and flotsam, suggests Whitman, especially in sections of "Song of Myself" and in the elegiac cluster of "Sea Drift," as a poetic analogue and perhaps even source for Day Lewis's effort to acknowledge and survive his own life-and-death crisis.

Although *Poems 1943–1947* contains many moving and expert poems, the tightening grip of Day Lewis's depression made it difficult for him to configure the volume, like its predecessors, around a long poem. Near the end of 1947 he wrote to his friend Rupert Hart-Davis that he had decided to discard almost all of a long poem, "the best part of a year's work wasted" because it "simply was not good enough" (Sean Day Lewis, 167). When assembling the collection the next year, he used as its centerpiece a recent work commissioned by the Third Programme of the BBC and read over the airways for the turn of the year 1948 by two professional actors. "New Year's Eve," in unrhymed quatrains accompanied by a prosy "Meditation," was a public statement in which his melancholy becomes freighted with Arnoldian sententiousness and abstraction. Written at "the zero / Between desire and resignation," the familiar sentiments ("To live the present then" as "the true seer"; "To witness the rare in the common, and read the common / Theme for all time appointed / To link our variations," [386]) have the somewhat formulaic sound of New Year's resolutions.

Much more successful and convincing is Day Lewis's celebrated translation of Paul Valéry's "Le Cimetière Marin" as "The Graveyard by the Sea." The English and French versions of the poem were published in 1947 in an elegant limited edition by Martin Secker & Warburg, and the next year Day Lewis closed his new volume with "The Graveyard by the Sea." By his account he reread "Valéry's great meditation upon death-in-life" in 1944 during London's second period of sustained bombing, this time by V1 flying bombs and V2 rockets: "I was possessed by the poem: I *had* to translate it; the compulsion was as great as with any personal experience I have ever sought to compose into poetry. Indeed, it *was* a personal experience" ("On Translating Poetry," 20.).

By Day Lewis's own testimony Valéry served him in the forties as "a technical corrective to the strong influence of Thomas Hardy" (20). In contrast to Hardy's inclination toward a balladlike directness and simplicity, "Le Cimetière Marin" presented the gradual accumulation of recurrent but shifting images "which are numerous, often enigmatic, and arranged in systems of constellations." But "the main technical problem," from the translator's perspective, "was that of stanza form. The original is in decasyllabic metre—an unusual one for French poetry, and the rhyme scheme is a–a–b–c–c–b, an even more unusual one for English poetry." To Day Lewis's sensitive ear, the effect, especially with a couplet beginning rather than ending the stanza, was "of initial confidence and simplicity broadening out in each stanza to something more complex, more tentative" (20). Each stanza, then, epitomized and recapitulated the total and cumulative registration of ambiguity in the poem.

However, like Wallace Stevens, Day Lewis was drawn to the last great symboliste poet principally for psychological and emotional reasons: "Le Cimetière Marin," like "Sunday Morning," stands almost as a paradigmatic statement of post-Romantic angst. The speaker stands in a cemetery and, ruminating on the split between mind and body endemic to the human condition, is helplessly transfixed by his consciousness of mortality: "What body drags me to its lingering end, / What mind draws *it* to this bone-peopled ground?" (410). But inexplicably he feels himself delivered from his convoluted "thought" by sight of the "celestial calm" of the vast sea spangled by the "grace of light": "Pure artifice both of an eternal Cause" (408). "Grace," of course, suggests both a religious reality and an aesthetic quality, and Valéry, like Stevens, deliberately blurs the distinction. Are they reducing religion to aesthetics, or elevating aesthetics to a quasi religion? Are they reducing God to the imagination, or sublimating the imagination into a power quasi-divine? What was the "eternal Cause" that made this scene, and is its "pure artifice" a revelation or an invention? Still, as sometimes in Stevens and in Day Lewis, the speaker surrenders with erotic relief to the sublime landscape and finds himself sublimated: "All is burnt up, used up, drawn up in air / To some ineffably rarefied solution. . . ." But, again, is this solution the final answer, or the final liquification into nothingness? If there is a "Cause," it "broods on itself" in "self-sufficient" "indifference" to the human dilemma (409–10). Consequently, the speaker rises to an articulation of his doom: "Life is enlarged" only by the "annihilation" of his consciousness and the "dissolution" of his mortal body. Yet is dissolution so attractive, so seductive a consummation? Is death the outlet of hopeless erotic desire ("'Love', shall we call him?"), or neurotic self-destructiveness ("'Hatred of self,' maybe?" [411–12])? "Death is a womb, a mother's breast"; but on the brink of annihilation the speaker pulls back in self-preservation and fends off death for the time being by resolving in the last stanzas to resume his isolate and alienated self.

Day Lewis excerpted the first line of the final stanza as the second epigraph to *Poems 1943–1947* to counter Hardy's grim fatality in the first epigraph: "I seem but a dead man held on end / To sink down soon. . . ." Valéry's words seemed to voice the will to survive: "Le vent se lève . . . it faut tenter de vivre!" (351). The stanza that follows this line, however, subverts the hortatory phrase "try to live" with apocalyptic images of dissolution in the violently triumphant and annihilating sea:

> The wind is rising! . . . We must try to live!
> The huge air opens and shuts my book: the wave
> Dares to explode out of the rocks in reeking
> Spray. Fly away, my sun-bewildered pages!
> Break, waves! Break up with your rejoicing surges
> This quiet roof where sails like doves were pecking.   (413)

By translating another poet's words and images Day Lewis gave his desperation aesthetic form, but Rosamond saw him near "breakdown."

• 8

A trip to Denmark with Laurie Lee helped to bring Day Lewis out of the severe depression of spring 1947, and in gratitude and in recognition of Lee's work, which Day Lewis had worked to promote, he dedicated *Poems 1943–1947* to his friend. In May of the next year he spent a fortnight in Italy with Rosamond, who had been invited by Bernard Berenson, the Renaissance art historian, to stay with him at his villa outside Florence.

This jaunt was even more restorative, and its literary results were the poems in *An Italian Visit*, almost all written in 1948 and 1949 right after the trip, though they would not be published, for reasons that will become clear, until 1953. Far removed from Brimclose, the panorama of Italy—as the pair wended their way from Rome through Siena to Florence and I Tatti—opened before his clenched heart like the land of Eros and seemed to display ravishingly and unashamedly what he had never found in the English countryside: "the lineaments of gratified desire" (443). The high spirits and prosodic ingenuity of the poems (including the suite describing Florentine artworks successively in the styles of Hardy, Yeats, Frost, Auden, and Dylan Thomas) make *An Italian Visit* a continuous delight whose panache gradually and charmingly reveals its serious purpose.

Even before the first page the epigraph from Jasper More's *The Land of Italy*, which also supplied the book's title, reminds the reader that on "a voyage of discovery" the "scenes and cities" mirror "the traveller's heart and mind" (415). The opening section, "Dialogue at the Airport," is a Horatian colloquy in which the poet's personae, Tom, Dick, and Harry, represent three versions of the poet trying to live in time. Tom is the more fleshly and sensual one, a Paterian hedonist who wants only to savor the present moment; Dick is an agonized Romantic who wants to compose the fragments of past and present into an intuitive mythical synthesis; Harry is a cool philosophical classicist, speculatively analyzing experience in search for an underlying system. What links these differing types of the poet is that each is in his own way bent on a moment of more-than-natural clarity and coherence:

TOM   Still, there is such a thing as simple impressionability,
        A sense in which form and colour are more than mere
                                    dreams of our senses,
        A moment—though rare—when the lily speaks for itself
                  alone
        And the babe's ephemeral laughter chimes with eternity.   (425)

DICK   If I could find that place where nymph and shepherd meet
        And the distance melts into deity, I would unearth my buried
        Heirlooms, my sealed orders. Genius of the place, remarry
            These sundered elements, make one circle at last complete!
                                        (429)

HARRY   Separation's my metier, then, sifting through form the
                              formless:
        Creation my end, to subdue and liberate time in the
                              timeless.
        I find the whole in elusive fragments: let one be caught
        And profoundly known—that way, like a skeleton key, the
                              part
        May unlock the intricate whole. What else is the work of art?
                                        (431)

The poet is, as often before, a traveler: but this time not toward the imagined utopia of the magnetic mountain beyond the horizon but rather within an Eden that seems to have survived the fall into history: "Earth a mere trusting step from Paradise" (450). But the tourist has brought with him the exile's premonition of merely passing through:

> A driven heart, a raven-shadowing mind
> Loom above all my pastorals, impend
>   My traveller's joy with fears
>   That travelling has no end.   (449)

As the bedazzled tourist begins to discern, beyond the first overwhelming impressions, that bright light casts strong shadows, he begins to piece out the paradox of Italy as both pageant and monument, renaissance and ruin, idyll and "glorious junk-heap" (437), lover and whore. In the end he comes to recognize what the residents already know; this lovely and faded place is no paradise recovered after all. "It's not the Florentine who pales beside / That vast, rank efflorescence. The pop-eyed / Tourist it is who rushes on his doom . . ." (453).

Journey's end was Berenson's Villa I Tatti in the Florentine suburb of Settignano. All the themes of the book come together in one of Day Lewis's supreme poetic achievements: "Elegy Before Death: At Settignano," dedicated "To R. N. L." The affinity between love and death sung lyrically and playfully in "Is it far to go?" expands here into a sublime meditation. "Elegy Before Death" celebrates their love in anticipation of its extinction, and for that reason R. N. L. prohibited its publication and held up the appearance of *An Italian Visit* for several years. The poem consists of twenty-five stanzas of nine loosely pentameter lines, with the third, sixth, and ninth lines of each stanza rhyming; the stanzas are grouped into three sections set off by asterisks. However, the triadic consistency of this prosodic scheme is played off against a number of destabilizing devices: the occasional and unpredictable lapse from pentameter into shorter lines, the additional rhymes interpolated irregularly without pattern, the caesuras that break up the lines into various phrasal and rhythmic elements of different lengths, the measured but conversational voice of the speaker enjambing lines and tercets, and the different lengths of the poem's three sections.

The first stanzas place the lovers in the famous orangery of the villa, looking out on the surrounding hills and the distant city at sunset, and the serenity of their peaceful harmony raises the poignant problem of living in time (which the bantering of Tom, Dick, and Harry had posed at the volume's outset). The failure to find "in a melting Now the formula / Of Always" makes Always "the word the sirens sing / On bone island" (461). The third stanza sums it up:

> Again again again, the frogs are screeling
> Down by the lilypond. Listen! I'll echo them—

Gain gain gain . . . Could we compel
One grain of one vanishing moment to deliver
Its golden ghost, loss would be gain
And Love step naked from illusion's shell.
Did we but dare to see it,
All things to us, you and I to each other,
Stand in this naked potency of farewell.   (461–62)

Can our consciousness of time's falling "grain" turn "Again, again, again"
to "Gain gain gain"? The verbs are conditional: "Could we compel / One
grain of a vanishing moment to deliver / Its golden ghost . . ." and "Did
we but dare to see it. . . ." But if we had the will, the moment would reveal more than a "golden ghost." "Illusion's shell" would split wide open
to "deliver" the goddess of Love, mother of Eros, for it is the very awareness of mutability that drives us to "see" and to "compel." Stevens said in
"Sunday Morning" "Death is the mother of beauty," and here Day Lewis's
repetition of "naked" in the phrases "Love step naked" and "this naked
potency of farewell" makes a joint revelation of eros and thanatos. Precisely because the clash of irreconcilables both makes and unmakes us,
"potency" and impotence are functions of each other. Lines near the end
of the first section repeat the diction of this passage, now with the clear
resolve "to make our flux / Stand and deliver its holy spark": "to tap the
potency of farewell" (463).

In a love-elegy like this one, the beloved (much to Rosamond's dis-
comfiture) embodies at once eros and thanatos. The remarkable middle
section of the poem goes on to perform the metamorphosis of Rosamond
into a love-goddess who is also a "ghost," "shade," "wraith" (464–65).
The psychologist Carl Jung would have recognized in Day Lewis's
apprehension of Rosamond here what he called the "anima"; in his psychic life and creative imagination, "she" mediates the twinned mysteries
of sexuality and spirit at the heart of "L'Amour/La Mort." So in the passage below Day Lewis moves into myth and symbol, hymning his beloved
as "all woman" and then as "all women": the archetype of woman within
whose cosmic "orbit" are "clasped and enhanced" "all creatures" and "all
hours, moods, shapes, desires" (465–66). The metamorphosis requires
extended quotation to let its visionary exaltation evolve and expand:

Her orbit clasped and enhanced in its diadem
All creatures. Once on a living night
When cypresses jetted like fountains of wine-warm air
Bubbling with fireflies, we going outside
In the palpitating dark to admire them,
One of the fireflies pinned itself to her hair;
And its throbbings, I thought, had a tenderer light
As if some glimmering of love inspired them,
As if her luminous heart was beating there.

Ah, could I make you see this subtle ghost of mine,
Delicate as a whorled shell that whispers to the tide,
Moving with a wavering watersilk grace,
Anemone-fingered, coral-tinted, under whose crystalline
Calm such naiads, angel fish and monsters sleep or slide;
If you could see her as she flows to me apace
Through waves through walls through time's fine mesh
                              magically drawn,
You would say, this was surely the last daughter
                              of the foam-born,
One whom no age to come will ever replace.

Eve's last fainting rose cloud; mornings that restored her
With orange tree, lemon tree, lotus, bougainvillea:
The milk-white snake uncoiling and the flute's light-
                              fingered charm:
Breast of consolation, tongue of tried acquaintance:
A tranquil mien, but under it the nervous marauder
Slithering from covert, a catspaw from a calm:
Heaven's city adored in the palm of a pictured saint:
My vision's *ara coeli*, my lust's familiar,
All hours, moods, shapes, desires that yield, elude,
                              disarm—

All woman she was. Brutalizing, humanizing,
Pure flame, lewd earth was she, imperative as air
And weak as water, yes all women to me.   (465–66)

The first stanza locates the beloved temporally and spatially—as the constellating center for a widening "orbit" that will become coterminous with the cosmos. As in a dream or fairy tale ("Once on a living night"), the intoxicating "warm-wine" atmosphere in the gardens of I Tatti casts a spell of dionysian-aphroditean magic, rendered in the erotic acceleration of participles and gerunds ("living," "Bubbling," "going," "palpitating," "throbbings," "glimmering," "beating"). The metamorphosis of Rosamond into "Rosamond" as archetype is signaled in the shift of pronouns from "you" (who, together with the speaking "I," makes the "we" of this magic moment) to the objectified and universal "she" described in the rest of the passage. At once carnal lover ("my lust's familiar") and blessed damozel, "Pure flame" and "lewd earth," the archetypal "she" comes to personify in herself the biological and psychological round. As the summation of these cyclic processes she makes changes and contrarieties consonant by holding them all within herself. In her apotheosis "she" is the ground and transcendence of change, "ghost" and goddess of all mortality. Consequently, she is hailed as the "foam-born," "shell"-borne lady of the moon-tossed waters, the lady of the beasts and of the paradisal garden, the lady of the hours and years and of the elements. She is linked with the snake both as the "milk-white" totem of the mother-goddess and as the "slithering" and "nervous marauder" who tempted Eve and brought death to the world. The phrase "Eve's last fainting rose cloud" makes the association with our first mother, and the epithet "*ara coeli* [heaven's altar]" from the "Litany of the Blessed Virgin" invokes the Mother of God, through whom the Fall was reversed and redemption achieved. But in this mythic dimension "Rosamond"'s name would be myriad—not just Eve and Mary but Aphrodite, Artemis, Demeter, Kore—so numerous that, all-named, she is better unnamed. On this "living night," her individual name reveals "her" universality: "rose of the world."

There is no other passage like this in all of Day Lewis's work—and few enough in all literature. Rosamond's uneasiness might well and rightly have to do with the sense that, despite its dedication to her, the poem left her far behind, had indeed turned her into a ghost, a figment of the poet's imagination. The speaker in Stevens's "Final Soliloquy of the Interior Paramour" says to the woman within: "We say God and the imagination are one . . . / How high that highest candle lights the dark" (*Collected Poems*, 524); and Stevens's title acknowledges that the dialogue with the anima is finally a soliloquy. In this passage Day Lewis was able to find in the figure of his beloved the figuration of erotic fulfillment in the "highest" psychological and religious sense that Bataille postulates. The poet found the words and images through which "she"—not Rosamond so much as the "rose of the world"—makes palpable the transcendent dimension in which desire going forth and returning meet. At that height he probably could not have distinguished even for himself whether he was finding the language for the experience of transcendence or finding transcendence in the experience of language.

Language for transcendence . . . or transcendence in language. Bataille tells of being challenged by a sympathetic but sceptical listener with an objection that cut to the heart of the quandary. All Bataille's talk about eroticism as the life force/death force driving mortal individuals to overcome discontinuity and merge with all of life seemed futile to the questioner because language failed at the ultimate orgasmic point where the individual consciousness would die into such total continuity. In response, Bataille both conceded the objection and sought to overcome it. Yes, Bataille admitted, existence involves the constant struggle and negotiation between the effort of individual consciousness "to reach continuity by breaking with individual discontinuity" and the counterdrive to maintain individual consciousness against the annihilation of continuity (*Erotism*, 144, 276). In Day Lewis's words, "the desire / Going forth meets the desire returning" (319). As the voice of that erotic drive, language propels us to the dangerous boundary before the no-man's-land where words inevitably fail and "there is no more speech"; and, yes, "in the end the articulate man confesses his own impotence." However, "sometimes," if we approach (but do not cross over) that "borderline" where "continuity and consciousness draw very close together," language can articulate "the sovereign moment at the farthest point of being where it can no longer act as currency" (*Erotism*, 276). At such rare and liminal moments language is the erotic elegy before death that sometimes contrives to say something about the unsayable.

The middle section of "Elegy Before Death" records, in rhythms and rhymes and metaphors, such an extraordinary point of meeting between the desire going forth and the desire returning, where language in extremis confesses not its "impotence" but rather, as the poem says, "this naked potency of farewell." In "The Homeward Prospect," the closing and retrospective dialogue among Tom, Dick, and Harry, Day Lewis has Harry gloss "Elegy Before Death" with these last lines of *An Italian Visit*:

> . . . I took our most cherished possession
> And offered her to death. I took a ghost for my glass
> And focused through it the inchoate, atomized face of
>   becoming.
> Then, from the tower in the sky to the tiniest flower in
>   earth's hem,
> All was distinct, illustrious, full-formed in the light of
>   necessity,
> Time's cocoon fallen away from the truth and kinship of all
>   things.
> For one immeasurable moment the world's hands stood still
> And the worm that ticks at the heart of the golden hoard
>   was silent.
> Losing my heart to this alien land, I renewed my true love:
> Lending my love to death, I gained this grain of vision.
> I took my pen. What I wrote is thanks to her and to Italy.   (475–76)

Day Lewis writes thankfully, because through Rosamond/"Rosamond" and Italy he had found adequate language at Bataille's "borderline," desire's cross-point. The penultimate line completes the word play on "grain" and "gain" early in the "Elegy" and encapsulates the "vanishing moment" in the orangery at Settignano: "Lending my love to death, I gained this grain of vision."

In *The Poetic Image*, the would-be believer in Day Lewis went beyond Bataille's sense of the limits of language and even seemed at times to propose a metaphysical motive and authentication for metaphor:

> It has been called the perception of the similar in the dissimilar: . . .
> but the perception would not cause pleasure unless the human mind
> desired to find order in the external world, and unless the world had
> an order to satisfy that desire, and unless poetry could penetrate to this
> order and could image it for us piece by piece. The poetic image is the
> human mind claiming kinship with everything that lives or has lived,
> and making good its claim.

(35)

Certainly "Elegy Before Death," in its large ambition and impressive realization, stands as one of Day Lewis's most successful efforts to "satisfy that desire." This singular, momentary reconciliation between desire going forth and desire returning is the climactic and concluding statement of his decade-long relationship with Rosamond Lehmann and his decade-long contention with eros.

THREE • "ON NOT

SAYING

EVERYTHING"

Poetry and
Thantos
1950–1972

IN MAY 1949, Day Lewis began writing "Elegy Before Death," memorializing his Italian visit and his relationship with Rosamond Lehmann, while
the two of them were on another jaunt to southern Europe—this time to
W. Somerset Maugham's villa at Saint-Jean-Cap-Ferrat. Years later she
would reflect: "I never thought at the time that it was more than a beautiful, romantic farewell to an idyll. . . . Though with hindsight it does seem
strange, as if he was already denying us a future together" (Sean Day Lewis,
178). She seems to have been correct in suspecting that, as the end of their
decade together approached, he had already, mentally and emotionally,
begun to detach himself in preparation for a final break. But anticipation
could not mitigate the pain of rupture, and when it came it was for him
another stormy "departure in the dark."

Afterward, he wrote to his son Sean, by then almost twenty years old
and doing military service, that he "could not stand any longer the mental
agony of trying to divide myself between two people, . . . of trying to live
a divided life." Mary's diary records her long hurt, still unreconciled to
the hollow routine of their marriage: "It is nearly a year since Cecil decided not to go, he has gone most of the way"; "I miss Cecil, but when he
is here his heart isn't"; "Cecil isn't really back"; "Cecil out when I'm in,
we haven't done one thing together, I'm only a bloody housekeeper" (Sean
Day Lewis, 195, 124, 177, 178). At the same time, Rosamond, though

never the housekeeper, began also to feel the ache of absence and sought desperately to explain Day Lewis's black-ice depressions as paternal concern for Sean's military service. Just a few years earlier Day Lewis had broached to Mary the possibility of a divorce so that he and Rosamond could marry. By 1949, however, though he felt as never before that his own survival depended on at last breaking the deadlock of his "divided life," Rosamond—perhaps because the force of her personality threatened to become overpowering (as it had been to other men)—seemed now an aspect of the dilemma rather than its solution.

In early February of 1950, Rosamond wrote in extremis to Mary, shocked by the word she had just received from Day Lewis. He had told her that he had been released from his "state of despair, of black melancholy" by falling passionately in love with a young woman named Jill Balcon. He brought the news to Musbury himself the next day, and his wife's diary entry reads: "Jill Balcon comes into the picture. Everything has the feeling of nightmare, I broke down" (Sean Day Lewis, 185–86). Jill Balcon was an actress and the daughter of Michael Balcon, the head of Ealing Studios later knighted for his distinguished career as a film producer. When she and Day Lewis met, she had already begun an acting career on stage, screen, and radio, and her combination of incisive intelligence, dark-haired and luminous beauty, and empathetic understanding pointed to a successful career. Always an avid reader of poetry and destined to become one of the most accomplished readers of poetry on the BBC and on platforms around Britain, she already knew Day Lewis's work well and admired it intensely when in January 1949 they read together on the BBC program "Time for Verse." Their acquaintance was renewed at the Festival of Spoken Verse in July 1949 and at this point quickened on both sides into love.

As could be expected, the announcement produced in Rosamond outraged and fuming disbelief at what she felt as Day Lewis's betrayal, and the session with Mary, the day after she had been forewarned by Rosamond's letter, was another "terrible ordeal." Since Jill was two decades Day Lewis's junior, both women, he told Jill, sought to misjudge their love as merely "the sort of infatuation for a girl that a middle aged man often falls victim to." Rosamond even maneuvered to make league with Mary to stop this "act of madness," this "fit of temporary madness," but to herself Mary shrewdly "wondered which of us was going to have Cecil if we did get him back" and declined to join forces with Rosamond (Sean Day Lewis, 186, 188). Once he had committed himself to Jill as the way out of an impasse painful to all, Day Lewis remained resolute and moved as swiftly as he could to make the break and put the pain behind them. He would recall later:

> During the ten years after 1940, . . . I was never long free from the sense of guilt, oppressive with disaster like the atmosphere before a storm that will not break, until I learnt how guilt may be a kind of self-indulgence,

or at least a futile surrogate for the moral action one cannot, dare not take.

(The Buried Day, 240)

"A clean break," he wrote to Sean at the time, "generally is preferable to a ragged wound—and an amputation to a limb dangling by a thread" (Sean Day Lewis, 195). A wound so deep and torn open so many times over the years was beyond healing, and under the desperate circumstances even amputation seemed "a clean break."

But amputations are bloody and life-threatening. After the final confrontation with Rosamond on March 20, 1950, he departed what had been his second home at Little Wittenham, drained and shaken by her withering fury. Because train service had ended for the night, he had to walk five miles through Oxfordshire darkness till he could find a hired car. He arrived at Jill's flat in Pimlico at three in the morning, looking, she would recall, "as though he had been tortured" (Sean Day Lewis, 188). Years later, in her memoir *The Swan in the Evening* (1967), Rosamond displaced her outraged feelings onto her daughter Sally, who had come to know Day Lewis as a second father during the forties and whose tragic death from polio at twenty-three in 1958 had cast an even darker shadow over the rest of her mother's life:

> She [Sally] was obliged to witness a catastrophe . . . at close quarters, and at an impressionable age. A pattern of relationships she wholly trusted in collapsed without warning; she saw the effects of this upon a person [Day Lewis] she had been accustomed to love happily.
>
> (The Swan in the Evening, 96–97)

Day Lewis's "treachery" and Sally's death became fused and confused in her mind. The passage from her memoir goes on to recall, from his poem "Love and Pity," the phrase "almost a mercy-killing": "[T]he poem in which it occurs is, if I remember rightly, a philosophical justification of ruthless destructiveness in certain relationships of love. I was particularly struck by the word 'almost'" (96–97).

Because the long-suppressed emotions remained bottled up even to the end, Day Lewis's departure from Musbury on September 11 was less visibly dramatic than the earlier one from Little Wittenham, but it was perhaps no less painful for that. Still, from this point on Day Lewis never wavered or looked back. By the end of the month Mary reluctantly agreed to his request that she sue for divorce, and six days after it became final—on April 27, 1951, Day Lewis's forty-seventh birthday—he and Jill Balcon were married. It was clear to his friends that he felt anything but a "victim" of his feelings for Jill, as Mary and Rosamond may in their shaken state have chosen to suppose. The fact that he had never known a mother had perhaps served to predispose him toward strong older women: Mary had been the mother, and Rosamond the lover. With the younger Jill he hoped that his wife would be both lover and mother of their offspring. He had been living not so much a double life as two half-lives, predicated on the very split in sensibility that bedevilled him at every turn. All his previous experience brought him to this last gamble with eros—a desire to prove eros not a death wish but a life force, not the sublime moment of annihilation but the sustaining condition for living in time. Bataille, in his Lacanian study *Erotisme* (1956), would judge as sadly unattainable precisely what Day Lewis during these same years was seeking: the erotics of married life. And those who had witnessed the years of stress and crisis felt that they saw an extraordinary transformation; by general testimony the couple radiated the tranquil excitement of the love that drew them together. In 1953 Lydia Tamasin Day Lewis was born, and in 1957, Daniel Michael Blake Day Lewis. In January 1958 the family of four moved to the lovely Georgian house at 6 Crooms Hill in Greenwich, downriver from central London, the house that became Day Lewis's home and haven until his death, with alternating work-weeks in his study there and in the editorial offices of Chatto and Windus near Trafalgar Square.

The Buried Day, written in the late fifties, brings Day Lewis's autobiography only through the thirties, but, as we have seen, the last pages of the closing chapter anticipate in generalized terms the combined shock of pain and ecstasy that the forties would bring. And the Postscript glows with the contentment he had found in his new life and the place where it was rooted:

> Yesterday was my fifty-fifth birthday. J. gave me a telescope. Now, sitting by the Thames, I can bring closer to me the great cargo-liners rounding the Isle of Dogs, the tugs and their strings of lighters, the wharves, warehouses, power stations, the skyline restless with cranes, the blue-diamond lights of welding and the indigo smoke from tall chimneys—all the river life which, here at Greenwich, overlooked by the palace and the park, enlivens their elegance with a workaday reality. I am happy, living in this place where old and new can be focused into a historic present. Heavy traffic between the Blackwall tunnel and the Rochester road may shake down one day my early-Georgian house; or the bomb will fall. But, fortunate beyond words in my wife and children—yesterday was also the eighth anniversary of my second marriage—I shall play my luck while it lasts. At least I am learning to live with myself, to view in some kind of focus and in some degree to reconcile the contradictory elements that make up the man of whom this book is a portrait.
>
> (*The Buried Day*, 239)

He would write more love poems, to Jill and to others, but with his second marriage the contention with eros that had generated most of his writing in the forties was over. His poetry would engage the issues of another time of life and another period in his life.

The beautiful passage from the Postscript suggests the contours and concerns of Day Lewis's later work, which contains some of his best and most moving poems. It is emotionally narrower, less turbulent, but more reflective and self-reflective; it is more local, grounded in the scene and in the realization of the moment, and at the same time more urgently focused, as he noted, on recovering the past in the immediate "historic present." It is in a certain sense more conservative in its concern with continuity and history rather than revolution or change, and that concern for the past and present rather than the utopian future reflects an older man's acute awareness of the fragility of the cultural present under the pressures of mass media, of the social present amidst the postwar politics of the Cold War and the Bomb, of the personal present in the face of advancing years. To any idealistically or ideologically "intolerant young" who might carp that he had made "a surrender to the *status quo*, a going over to reaction, complacence, hypocrisy," he replied unapologetically that the seeming circumscription of outlook was in fact a blessed and long-sought concentering, a hard-earned clarification of the qualities and values essential to self-knowledge and human relationships (*The Buried Day*, 240). As the end of the long passage above indicates and as Day Lewis's Preface to the *Selected Poems* published by Penguin in 1951 puts succinctly, the "unbroken thread" running through the dramatic shifts of focus in his work is "the search for personal identity, the poet's relentless compulsion to know himself" (11).

Day Lewis did not live to old age like Yeats and Eliot, much less to the great old age of Hardy or Graves or, as it turned out, Spender. Aging came early and cut his life short. A hemorrhage from the nose that could not be stopped for days almost killed him just after Christmas in 1964, and thereafter he suffered from one physical ailment after another till his death in May 1972, a month after he turned sixty-eight. "[T]he pains and physical ignominy of old age," which in the Postscript to *The Buried Day* he innocently saw as "still distant" (239), afflicted him prematurely. Those afflictions would sharpen the focus of his later poetry on living in time, the unbroken theme of his life's work. During the years in Greenwich he had to ponder, sooner than he had anticipated, how the inescapable encroachment of death defined—that is to say, both delimited and gave meaning to—the terms of living and, for the poet, the vocation of versing.

• 2

In June 1951, Day Lewis delivered "The Poet's Task," the inaugural lecture of his five-year tenure as Professor of Poetry at Oxford. It gave him particular pleasure that he succeeded C. M. Bowra, his revered tutor from Wadham, and that in turn Auden succeeded him in the chair. In part no doubt because of the prestige of the professorship, following upon the Clark lectures he had given at Cambridge in 1947 as *The Poetic Image*, he was also invited to give the Chancellor Dunning Trust Lectures at Queen's University in Kingston, Ontario, and in January 1954, he made his first trip to North America to deliver lectures on Emily Brontë, George Meredith, and W. B. Yeats. They were published that year under the title

Notable Images of Virtue, and, besides being perceptive essays on three of his favorite poets, they began a more extended consideration of the poet's task. In fact, Day Lewis took those poets as mediators through whom he sought to reorient and redefine himself in the new phase of his life and work.

In the Preface to the published version of the lectures Day Lewis identified the source of his title: "Philip Sidney said it was the poet's task to 'feign,' that is, to compose, 'notable images of virtue'" (xi). He took Sidney's phrase to mean not so much "virtue" as the classical sense of *virtu*, the distinctive and energizing signature of a poet's life and character as reflected or constructed in his works. Pound uses the term in the early cantos to characterize the particular integrity of heroes he admires. This Romantic/Modernist appropriation of a classical term for the individual's defining character runs counter to the current Postmodernist talk about the death or disappearance of the author and about art as a socioeconomic construction. In Day Lewis's case, the criterion of *virtu* confirms his abiding humanistic conviction of the ethical efficacy of art, conceived now more flexibly and personally than in the political poetry of the thirties. Experience had taught him to conceive "poetic virtue" as the function and consequence of the "personal mythology" that he speaks of at the end of *The Buried Day*: the configuration of a writer's work "which, because it modifies him, does become representative truth" (*The Buried Day*, 243). As Keats said, the poet writes his personal experience into the allegory of his life. Poetry expresses "representative truth" through the open interplay of art and life, so that the "feign[ing]" of experience into poetry shapes the poet in his own image, and this representation of himself speaks to the effort at self-representation in which we are all engaged.

The titles of the first two essays—"Emily Brontë and Freedom" and "George Meredith and Responsibility"—view the parameters of freedom and of responsibility from different, almost opposite perspectives. Brontë's radical pursuit of absolute personal freedom is a Romantic "protest against the limitations of our human nature": in her case particularly, a refusal to accept "the limitation of material existence" and "the limitation of not being a man" in a patriarchal society (*Notable Images of Virtue*, 2, 19). Powerfully moved though Day Lewis is by the strength of Brontë's vaunting will and the force of her poetic *virtu*, he finally pulls back from the "furious individualism" of an "intransigent Protestant unorthodoxy" so antinomian that it alienated her from community and society, even from "the Nature which she loved" in the hills and moors around Haworth. So antinomian, indeed, that in the end she "confused, almost identified" God with her own imagination (23, 24, 21).

Consequently, Day Lewis finds Brontë's poetry a seductive but destructive siren call: it stands as the "notable image" of "freedom without responsibility." Her fatal limitation lies in her manichean refusal to accept either the material and social world or personal limitation: "[S]he felt responsible to no one but the God within her breast." However compelling to the individual aching with desire for completion, the hubris of that identification with the divine leads not to liberation but to a death wish: "[W]hat her poetry gives us, finally, is not an image of freedom but an image of man's inveterate, vain yearning for it; not the unbounded empyrean, but the beating wings" (24, 25).

Unsatisfied desire drives us to the boundaries of experience and tempts us to transgress them, but Orpheus the poet has to learn that once desire crosses the threshold it enters the realm of Hades and cannot return. During the forties Day Lewis had come as close as he would or wanted to come to that suicidal transgressiveness of Romantic desire:

> Whether we think of freedom as the knowledge of necessity [as the rationalist philosophers and the Marxists believe] or as the gift of a Supreme Being in whose service is perfect freedom [as Christians and other religious believers believe], it remains an ideal which we can fully realize only though acceptance of its limitations.
>
> (24)

Nevertheless, the power of Brontë's *virtu* comes from her "right instinct for rooting her work in the most vulnerable, most wounded part of herself—in the deep cleft between the opposed sides of her nature" (25): namely, in her outraged awareness of the limitations she is driven to resist, even to her death.

The essay ends by citing the last two stanzas of Day Lewis's "Emily Brontë," which had appeared in *Poems 1943–1947* in the midst of his own erotic adventure. The monologue shows Day Lewis's susceptibility to the Romantic desire he resists in Brontë by speaking through her as she imagines her partner in erotic death. His lines are at once an evocation and a catharsis of Brontë's *virtu*:

> Is there one whom blizzards warm and rains enkindle
> And the bitterest furnace could no more refine?
> Anywhere one too proud for consolation,
> Burning for pure freedom so that he will pine,
> Yes, to the grave without her? Let him mingle
> His barren dust with mine.

> But is there one who faithfully has planted
> His seed of light in the heart's deepest scar?
> When the night is darkest, when the wind is keenest,
> He, he shall find upclimbing from afar
> Over his pain my chaste, my disenchanted
> And death-rebuking star. (388)

George Meredith's autobiographically based *Modern Love* was a poem that drew both Day Lewis and Rosamond Lehmann. As we have seen, the last poem in the sequence supplied the title of her first novel, *Dusty Answer*, and of Day Lewis's autobiography, and he wrote a perceptive introduction to an elegant new edition of *Modern Love* that appeared as their affair was drawing to a close. What shocked the Victorians and spoke to Lehmann and Day Lewis was Meredith's candid and unsparing anatomy of the failure of a marriage through the adulterous infidelities of both spouses with disastrous consequences for both: death for the wife and embittered disillusionment for the husband.

Day Lewis's lecture in Kingston followed up the introductory essay to ask why Meredith's poetry after *Modern Love* became so "impatient, hurried, botched" (48), merely "smart, flashy, flippant" (43). His answer to that question reveals the reasons that Meredith continued to stalk his conscience as he set about taking up a new life in the wake of the rupture and divorce that made it possible:

> The hideous and long-drawn suffering which produced *Modern Love* devastated him . . . in two ways: it left a large area of scorched earth behind it; but also it forced Meredith to withdraw to a position in which he could never be so badly hurt again. In making this withdrawal, he cut away, surrendered, too much of himself: it was a major operation which left his poetry permanently invalid.
>
> (51)

The surgical metaphor gives a dismal gloss on Day Lewis's wishful assertion to Sean that after all "an amputation" was preferable "to a limb left dangling by a thread."

The poem "George Meredith, 1861," also written during these transitional years, develops the trope of the earth scorched by combat:

> He'd been the battlefield long enough
> As well as the combatant, when he withdrew
> Scorching the earth behind him thus,
> To whatever was left of integrity.
> If they merely say that he saved his own skin,
> They miss the point. Though he could not be
> Occupied, utterly possessed again,
> He has bought invulnerability
> Too dear: such broad areas blackened, deadened—   (505)

"He'd been"—not seen—"the battlefield." The first lines above present compassionately Meredith's withdrawal from the contest within and without, but the real "point" of the lecture and the poem is that the withdrawal became, in his case at least, a "deadened" inability "to accept relationship, responsibility; to be involved" (51). Paradise, "mortgaged by our ancestral sin," dwindles and recedes, more and more lost

> Each time, however needfully, we sell
> Some share of it, buying with certain loss
> Uncertain reprieve for our dwindling demesne. . . .   (505)

Thus where Brontë warned Day Lewis against the self-destructiveness of refusing to accept human limitations, including the risks and hurts of human relationships, Meredith demonstrated the opposite error, in its own way just as fatal: the self-destructiveness of imposing unnecessary and crippling limitations on erotic desire and aspiration. Both courses in opposite ways fall into solipsism and fail the "responsibility" of "relationship" to loved ones and to community. "Betrayal," Day Lewis speculated gloomily in the Meredith poem, obviously worrying about himself, "is always a self-betrayal / Where love is concerned" (505).

Moreover, the prose passage above mentions "two ways" in which Meredith's scorched-earth course left him the victim of his own devastation. The second, a consequence of the personal failure, consists in a "failure in responsibility to his art":

> When the youthful lyrical impulse has withered, a poet must attempt more conscious investigation of experience: for this purpose he may have to develop new techniques: but what he must never do—and what, I think, Meredith did—is to lose patience with the medium, to spur and whip words in pursuit of ideas, to abandon the loving care for technique which reflects the poet's perpetually-renewed self-dedication.
>
> (48)

For Day Lewis, the reason that the human failure registers at the level of language is that the exploration of the medium is not just a technical skill but a cognitive act, "not only the conscious ordering of words and rhythms" but "The Poet's Way of Knowledge" (the title of the Henry Sidgwick Memorial Lecture he would give at Cambridge in 1956). The linguistic ordering provides a concentration of focus on two levels at once: an intellectual and an emotional clarification in the verbal construction. For a poet like Day Lewis—and here again he is part of the Romantic-Modernist consensus, opposed by contemporary Postmodernist deconstruction—technique functions, in a culture increasingly uncertain about metaphysical certitudes, as "the discipline of creative meditation" through which the poet comes to a realization of self in relationship (48–49).

In "W. B. Yeats and Human Dignity" Day Lewis tries to find a life's course that might steer between the Scylla and Charybdis that Brontë and Meredith presented. Yeats offers another cautionary and admonitory instance of *virtu*. Day Lewis had negotiated the transition (he did not see it as a retreat) from Marxism to the liberal humanism of Hardy, his avowed hero, and E. M. Forster, to whom he had dedicated *Overtures to Death* in 1938. However, Yeats, the other undisputed master of modern British and Irish poetry and an influence on Day Lewis's poetry from the start, presented a challenge that required him to reexamine his politics from a different perspective from Hardy's. After all, "Yeats was a poet—perhaps the last poet—in the aristocratic tradition" (55), and although Day Lewis in the thirties was not alone in being a leftist still attracted to that tradition, he could see, all the more clearly after the Second World War, that Yeats also showed the susceptibility of rightists to the delusion that "the aristocratic tradition could best be carried on, *faute de mieux*, by a Fascist movement" (71). Could such a tradition still espouse an ideal of "human dignity" after Belsen and Auschwitz? Could Day Lewis—no longer a Communist but still a democratic socialist—countenance totalitarian inclinations, left or right, "in an age whose most powerful figures have been Lenin, Hitler, and Stalin" (73–74)? Some might take it merely as confirmation of Day Lewis's drift to the center, but he was convinced that the complementary notions of hero worship and ancestor worship at the "core" of Yeats's idealism were separable from aristocratic or totalitarian politics and could be reconceived as the basis for an ethics and a poetics desperately needed as an antidote to postwar pessimism (76).

From the beginning of his career, Day Lewis acknowledged his muddled generation's need for some mode of belief and worship. The hero that Day Lewis extrapolated from Yeats is no totalitarian absolutist in thought or action but, on the contrary, a liberal-humanist seeker of psychological and moral realization: "the abundance of his personality, the full expression of his own spirit." Moreover, Day Lewis construed ancestor worship as supplementing hero worship by enmeshing the individual quest in a larger pattern. Thus, "just as the heroic view of life gives man images of virtue, by representing him at his loftiest, most intensely living moments, so ancestor-worship helps him to discover his own identity" beyond personal limitation through empathetic identification with others (74–75):

> I take "ancestor-worship" to mean that feeling of affinity for another person, whether dead or alive which reveals to a man some truth about himself, and rouses him to emulation. An ancestor, in this sense, may be a friend or enemy—the living image of oneself, so to say, or its extreme opposite. All that matters is the sense of affinity, and the power it gives us to recognize our own selves by the intimate identification with another.
>
> (75)

Day Lewis no longer sees the individual defined through participation in the People, abstract and anonymous, but he continues to postulate individuality as defined only through an interchange with others, past and present, whom one knows, lives with, knows about. In contrast to the self-isolation of Brontë or of Meredith, Day Lewis's refiguring of Yeats summons the individual to selfhood in and through relationship to a community.

Specifically for a poet, Day Lewis adds, "ancestors are those other poets who, from time to time, provide the medium through which he can realize a new theme, explore a virgin field of subject-matter. They are what the literary critic calls 'influences'" (75). What Day Lewis seems to envision is something like the ethos that Keats, another poet for whom hero worship and ancestor worship offered ethical and aesthetic models, formulated for himself. Keats rejected the egotistical sublime of Wordsworth and instead sought to cultivate his identity, paradoxically, through "negative capability"—that is to say, through the empathetic affinities that extend consciousness into an imaginative assimilation of other existences. In this extended humanistic formulation, hero worship and ancestor worship served Day Lewis, like Keats, as a post-Christian (and, for Day Lewis, post-Marxist) faith: an ethos for the pursuit of selfhood in a social, historical, literary world, though not the specific world to which Yeats gave his imaginative allegiance.

In the 1951 Preface to his Penguin *Selected Poems*, Day Lewis issued to readers a mock warning that "in the view of some critics, my verse has deteriorated since the early 'school of social consciousness' days into an anti-social or at any rate a-social preoccupation with the past and with traditional forms" (7). And certainly Day Lewis had come a long way from his stance in the thirties when, in the Yeats essay, he asked rhetorically whether we wish merely "to measure human dignity by the average rather than by the best, . . . to render the Common Man's self-esteem more complacent still by praising 'the new narcissism of the also-ran'" (76). But the point here is less about class than about the numbingly complacent conformity of modern mass culture. He, like Arnold a century before, wanted to insist that the decline of old aristocratic notions did not leave us without criteria of excellence and value, without norms of action and behavior in the mass society that Arnold feared and that eventuated in the postwar welfare state. In public life Marxism had not proved a sustainable substitute for the Christian faith he had lost in adolescence, nor had eroticism proved a sustainable substitute in private life. But Day Lewis continued to reformulate the secular humanism that in one form and another has grounded art and culture from the Enlightenment (at least till the Postmodernism of the last few decades).

Though at times Keats would feel compelled to conclude resignedly that poetry "is not so fine a thing as philosophy—For the same reason that an eagle is not so fine a thing as a truth," his life's vocation actually proceeded from the postulation of another, admittedly less absolute, more relative source of truth: "I am certain of nothing but of the holiness of the Heart's affections and the truth of Imagination—What the Imagination seizes as Beauty must be truth" (*Letters* 1: 184 & 2: 81). Keats goes on to reiterate the point in another letter: through the empathetic creativity of the Imagination each person's life composes "a continual allegory," "figurative" of its own "Mystery." The moral and psychological function of the Imagination, then, is to turn the world of experience from "a vale of tears" into a "vale of Soul-making." Moreover, Keats goes on to speculate, this process whereby we come to "acquire identities, till each one is personally itself" may envision "a grander system of salvation than the chrysteain [*sic*] religion" (2: 67, 102).

More than a century after Keats, Day Lewis felt uncomfortable with spelling imagination with a capital "I" or mystery with a capital "M" or soul with a capital "S." Nevertheless, these remained resonant words for him, and, however reduced the terms of negotiation, he remained committed to the process of soul making through engagement with the world in language. In one of his last major public addresses on poetry, at the University of Hull in 1968, he quoted several passages from Keats's letters, including the description of the poet's negative capability and the expression of faith in "the holiness of the Heart's affections and the truth of Imagination," with the telling comment: "[I]n his letters [Keats] came to the very core of a poet's nature and of the kind of poetry with which we, still in the shadow of the Romantic Revival, are most familiar" (*A Need for Poetry?* 10). As Day Lewis moved through and past his middle years, this "Churchy agnostic" was drawn more and more strongly to "the discipline of creative meditation" that mediated "the truth of Imagination" and to associate such mediation with the craft of poetry.

• 3

Looking both ways, the poetry that Day Lewis began to write in the fifties tested out the possibilities of such mediation and meditation as it assessed the permanent scars and lingering pains left by the recent, still smarting amputations. The publication of *An Italian Visit*, waiting for years upon Rosamond Lehmann's reluctant permission to include the sequence's central piece, "Elegy Before Death," had to be delayed until January 1953, and the *Collected Poems 1954* honored Day Lewis's fiftieth birthday by bringing together (except for his excision of the last part of "A Time to Dance" and all but two choruses of *Noah and the Waters*) twenty years of work from *Transitional Poem* through *An Italian Visit*. But during these years poems for the next volume were beginning to accumulate and coalesce into *Pegasus and Other Poems*, published in 1957 with a dedication "To Jill."

Meanwhile, publication of Day Lewis's translation of *The Aeneid of Virgil* in 1952 had preceded these books. Productive reengagement with Virgil provided a welcome focus during the traumatic years just before and after the divorce from Mary, the breakup with Rosamond, and marriage to Jill. In 1949 the BBC had approached him about following up his successful version of the *Georgics* with passages from the *Aeneid* for radio broadcast. By the next year the project was extended into a verse translation of the entire poem for broadcast, one book at a time, in dramatic readings by a cast of actors on the BBC's Third Programme. The extravaganza was conceived as an event in the yearlong Festival of Britain. The epic and nationalistic character of the poem seemed suitable to this all-out effort to herald Britain's economic (and cultural) emergence into the booming postwar world. Day Lewis could be ironic in letters and conversation about his contribution to this nationwide huckstering, but in fact the translation of the *Aeneid* allowed Day Lewis's genuinely patriotic feelings (which the

Georgics had served to clarify at the beginning of the war) and his long-standing love of the heroic to express themselves at a time when the dislocations in his personal life had created some interference with lyric expression. By the time he began his life with Jill Balcon, he was already working steadily on the line-for-line translation into loose English hexameters, consulting regularly with the classical scholar W. F. Jackson Knight (to whom he dedicated the translation), and he had completed the remarkable feat of rendering all twelve books before broadcasting began in June 1951. Over the years, Day Lewis's version, in several published editions, has become probably the most widely read translation of Virgil's epic in the century.

The autobiographical resonances at least of the early books of the *Aeneid* could not have been lost on the translator. The stormy scenes between Aeneas and Queen Dido—she distraught with the proud outrage of rejected love, he steeled at last in his determination to abandon her—must have recalled the recent confrontations with Rosamond Lehmann, though in fact Day Lewis wrote Dido's lines with Jill Balcon's voice in mind. In the production, however, she was cast, more appropriately perhaps than the director at the BBC knew, in the role of Venus, the goddess of love, who as Aeneas's mother and patroness maneuvers to rescue him from punishment by his enemy Juno, whose vengeful ire against him has been deepened by her sympathy for Dido.

The translation of the *Aeneid*, therefore, comes at a turning point in Day Lewis's personal and poetic life. Steeped as he was in the epic narrative and its classical context, he found himself drawn to narrative poetry and wrote a suite of four poems whose mythological themes allowed him the frame to examine the traumas of the previous period. The poems, each three to four pages long in loose pentameters reminiscent of the loose hexameters of the *Aeneid*, compose Part One of the *Pegasus* volume and, in effect, open the way into the new phase of his poetry. The poems are not translations or academic exercises in versified paraphrase. On the contrary, the ways in which Day Lewis adapted the myths—omitting, adding, shifting perspective—reveal the thematic point of his telling. For Day Lewis, as for Pound and H. D., myth served as a strategy for distancing—and thence for handling—volatile autobiographical materials. For them mythological figures embodied states of mind and feeling, and mythic stories were psychodramas seeking to resolve their moral and emotional conflicts. Day Lewis's Ovidian legends present four cautionary tales on various kinds of "marriage" and explore aspects of the erotic theme that had become the obsessive concern of the poetry of the forties. In important ways their thematic development prefigured and set the course of the next two decades.

In a poem from *Pegasus* cited in the previous section Day Lewis said through the persona of George Meredith: "Betrayal is always a self-betrayal / Where love is concerned" (505). "Ariadne on Naxos" pursues the twists of betrayal and self-betrayal to a possible resolution. Ariadne has

betrayed her own father through her passion for Theseus and then con-
nived with Theseus to slay her half-brother, the dreaded and monstrous
Minotaur, only thereafter to be abandoned by Theseus on the island of
Naxos. Most of the Ariadne poem is the monologue of her lament and
self-accusation: violence begetting violence, victor victimized in turn. Con-
templating the self-perpetuating succession of human betrayals, Eudora
Welty invoked another myth to exemplify this pattern: "Endless the
Medusa, and Perseus endless" (*The Golden Apples*, 243). But here, in contrast to the tragic fatality of Welty's phrase, Day Lewis is intent on imagining through Ariadne the possibility of breaking the chain of violent
betrayals. The very first line of the poem deliberately places her monologue "between the hero's [that is, Theseus's] going and the god's [that is,
Dionysus's] coming" to rescue her (494). For in the crucial "between" of
the poem Ariadne undergoes a redemptive change that allows Dionysus's
arrival at the end. Ariadne's tragedy as perpetrator and victim, far from
confirming her in blood-vengeance, arouses in her instead an understanding
that enables forgiveness and self-forgiveness:

> What is this word
> The bushes are whispering to the offshore breeze?
> 'Forget'? No. Tell me again. 'Forgive.' A soft word.
> I'll try it on my tongue. Forgive. Forgive . . .
> How strangely it lightens a bedevilled heart!   (496–97)

The need to forgive and be forgiven for betrayals and self-betrayals, for
injuries done and received has haunted Day Lewis's poetry for over a decade, as in this final stanza of "It Would Be Strange" (from *Word Over
All*):

> It would be more than strange
> If the devil we raised to avenge our envy, grief,
> Weakness, should take our hand like a prince and raise us
> And say, 'I forgive'.   (330)

The lines from "Ariadne on Naxos" echo the ones above and bring them
to fulfillment. "It Would Be Strange" speaks from the erotic contortions
of the early forties, but in the later poem, written for his new wife, Ariadne
is his persona in coming to a realization of the redemptive possibilities of
forgiveness. She sees that the "dead, piteous monster," despite the yearly
"slaughter of the innocents" in his cave, was himself a victim who needed
and deserved to be loved, her blood brother and now, through her treachery, her brother in blood:

> Come, lay
> Your muzzle on my forsaken breast, and let us
> Comfort each other. There shall be no more blood,
> No more blood.   (497)

William Faulkner's *Light in August* speaks of the need for all sinful mortals to strive for "that peace in which to sin and be forgiven which is the life of man" (461). Ariadne has come to a similar understanding when as sister-turned-mother to the Minotaur she says to the grotesque form she imagines cradled in her embrace:

> Our lonely isle expands
> Into a legend where all can dream away
> Their crimes and wounds, all victims learn from us
> How to redeem the Will that made them so.   (497)

As in Greek drama, the Will that seems like Fate, cursing generation after generation, may in fact be changed by nothing more than a frail and guilty individual's change of heart or will. Ariadne at least reaches a peaceful sleep, "between death and birth," in which "no victim cried / Revenge," and the crepuscular "between" shifts to a daybreak in which she wakes to her own hierogamy, "seeing the god bend down / And oVer a hoop of stars, her bridal crown" (497). Ariadne experiences what the poet hopes for: a catharsis that will release him into a wiser, humbler selfhood in his new marriage. The poem, therefore, strategically ends with the hierogamy with Dionysus and excises the aftermath. In the myth, after rescuing Ariadne from Naxos, Dionysus abandons her to her own fate. However, in omitting a conclusion that would seem to conWrm Welty's fated repetition of violence, Day Lewis is leaving the outcome open to Faulkner's ameliorative forgiveness.

"Baucis and Philemon" is adapted from Ovid's *Metamorphoses*, and, in the configuration of Day Lewis's four marriage myths, it presents, in explicit contrast to Ariadne and Theseus and in unacknowledged but implicit contrast to Ariadne and Dionysus, a true marriage that has sustained the humble, compassionating couple through long years of domesticity: "There was love in the shine / Of the copper pans, the thrift of a mended coverlet, / The scrubbed and sabbath face of the elm-wood table" (490). The line, early in the poem, "In this evening light their wall is a hoop of gold" makes the connection back to the "hoop of stars" that crowned Ariadne's epiphany and changes it to the marriage bond of Baucis and Philemon. In fact, after basking in the glow of their hearth, the visiting gods reward the enduring love of the Hardyesque couple by joining them in death as a pair of trees, root and branch forever intertwined outside their cottage. For the fifty-year-old Day Lewis, the myth idealizes a settled domesticity that his younger self found wanting with Mary at Box Cottage and Brimclose, but that he now sought in his second marriage.

However, Day Lewis unsettles the outcome by interpolating an extraneous "modern" theme, counterpointing the sanctification of domesticity with the existential angst of the aging mortal at the seeming futility of human striving. Before the arrival of the divine visitors, Baucis intuits her husband's unspoken despair that despite their love "the works and days of his hands" have made only "a beaten path / Leading nowhere and soon to

be overgrown" (490). Day Lewis has the disguised Zeus reconcile Philemon
to living in time because memory holds and restores to consciousness "the
good works and days of your own hands." (The phrase "works and days"
recalls Hesiod's ancient poem and implicitly his *Theogony*.) Philemon
undergoes an instantaneous and unconvincing metamorphosis; he says that
the power of memory to retrieve the past from oblivion changes his "despair into a cup full of blessings": "Oh, chime and charm / Of remembered Junes, of killer frosts returning / To smile and be forgiven!" (492–93).
Mutability and the vanity of time are age-old themes, but here, invested
with the aura of twentieth-century disillusionment, they complicate the
simple moral of Ovid's story without addressing or resolving the complications they introduced. Day Lewis has to rely on the device of the deus
ex machina to banish Philemon's depression, but the need to interject it
in the poem indicates Day Lewis's awareness that even a happy marriage
does not exempt him from the necessity of coming to his own terms with
dying: an eventuality he would confront sooner than he knew when writing this poem.

Experience up to this point had taught Day Lewis how hard it is for
errant love to find a home. Consequently, where "Baucis and Philemon"
is a parable about the stability—in fact, immortality—of domestic love,
"Psyche" is a more foreboding parable, drawn from Day Lewis's experience of the forties, about the evanescence of erotic consummation, even a
warning against the tragic overreaching of erotic love in seizing the sublime object of its desire. Here Psyche, the poet's female persona and emblem of the soul, experiences Eros in his very person but, by ordination of
Eros himself, only under the cloak of darkness. Wanting to know Eros
totally, Psyche violates the prescribed limits of human experience and lights
a candle to see him as he sleeps at her side. The outcome inverts her aspirations: sight removes what she, unseeing, saw. Psyche knew Eros in sight-
less consummation, but light/sight, violating "this maidenhead of dark,"
alienates and divides her from Eros. Paradoxically, the light closes rather
than opens—"a clear, impassable window / Through which her love could
gaze but never go"—and she finds herself not joined but "estranged in
revelation" from his "rod and fount of passion" (487–88). The drive to
carnal knowledge, as Bataille was not the first to note, is psychologically
associated with the soul's (or Psyche's) yearning for the absolute, a consummation that exceeds human grasp. Too late Psyche realizes that in
"breaking my faith" and demanding to know what humans cannot know,
"myself I have betrayed": where "once you were mine, were me, for me
alone," now "we that were one are two. Thus am I doomed."

Without any explicit Christian allusion, the language of Day Lewis's
retelling of Apuleius's late-classical fable is overlaid with suggestions of
Eve's fall from love into a "self-love" that is just "lust": possessive and
therefore dispossessing. The homonym of "eye" and "I" links insight and
individuation, consciousness and ego, identity and separation. Psyche has
fallen from limited intimation of presence to isolated consciousness of

absence, exiled in "the busy, barren world of mend and make." Now only "her need" for what she lost "proves and touches the Divine" (489). Is the beloved, then, only the shade of desire? The following stanza—by stretching the rhyming syllables of the first two lines into next three (a-b-a-a-b)— closes round Psyche's consciousness of that question:

> So he passed from her, and at last she learnt
> How blind she had been, how blank the world can be
> When self-love breaks into that dark room meant
> For love alone, and on the innocent
> Their nakedness dawns, outraging mystery.   (489)

"Dawn" in "that dark room" spells "doom." But where Day Lewis cut off the story of Ariadne before Dionysus betrayed their conjugal union, here he chooses not to extend his account to the eventual reunion of Psyche and Eros. Instead, Psyche's didactic plea at the conclusion of the poem— "Dear souls, be told by me"—underscores the poet's hope that he has learned from sad experience the limits of love as he seeks to renegotiate his life between the reach of desire and the circumference of possibility.

As always with a poet, these matters are mediated through language. The title poem of *Pegasus* (dedicated to the memory of Lilian Bowes Lyon, a friend from the thirties for whose selected poems Day Lewis provided an introduction in 1948) pursues the marriage theme as a figure for aesthetic creation, and it has been acclaimed as one of his best poems. From the many episodes of Bellerophon's story Day Lewis focuses exclusively on his contest with Pegasus. The interplay through which the winged horse eludes all of Bellerophon's wiles but then submits to the controlling bridle of an humbled master is a time-honored parable for the hard-earned combination of skill and submissiveness that a poet needs to ensnare elusive inspiration in linguistic and prosodic constraints, to catch unconscious intuition in conscious form. Day Lewis's redaction of the episode at this strategic point in his development proposes a poetics of limitation, which, as we shall see, will become a major concern of his later years.

The poem recalls that Pegasus "was born from the blood of uncanny / Medusa, the nightmare-eyed" (484). In the previous chapter we examined "The Image," a sonnet written some ten years earlier than "Pegasus," in which the slaying of the Medusa, with its overtones of erotic conquest, becomes a trope for mastering the violence of experience in aesthetic form. There Perseus is a trope for the poet, and his reflective shield a trope for the imaged poem. Now in "Pegasus" Bellerophon the "invincible hero" becomes Perseus's avatar in confronting the winged offspring of the Medusa's decapitation. Again, the erotics are explicit; Pegasus is the object of Bellerophon's mastering—and as a poet his phallogocentric —desire: "his naked lover," "as if it [the horse] were some white girl / To stretch, mount, master, exhaust . . . " (483, 485). The pun on "bridal"/ "bridle" sustains the link between erotic consummation and aesthetic constraint.

But the point to be stressed is that, for all the similarities between "Pegasus" and "The Image," both the erotic and the aesthetic stance of the two poems turns out to be significantly different. For in the course of his aggressive pursuit of his "bride" with his "bridle," Bellerophon undergoes a reversal of roles when he comes to realize that "he, not the winged horse, was being broken" and trained for a different kind of encounter. In the sudden vulnerability of his new perspective he sees the horse no longer as "some white girl" to be mounted but, on the contrary, as "his lode, his lord, his appointed star" (485); outwitted, he gives in and accepts Pegasus's untrammeled victory. But of course the episode does not end with Pegasus's vanishing flight; on the contrary, the denouement brings consummation within the constraints of a reciprocity that is both escape and capture, freedom and surrender for both Bellerophon and Pegasus. In the dream that comes to Bellerophon after his impotent surrender, he receives from Athena, the most androgynous of goddesses and his patron, a golden bridle that becomes the sign and means of his empowering metamorphosis. This "mesh of immortal fire and sensual earth" portends the reconciliation of opposing elements; moreover, the bridle that the awakened Bellerophon finds at hand is a sign that such reconciliation can actually occur. He finds Pegasus waiting to "receive the visionary curb" with these reconciling words: "I am brute / And angel. He alone who taps the source / Of both, can ride me. Bellerophon, I am yours" (486). Who, then, is bride and who is bridled? The distinction is superseded: "It was all brides, all thoroughbreds, all pent passion" (486)—both earth and fire, animal and spirit.

Bellerophon wakes to find his dream come true. Then is such consummation possible this side of death, in the broken "world of mend and make"? "Psyche" says no, but "Pegasus" seems to allow it within the circumscription of the bridle. Circumscription, literally a "writing around," reminds us, however, that this poem is about the erotics of poem-making. The poem is the manifest of the waking, or awakened, dream—or, it would be more accurate to say, it can be on those rare occasions that validate the poet's life when he manages to catch the stretch of desire in the net of language, when he inexplicably succeeds in fusing "immortal fire and sensual earth" in the poem's "mesh." In the Harvard lectures, which the next section of the chapter will examine, Day Lewis returned to the legend of Pegasus and Bellerophon as "an image for the creative process" and glossed the "Pegasus" poem from the practical perspective of the working poet:

> With our own human problems, how often we are told to 'sleep on it'. But we have to play an active part first. . . . Bellerophon would not have been granted the bridle if he had not spent all his energy and skill attempting to catch Pegasus. . . .
>
> (*The Lyric Impulse*, 130–31)

In other words, as the poem itself suggests, the poet must assume his own kind of bridle, disciplining and training himself in the strategic maneuvers of poetic craft. By dictionary definition, "craft" denotes both "shrewdness, even cunning, in planning strategy" and "skill in making." The poet will never bridle Pegasus without learning to play the game and becoming an expert horseman, but, as Bellerophon had to learn, the arrogance of craft alone will never catch Pegasus. "Why is it that in one poem a good poet can capture the inspiration and go soaring up on it, whereas the next poem he writes, though as much skill and energy have gone into it, never leaves the ground?" (*The Lyric Impulse*, 131). The winged inspiration derives not from "conscious art" but, as Pegasus instructs Bellerophon, from tapping the "source" or ground of our divided being and releasing the uncontrolled energies so that, through the instrumentality of the bridle, "conscious art" can then rein in those soaring energies and coordinate their flight pattern toward final destination (484, 486). No wonder that the opportunity to ride the winged horse presumes the requisite technical training but requires besides "a gift of the goddess," "a moment, if you like, of grace" (*The Lyric Impulse*, 131).

Day Lewis calculatedly extends the theological term "grace" into the aesthetic dimension to signify the consonance of insight with technique, the registration of spirit in form. The six-line stanza in which the narrative of "Pegasus" unfolds is an excellent instance of such formal grace: a quatrain with alternating rhymes, a-b-a-b, brought to rest in the closing couplet, c-c. The last two stanzas show how the movement fulfills the form while the form manages the movement:

Wings furled, on printless feet through the dews of morn
Pegasus stepped, in majesty and submission,
Towards him. Mane of tempest, delicate mien,
It was all brides, all thoroughbreds, all pent passion.
Breathing flowers upon him, it arched a superb
Neck to receive the visionary curb.

Pegasus said, 'The bridle that you found
'In sleep, you yourself made. Your hard pursuit,
'Your game with me upon this hallowed ground
'Forged it, your failures tempered it. I am brute
'And angel. He alone, who taps the source
'Of both, can ride me. Bellerophon, I am yours.'   (486)

The expansive pressure of various polarities—"wings," "feet"; "majesty and submission"; "Mane of tempest, delicate mien"; "all brides, all thoroughbreds," followed by the oxymoron "all pent passion"; "found," "made"; "brute / And angel"; "taps," "ride"—is reined in by rhymed couplets whose terms reiterate the interplay of restraint and inspiration, form and substance: "superb"/"curb"; "source"/"yours."

"Final Instructions," which concludes Part Two of *Pegasus*, recapitulates these points and provides its own gloss for the "Pegasus" poem. Its didacticism is masked as a dramatic monologue with a classical setting in which an older temple priest prepares an ephebe for the sacrificial rites. The lesson of experience is to absorb the proven techniques until they become second nature and then wait in hope but not expectation for the unpredictable descent of the god:

> So luck is all I can wish you, or need wish you.
> And every time you prepare to lay yourself
> On the altar and offer again what you have to offer,
> Remember, my son,
> Those words—patience, joy, disinterestedness. (512)

In Day Lewis's commentary the three final words sum up "the human qualities which are required if the workings of the creative spirit are to go forward unimpeded" ("The Creative Spirit," 2). The joy that can overwhelm patient exercise of the craft requires the disinterested recognition that the poet-priest's successes—most especially his sublime successes—are not just personal triumphs or technical achievements. It is noteworthy that Day Lewis again connects poetry writing with religious ritual and worship; and the fact that he cited "Final Instructions" in so many lectures and discussions about how to write a poem indicates how basic those instructions were for him.

The poems in Part One of *Pegasus* provide a mythological distancing for the transitional themes that are then developed autobiographically in the poems of Parts Two and Three. Part Two contains a number of poems from the late forties and early fifties describing the scorched earth—the metaphor, as we have seen, comes from "George Meredith, 1861"—that was the psychological and moral terrain of the tortuous break with Mary Day Lewis and Rosamond Lehmann. One of the best is "Love and Pity," which uses the structure of the sonnet to contrast "love without pity" and "pity without love." They are characterized separately in succeeding quatrains through a pummeling succession of violent metaphors; then they are compressed and juxtaposed in the split halves of the third quatrain, and the contrast is summed up in the closing couplet:

> Love without pity is a child's hand reaching,
> A behemoth trampling, a naked bulb within
> A room of delicate tones, a clown outraging
> The heart beneath the ravished, ravisher skin.
> Pity without love is the dry soul retching,
> The strained, weak azure of a dog-day sky,
> The rescuer plunging through some thick-mined region
> Who cannot rescue and is not to die.
> Pitiless love will mean a death of love—
> An innocent act, almost a mercy-killing:
> But loveless pity makes a ghost of love,
> Petrifies with remorse each vein of feeling.
> Love can breed pity. Pity, when love's gone,
> Bleeds endlessly to no end—blood from stone. (507–8)

The poem has the shocking impact of some of Shakespeare's dark sonnets or Hopkins's terrible sonnets. As in other painfully personal poems, Day Lewis assumes a certain objectivity of presentation (though the bruising barrage of violent metaphors gives away his deep engagement), and he did not specifically associate pitiless love with his own feeling for Rosamond and loveless pity with his feeling for Mary. But Rosamond acknowledged the connection when in her autobiography she recalled the poem with bitter scorn for what seemed to her his self-exoneration and cites the phrase *"almost a mercy-killing"* in italics for emphasis (*The Swan in the Evening*, 97).

But self-exoneration is not finally what these poems seek and express. "Almost Human" is a punishing self-caricature, presented in the relative remove of the third person, and calling to mind E. A. Robinson's mordant sketches in ballad quatrains of "Richard Cory" and "Miniver Cheevy." The subject in "Almost Human" is a tweedy, much-admired writer, publicly "assured and kind" in his smooth articulateness but within "an outlaw and a cripple" with "an incurable / Sickness upon his mind" (503):

> A woman weeps, a friend's betrayed,
> Civilization plays with fire—
> His grief or guilt is easily purged
> In a rush of words to the head.   (504)

Day Lewis is not the first artist to charge that the artist's compulsion to appropriate human emotions as the material for his art points to a strain of the "moral desperado" in him (Sean Day Lewis, 231–33):

> The newly dead, and their waxwork faces
> With the look of things that could never have lived,
> He'll use to prime his cold, strange heart
> And prompt the immortal phrases.   (504)

This man might be the not-quite-human figure in Lehmann's memoir. But Day Lewis is no moral desperado, and the last two quatrains ask the reader, before condemning "this eminent freak / As an outrage upon mankind," to look deeper and see him as all too human: "something there is in him" that seeks to break out of isolation and share in human love, but that thwarted aspect of himself (in an image from "The Little Mermaid," Hans Christian Andersen's fable of longing and betrayal) "walks on knives, on knives" (504).

"Almost Human" is an act of self-accusation (and, Day Lewis perhaps hoped, of exorcism preparatory to a different love-commitment), but not of exoneration from responsibility. The literary exploiter in "Almost Human" is only a tourist through life (see "The Tourists," 508–9), not (as Day Lewis often figured his purpose) a traveler who becomes the "fabric of the road" he journeys (325). At this midlife juncture Day Lewis cannot but ask himself about his present direction. "The Wrong Road" even questions the "easier walking" that his second marriage seemed to have brought him. Though he felt "at home" at last, did its "lack / Of grit and gradient" make it for that very reason the wrong road for him? It was, in any case, the road before him; there did not seem the choice that Frost faced in "The Road Not Taken." The challenge, then, was to be not a mere sightseeing tourist but as wholly human a journeyman as possible:

> For this lost traveller, all depends
> On how real the road is to him—not as a mode
> Of advancement or exercise—rather, as grain
> To timber, intrinsic-real.
>   He can but pursue
> His course and believe that, granting the road
> Was right at the start, it will see him through
> Their errors and turn into the right road again.   (502)

"Their errors": the word includes the road's meanderings and his own transgressions.

The momentary hesitation about the future was resolved by poem's end. In fact, the road ahead would provide its own grit and gradient, but in the fifties he let himself enjoy the slower pace of the level stretch, and his meditations savored the autumnal fruits of domesticity, bittersweet because late coming and seasoned by the awareness of spring-in-fall. In Part Three of *Pegasus*, a translucent serenity, not free of conflict but instead distilled from it like an essence, begins to suffuse many of the poems of his last two decades: something of Edgar's essential wisdom in *Lear* that "Ripeness is all" (V, ii, 11). "On a Dorset Upland" (from Part Three of *Pegasus*) is a superb instance of this plangent lyricism. It memorializes the many radiant sojourns he and Jill enjoyed in the Dorset countryside around Dorchester during the early years of their marriage:

> The floor of the high wood all smoking with bluebells,
> Sap a-flare, wildfire weed, a here-and-gone wing,
> Frecklings of sunlight and flickerings of shadowleaf—
> How quickly, how gustily kindles the spring,
> Consumes our spring!
>
> Tall is the forenoon of larks forever tingling:
> A vapour trail, threading the blue, frays out
> Slowly to a tasselled fringe; and from horizon
> To horizon amble white eternities of cloud,
> Sleepwalking cloud.
>
> Here in this niche on the face of the May morning,
> Fast between vale and sky, growth and decay,
> Dream with the clouds, my love, throb to the awakened
> Earth who has quickened a paradise from clay,
> Sweet air and clay.

Now is the chink between two deaths, two eternities.
Seed here, root here, perennially cling!
Love me today and I shall live today always!
Blossom, my goldenmost, at-long-last spring,
My long, last spring!   (521–22)

Day Lewis's knowledge of music and song and his own experience of singing songs (Tom Moore was a favorite) inform a poem like "On a Dorset Upland" and make it not so much a text awaiting musical setting (though some of Day Lewis's poems have been set) as an incorporation of lyricism into what Day Lewis called the "singing line" of spoken verse (*The Lyric Impulse*, 132). The rhyming of the second, fourth, and fifth lines of the five-line stanza quickens each unit and intensifies its euphony, only to cut it short with the contraction of the five-stress lines to two concluding stresses. The poem celebrates his marriage by transforming the Dorset countryside, already associated with Hardy and now intimately familiar through the couple's visits there, into the landscape of their love. The opening phrases of the stanzas particularize the time and place: "The floor of the high wood," the "tall" sky overhead, "Here" and "Now." The intensity of their love, reflected by the countryside, is muted by conscious-ness of its brevity. The incandescence of "Sap a-flare, wildfire weed" is matched, in the second half of line two, by "a here-and-gone wing"; "kindles the spring" collapses immediately into "Consumes our spring"; "larks forever tingling" disintegrate into "a vapour trail," with the allit-eration of "forenoon," "forever," "frays," "fringe," and "from" tracing out the unravelling. "Eternities of cloud" becomes, with the turn of a line, "Sleepwalking cloud." But, in the last two stanzas, mutability serves to concentrate and focus the present: the upland is made "fast"—that is, both fixed and short-lived—"between vale and sky" in the cycle of "growth and decay," and the moment is framed and delimited between the "two deaths, two eternities" of before and after. The poem issues imperatives ("Dream," "throb," "seed," "root," "cling," "blossom") that strive to prolong the in-between into the perennial, to elide "love" into "live," "today" into "always" ("Love me today and I shall live today always"), to reclaim "paradise" from "clay." But the affirmative exclamations are chas-tened by the slight but decisive modulations of the closing rhymes of each stanza; in particular the very last rhyme holds in tense consummation the postponed momentousness of my "at-long-last spring" and the prolonged finality of "my long, last spring." The declension from "at-long-last" to "long, last" is the decisive difference between a connective hyphen and the disjunctive comma that changes "at-long-last" into "long, last."

What makes the lyric achievement of a poem like this all the more remarkable is that its formal intricacy is enhanced rather than diminished by the immediacy of the spoken voice, which can even turn the flatness of "Love me today and I shall live today always" into song. As we have seen, Day Lewis, like others in the Auden circle, was seeking from the late twen-ties on to combine prosodic ingenuity with a flexible meter and run-on

lines that registered the timbre and rhythms of speech in a modern register. It was his strategy for defining a modern poetry between the nine-
teenth-century fustiness of the Georgian adherence to convention and the
Modernist subversion of the distinction between verse and prose. Day
Lewis's kind of colloquiality and even prosiness would be metered and
rhymed in complicated stanzas with singing lines. The prosy inflections
would make meter a supple medium for the modern sensibility, and meter
would lift contemporary speech into lyric intensity and concentration.
Poems like "On a Dorset Upland" and others we have examined and will
be examining demonstrate the assurance that made Day Lewis a virtuoso
in fulfilling his own model of the modern. For it is important to recognize
that in his criticism and poetry Day Lewis was deliberately proposing and
exemplifying a modern alternative to poetic Modernism for cogent intellectual, aesthetic, and social reasons.

"The Wrong Road" was only one of many Day Lewis poems, earlier
and yet to come, that treat the dialectics of "home" and "road"; houses
were signposts of the journey: Box Cottage, Brimclose, Little Wittenham.
But 6 Crooms Hill, the gracious Georgian residence of the Day Lewis family
from New Years Day, 1958, till his death, became home in a way he had
not previously known. From that base the poetry of the fifties and sixties
turned from the erotic quest of the forties to draw in and constellate the
circle of family and friends around the lodestar of home. Part Two of
Pegasus had settled the old scores sufficiently for Part Three to open the
new phase, beginning with "The House Where I Was Born" and ending with "Last Words." In between, poems deal with relationships between parents, especially fathers, and children, especially sons, so that
the poet as both son and father becomes the pivot of generations, turning and looking both ways.

In the first poem of Part Three, the poet imagines himself into a photograph of "The House Where I Was Born," summoning back the mother
he could not know and the father he did not know in life to "ask the questions I never could ask them / Until it was too late" (514). In the reversed
perspective of "Father to Sons" the poet broods over the lost childhood of
Sean and Nicholas at Box Cottage and wonders what they in their middle
age will "think of me, say of me, . . . When I am dead?" (515). He seems
by hindsight the "serpent" whose "unreason / Or too much reason" ruined what should have been his boys' "garden idyll" and so "made your
Eden / A state you could not be sorry to slough." The word "Forgive" is
again suspended in the need to absolve and be absolved: "I still had much
that even / A god only gets at through mortal stuff / To learn about love"
(515). In "Son and Father," the poet, now son once more, links his own
fall from grace retrospectively with his self-protective resistance to the demanding possessiveness of Frank Day-Lewis's love. Did the son's rebellion
against the ordained man of God so closely identify God and man as to
forfeit the son's faith as well and unwittingly cripple him emotionally and
spiritually for life?

> Did I thus, denying him, grow
> Quite dead to the Father's grace, the Son's redemption?

> Ungenerous to him no more, but unregenerate,
> Still on a frozen earth I stumble after
> Each glimmer of God, although it lights up my lack,
> And lift my maimed creations to beg rebirth.   (516)

"The Great Magicians" describes this "lack" as "the hollow in the breast / Where a God should be" and brands this "fault" beyond absolution or remedy (524). But "Christmas Eve" (issued separately by Faber and Faber as an Ariel poem in 1954) pursues the almost Arnoldian or Dickensian sentiment that even for questing unbelievers the commemoration of "incarnate Love" at Christmastide "can keep / Expectation alive." If, as he feared, his fall from grace is a consequence of the son's rejection of the father, then perhaps "Love's mystery" may be "revealed" in the counterturn when the secular son-turned-father "becomes the child" (517–18).

Become a child again himself? Become the Christ-child? Would either move be possible for him? If not, perhaps the offspring of his married love augured rebirth. The desire to recover something of the lost self in the child, therefore, looked forward as well as backward, trying to complete the circle of self. By the time the American edition of *Pegasus* appeared a year after the British, Day Lewis had interpolated into Part Three two poems written for and dedicated to the daughter and son of his "long, last love." But did the child offer the prospect of forging a new set of possibilities or simply of re-enacting the old heartbreaks? Within the circle of time was "expectation" of a change of terms and outcome merely a sentimental delusion?

"Getting Warm—Getting Cold" describes the baby Tamasin's excited search for a hidden present, while her parents try to guide her to it with hints of proximity or distance. The poem turns this familial game into a poignant recognition of the child's still warm belief in life's mystery before the chill of mortal loss:

> May she keep this sense of the hidden thing,
> The somewhere joy that enthralled her,
> When she's uncountable presents older—
> Small room left for marvels, and none to say
> 'You are warmer, now you are colder.'   (545)

As in John Crowe Ransom's poems about the child's doomed innocence ("Janet Waking," for example, or "Dead Boy"), the wit of the adult observer is meant to cut the sweetness of the sentiment. In this last stanza the puns on "uncountable presents older" (as the "gifts" but also the "passing moments" of a lifetime) and on "enthralled" (as "held in awed wonder" but also "held in bondage") implicitly acknowledge the speaker's ironic awareness of the futility of the prayer he finds himself pronouncing with all his heart.

Within the cluster of autobiographical poems in Part Three of the American *Pegasus*, "Getting Warm—Getting Cold" is placed just before "Christmas Eve"; and its companion piece, "The Newborn," comes just after. In explaining to the infant Daniel why "your birthday" is also, among the family feasts, "our thanksgiving" (542), "The Newborn" again posits the potential for transformation nascent in any manifestation of life:

> This morsel of man I've held—
> What potency it has,
> Though strengthless still and naked as
> A nut unshelled!
> Every newborn seems a reviving seed
> Or metaphor of the divine,
> Charged with the huge, weak power of grass
> To split rock. How we need
> Any least sign
> That our stone age can break, our winter pass!   (541)

The breakup of our stony, wintry condition requires the breakthrough of parturition. The grass seed is an organic and Romantic symbol (Whitman comes most quickly to mind, but also Williams's "A Sort of Song" in which the saxifrage's name asserts its power to split rocks) for the correspondence between nature and human nature as a "metaphor of the divine." But the language of the passage deflates such assurance repeatedly in the lapse from "potency" to "strengthless," from "huge" to "weak," from "power" to "need." Is the passage offering a "sign" of "power" . . . or only of "need"? A "metaphor of the divine" or, as in a post-Romantic like Stevens, just a metaphor for the divine? Does it signify presence or absence? The last stanza of "The Newborn," following the one above, reiterates that the boy's birth arouses hope for renewal in "time-worn folk," but even here the affirmation is qualified by a clause that melds hope with wish fulfillment: "as though mankind's begun / Again in you." Frost spoke for Stevens and Day Lewis and many of the moderns when he said "All virtue in 'as if'" (*Selected Prose*, 67). Honesty about the "as if" unsettles the conclusion of a poem like this one (and poems by Frost), but saves it from a falsifying sentimentality.

The "need" for a breakthrough is voiced again and again, as in this stanza from "The Years O":

> Far back, through wastes of ennui
> The child you were plods on,
> Hero and simpleton
> Of his own timeless story,
> Yet sure that somewhere beyond
> Mirage and shifting sand
> A real self must be.   (518)

Once again, however, the language wobbles. The passage plays its declarative statement against the underlying disparities between "mirage and shifting sand" and "real self," between "hero" and "simpleton," "wastes of ennui" and "timeless story," "sure" and "somewhere," "plods on" and "beyond." These lacunae shift the poem from statement to question. Is the father's hoped-for "second childhood" a sign not of rebirth but of senility? Does the circle of life close, as the recently dead Dylan Thomas found, on the parched frustration of unslaked desire?

> Is it a second childhood,
> No wiser than the first,
> That we so rage and thirst
> For some unchangeable good?
> Should not a wise man laugh
> At desires that are only proof
> Of slackening flesh and blood? (519)

But the last stanza borrows an image from Valéry to strike a note that will become more and more urgently felt in Day Lewis's later poetry; for it makes all the difference if, as this stanza claims, the approaching death of desire can invest old age with an intensified potency rather than impotence:

> Faster though time will race
> As the blood runs more slow,
> Another force we know:
> Fiercer through narrowing days
> Leaps the impetuous jet,
> And tossing a dancer's head
> Taller it grows in grace. (519)

Time's narrowing swirl can serve to put tumescent pressure on the passing moments, and the combined phallic and vaginal aspects of the image of the jet provide a more orgasmic version of what Stevens meant in "Sunday Morning" when he said that "Death is the mother of beauty" who impels her sons "to pile new plums and pears / On disregarded plates" for her daughters to "taste / And stray impassioned in the littering leaves" (*Collected Poems*, 68–69).

Paradoxically, however, the discipline of living under the pressure of time also requires acceptance of going with the flow, willingness to relinquish even moments of consummation. "Time to Go" commemorates an almost paradisal Italian visit that the Day Lewises made in 1951, the first after their marriage, and particularly their stay with Stephen and Natasha Spender in Torre del Benaco. The necessary moment of departure is cast, with Miltonic overtones, as an expulsion from a lapsed Eden:

> . . . time to go. They turned and hurried away
> With never a look behind,
> As if they were sure perfection could only stay
> Perfect now in the mind. . . . (521)

The couple, children of Adam and Eve, accept expulsion as a fate long since accomplished; they are not residents of Eden but travelers in exiled journey through a fallen world in which even "felicity" demands closure and terminus:

> release from its own charmed sphere,
> To be carried into the world of flaws and heartaches,
> Reborn, though mortally, there. (521)

The worldly wisdom of their free acceptance of exile, "cherishing their brief vision," shows its consolatory beneficence when St. Michael, the archangelic emissary charged with turning them out, sees that he can sheath his "flaming sword, his mission / A pure formality" (521).

"As if they were sure perfection could only stay / Perfect now in the mind"; "all virtue," as Frost said, "in 'as if.'" But of course the poet did not carry the "brief vision" into the "world of flaws and heartaches" perfected "in the mind" only. The writing of these words into a poem constitutes the "as if" that aspires to a "pure formality" of aesthetic invention to hold the moment within and against the erosions of time and memory. In fact, as we shall elaborate in the next section of the chapter, Valéry meant the fountain's jet as an image of the concentrated intensity that formal conventions can impose on the inchoate flow of experience and flow of words. Valéry's image sums up much about modern and Modernist aesthetics. Pound also invoked the fountain (this time from Verlaine's "Clair de Lune") at the end of Canto 74, as he seeks to give direction and focus to the articulation of his own scattered memories. He conceives all twenty-five pages of this first, longest, and baggiest of *The Pisan Cantos* as a whole held "serenely in the crystal jet / as the bright ball that the fountain tosses / (Verlaine) as diamond clearness"; and he too locates the source of the canto's force and direction in the imagination's control of its medium: "This liquid is certainly a / property of the mind" (*The Cantos*, 449).

When "The Years O" concludes that the fountain, "tossing a dancer's head" and springing "taller," "grows in grace," this last word, a recurrent one in Day Lewis's verse and prose reenforced here by the alliteration, serves again to deflect the religious fulfillment of desire into poetic fulfillment. The title of "Dedham Vale, Easter 1954," dedicated to Elizabeth Jane Howard, connects aesthetic "creation"—this time the Romantic paintings of Dedham Vale by John Constable—with the annual canonical season of rebirth. Constable perfects his passion for the pastoral countryside and luminous skies around his native Flatford and the river Stour by figuring them in paint as his own "landscape of the heart":

His sunburst inspiration
Made earthly forms so true
To life, so new to vision,
That now the actual view
Seems a mere phantom, through
Whose blur we glimpse creation.   (523)

So, for Day Lewis in *Pegasus*, poems celebrating a marriage trip and the birth of a child finally say that rebirth in time is an aesthetic "creation": our closest approximation on earth to paradise regained. The poem is jet and fountain, instrument and end, "where all is / Movement and all at peace" (523). In the poetic round at least, the desire going forth meets the desire returning home.

All movement and all at peace: Day Lewis pointedly gathered together at the end of Part Two of *Pegasus* a number of poems about artistic creation, climaxing in "Sheepdog Trials in Hyde Park" (included in the American edition and discussed in the next section) and "Final Instructions" (discussed earlier in this section). In order to bridge the transition from the "scorched earth" poems of Part Two to the autobiographical meditations of Part Three, this succession of poems about poetry must itself move from negation to affirmation. "Elegiac Sonnet" mourns his musician friend Noel Mewton-Wood, whose suicide in 1954 posts a warning about the vulnerability of the artist and the fragility of his purpose. For in his case "the stern ordeal of art" was not strong enough to maintain "the transport of his April force" against "the simple exercise of human loss," and so, all prematurely, "a fountain plays no more: those pure cascades / And diamond plumes now sleep within their source" (510). Similarly— and again with the trope of the dancing fountain—"In Memory of Dylan Thomas" begins with the lament "*Too soon, it is all too soon*" for another artist, who "danced on a plume of words, / Sang with a fountain's panache" but, again prematurely and almost willfully, was dead before forty in 1953.

But Day Lewis had always felt that Thomas's wrongheaded and profligate rage against mortality revealed the death wish it sought to deny, and now his elegy for Thomas works to retrieve from the wreckage a tempered assertion of the poet's high purpose:

A poet can seem to show
Animal, child and leaf
In the light of eternity, though
It is but the afterglow
From his consuming love,
The spill of a fabulous dawn
Where animal, leaf and child,
Timelessly conceived,
With time are reconciled.   (509)

The giveaway word "seem" in the first line sets into motion the deconstruction of "the light of eternity" into the "afterglow" of the poet's "consuming" desire. The single long sentence winds down the enjambment of verses past the irregular rhymes through the subversive "though" clause in the middle. But the end of the sentence recoups something of the loss and winds itself up again to the final period: "animal, leaf and child, / Timelessly conceived, / With time are reconciled." That is to say, the poet can show something; even if it is just the radiant reflection and conception of his own desire and need, that "afterglow" becomes "a fabulous dawn"— "fabulous" in the sense of "fabled" and "marvelous" but also in the sense of "fabling" or (Stevens's word) "fictive." The poetic offspring of the imagination's desire reconciles existence to its mortality. When Eliot wrote in "Burnt Norton," "Only through time time is conquered," he was speaking from a Christian perspective that sees time's shadow "in the light of eternity" and thus conceives time as a process necessary for but preparatory to transcendence. For Day Lewis "animal, leaf and child" are "timelessly conceived" not "in the light of eternity" but in the poetic measure that composes and thereby reconciles contingencies into its own artificial (or art-making) time, whose recorded movement is impervious to clock time. That is to say, for Day Lewis only through metrical time is chronological time conquered. His poem for the composer "Edward Elgar" reiterates this axiom unequivocally: the artwork, "beat to its own time, timelessly make[s] heard / A long-breathed statement or a hesitant phrase" (573).

Because *Pegasus* is a transitional book, composed from poems written over almost a decade and executing a painfully wrung reorientation, it is in its organization and development the most complex of all Day Lewis's volumes of poems. Most of the issues raised in the process converge in "Last Words." This concluding poem of the volume attempts to imagine a lifetime and a life's versing concentered in the consuming and consummating moment of thanatos:

Suppose, they asked,
You are on your death-bed (this is just the game
For a man of words),
With what definitive sentence will you sum
And end your being? . . . Last words: but which of me
Shall utter them?

—The child, who in London's infinite, intimate darkness
Out of time's reach,
Heard nightly an engine whistle, remote and pure
As a call from the edge
Of nothing, and soon in the music of departure
Had perfect pitch?

—The romantic youth
For whom horizons were the daily round,

Near things unbiddable and inane as dreams,
Till he had learned
Through his hoodwinked orbit of clay what Eldorados
Lie close to hand?

—Or the ageing man, seeing his lifelong travel
And toil scaled down
To a flimsy web
Stranded on two dark boughs, dissolving soon,
And only the vanishing dew makes visible now
Its haunted span?

Let this man say,
Blest be the dew that graced my homespun web.
Let this youth say,
Prairies bow to the treadmill: do not weep.
Let this child say,
I hear the night bird. I can go to sleep.   (529–30)

The poem sets a breezy tone at the opening: a verbal "game" to challenge this "man of words" to imagine his deathbed pronouncements. And the verbal play keeps the pace of the "game" lively: "definitive sentence" as "final declaration" and "writ of execution"; "you sum ["sum" is Latin for "I am"] . . . your being"; "infinite, intimate"; "horizons"/"the daily round"; "web / Stranded"; "boughs"/"bow"; "vanishing"/"visible"; "haunted span"/"homespun." And the prosodic form seems whimsical enough. Five six-line stanzas, with the second, fourth, and sixth lines of each in loose and approximate rhymes; each stanza has three five-stressed lines and three two-stressed lines, but the mixture of five and two varies from stanza to stanza as the perspective shifts. For the middle stanzas go back in time to plot out in three stages the poet's broken progress to his deathbed: the lonely boy in the vast city, recalled from earlier poems like "Cornet Solo" and "The Chrysanthemum Show"; the "romantic youth" vainly searching the horizon for the object of his desire first through radical politics in the thirties and then through erotic adventure in the forties; the aging and unappeased ex-traveler awaiting the end.

By the end of the fourth stanza it is clear that the playfulness of the "game" masks its mortal stakes, moving on a direct linear track from "the edge / Of nothing" to the brink of oblivion. But the last stanza turns the trajectory into a circle. Formally the fifth stanza returns to the pattern of the first: a regular alternation of three two-stressed and three five-stressed lines. In addition, the first, third, and fifth lines, unrhymed in the other stanzas, here all repeat the word "say," bringing the poet's life around to closure in deathbed declarations not of rage or resignation but of benediction and acceptance. The poet's consciousness has drawn the circle of containment, and within its conception and execution he is reconciled. The "man of words" dies and survives in the formal verbal construction of his identity. He re-members, re-calls, re-collects himself in the "graced," metered, rhymed symmetry of three "definitive sentence[s]."

• 4

The several different *Selected Poems* (the British Penguin editions in 1951, 1957, and 1969 and the American Harper and Row edition in 1967) and the *Collected Poems* published jointly by the Hogarth Press and Jonathan Cape in 1954 for the poet's fiftieth birthday provided occasions for Day Lewis to reflect on the course of his career. The tone of the prefaces to these volumes is sometimes too self-critical, as though he were responding to criticisms that he, as an established and many-laureled literary figure, had begun to receive. During the fifties and sixties "established" came to be taken automatically—and unfairly, he felt—as "establishment." As a result, his very success and popularity left him vulnerable to the sniping of old enemies and a new generation of poets jousting to establish themselves. Nevertheless, despite their modesty the prefaces and other self-critical statements of the period offer accurate observations about the "allegorical" intention and design of his poetry (in the Keatsian sense of allegory discussed earlier).

Looking back in the 1951 *Selected Poems* over twenty-odd years of verse, the poet is "struck . . . by its lack of development—in the sense of one poetic phase emerging recognizably from the previous one and pointing to the next"—yet at the same time he is struck just as forcibly by the persistence of "change," "a series of fresh beginnings" (7). So strong is the sense of discontinuity that, although poets like Auden and Spender "can rewrite and improve their early work," he cannot: "I could no more reconstruct an old poem than I could reassemble the self out of whom it was constructed: I can only write another poem, feeling my way along the same themes with the self I now am" (*Collected Poems*, 9). Yet the evolving self persists through temporal change, and the continuity within the discontinuities consists of "certain themes, certain obsessive states of mind, recurring throughout my verse: admiration for the heroic, a sense of life's transience, the riddle of identity" (Foreword, 1967 *Selected Poems*, ix). And these dominant themes are associated with the overlapping concerns of the three sections of this book: politics, eros, and thanatos.

The underlying and subsisting impulse is, as Day Lewis said on a number of occasions, the effort "to solve the riddle of personal identity" (*The Poet's Task*, 10), but he was suspicious of the self-indulgent narcissism of "confessional poets" like Robert Lowell and Allen Ginsberg, who were receiving much attention on both sides of the Atlantic. He insisted that even poems about identity, if they are successfully objectified as poems, are "not—except in a very limited sense—a form of self-expression. Who on earth supposes that the pearl *expresses* the oyster?" (1967 *Selected Poems*, x). Without the stimulus within the oyster, no pearl, but the pearl as artifact exists independent of and extrinsic to its maker: "Of course, many poems we write will be 'personal' poems: but however intimate the experience out of which we write, in the act of making a poem from it, that experience must be distanced, out there, a piece of the Other" (*A Need for Poetry?* 5). Even if "we write in order to understand" (1951 *Selected Poems*, 9), that understanding is mediated, since words are not persons or things or experiences but their symbolic displacements. No Modernist or New Critic could put it more clearly or succinctly than Day Lewis: "A poem is an object, with a reality of its own which depends on just those words, and none other, having been used to construct it. If you alter its words, . . . you get either no poem or a different poem: the meaning, however slightly, has been changed" (*On Translating Poetry*, 3).

At the same time, Day Lewis always assumed that mediation had the positive function of clarifying and defining (in contrast to the Poststructuralist assumption that mediation results in the deconstruction and endless deferral of meaning). For Day Lewis, the poet would not "want to compose a poem out of experiences which he altogether comprehended," because he resorts to the mediation of language precisely in order "to gain fuller knowledge of the experiences" that require clarification (4). The erotic impulse "to explore reality and make sense of his own experience" is completed in the craftsman's ability "to create an object in words," and it is the verbal construct with "reality of its own" that offers the most satisfying opportunity for fulfilling the poet's "desire" ("Making a Poem," 1; *On Translating Poetry*, 4). In the erotics of creation "a poem is an organic outgrowth in which the theme only reveals itself through the growing pattern" (*The Poet's Way of Knowledge*, 20), but for that very reason the poem cannot be reduced to extractable message, as "many of the Victorians . . . and the devotees of our political poetry of the Thirties" assumed (*Enjoying Poetry*, 3). Poems not only contain but also "*give* experience" (1969 *Selected Poems*, 15).

In the complete poem form and content are "inseparable" not in the sense that the medium has imprinted coherence on the incoherent material but rather in the sense that language acts as the enabling "instrument of poetic investigation" (*The Poet's Way of Knowledge*, 20). The poem is its meaning and the meaning is the poem because "the techniques of putting words together" create "things which in a sense do not *exist* till they are born (or reborn) in poetry" (*Enjoying Poetry*, 4). Stevens's version of this understanding was: "A poet's words are of things that do not exist without the words"; "Poetry is a revelation in words by means of the words" (*The Necessary Angel*, 32, 33). So in Day Lewis's trope of birthing the poem, language is both the obstetrical instrument and the delivered outcome. Like other moderns—Pound and Williams among them—Day Lewis mixes Romantic metaphors of erotic desire and organic growth with Modernist metaphors of instrumentality and construction for the creative process with the double purpose of validating the symbiotic authority of both poet (maker) and poem ("outgrowth"). As the poet writes the poem, the poem writes the poet; the words authorize the author of the words.

As we have seen, Day Lewis's critical writings keep shifting focus between the subjective genesis of the poem and its objective realization in language. Never an absolutist, he always saw poetry as an act of mediation between subject and object: the creative process through intuition and inspiration constructed the completed text. Moreover, in his particular in-between literary situation, he wanted to avoid the extreme impersonality of the Modernist artifact, on the one hand, and, on the other, the extreme personality of some Romantic poetry and of the contemporary confessional poets. Toward this end, metered form—its requirements and possibilities, its fixities and flexibilities, its conventions and variations—became his mediating device for striking that balance in a poem that clarified his own experience and made it not only clarifying to himself but relevant and communicable to his reading audience. Indeed, over the years he became more and more committed to a poetics of limitation as the operative mode that fuses subjective perception and objectifying expression: "I myself have always been challenged and captivated by problems of form. More and more I have come to realize that, for me at least, strict verse-forms are active discoverers of meaning. I believe they are liberating and felicitous, rather than constricting and deadening" (1969 *Selected Poems*, 15).

"Captivated" sums up the paradox of his being enthralled by form—at once held fast and carried away. On several occasions he cited Valéry to corroborate his deepening conviction that delimitation served as an enabling stimulus, and his most expansive statement came in his concluding Harvard lecture, "The Golden Bridle":

> What about its restraining function? . . . Paul Valéry wrote somewhere: "Why do I use strict form? To prevent the poem saying everything". That is an extremely profound remark. A poetic form . . . provides the poet with a system of checks and balances external to the memories, thoughts, images, which an incipient poem catches, and which—if not controlled—may run away with it. The form is a discipline which helps to select from an incoherent mass of material those data that are relevant to the poem's still undecided purpose. But the form is not always merely selective and disciplinary: many poets must have observed in their own work, as Valéry did, that the need for a rhyme in a certain place, or the exigency of a metre, has thrown up a revealing phrase, a creative idea, which might well not have come into existence without the prompting of the formal agency. Form, in a word, not only restrains but stimulates.
>
> (*The Lyric Impulse*, 149)

Introducing his 1967 *Selected Poems*, Day Lewis alliterated the requisite "lucidity" with "the limiting and liberating nature of poetic form" and cited his recent poem "On Not Saying Everything" (x).

To the end Day Lewis was intent on asserting the efficacy of "strict" or closed form against Modernist fracturing of form. "Modern poetry" is not the function of a single poetic ideology but "is every poem, whether written last year or five centuries ago, that has a meaning for us still" (1951 *Selected Poems*, 9). Admittedly, Modernist experimentation had intensified the "horizontal enlarging" of modern poetry that could "treat a much greater variety of subjects in a greater variety of ways," as well the "vertical development" that exerted "greater imaginative or emotional pressure" on words individually and in combination (*The Lyric Impulse*, 15). But Day Lewis would, like Stevens, make a distinction between being modern in matter and modern in experimental technique, and his complaints about Modernist experimentation are the same as they were in the thirties. Yes, the "innovation in language," the "violent juxtapositions," the "deliberate discords" achieved greater "complexity, intellectual toughness, irony," but the rupture of form and the disregard for shared conventions sacrificed the potential audience for poetry and shirked the poet's social and moral—and in this large sense political—responsibility to communicate (*The Lyric Impulse*, 44, 2, 49). Taking the Harvard lectures as an opportunity to address the American critical establishment that had canonized the avant-garde, he inveighs against the dereliction of Modernism again and again: "[W]e cannot be pleased with a state of affairs where poetry is nothing but a closed circuit" within which poets "are secretly quite happy to write for other poets alone"; "we are so inured nowadays to accepting poetry as an art for the minority that it is difficult to put ourselves in the minds of people who knew it as a popular art" (51, 50, 60).

In reaction, the thirties generation sought, not so naively as some would claim, what Day Lewis dubs "the Common Muse." The aim was to avoid "the ingrown, subjective poetry" of the late-Romantic, Georgian traditionalists, on the one hand, and the Modernist experimentalists, on the other, in order "to reach out beyond the cliques of the 'poetry-lovers' and the intellectuals" (99). Even after the political intention receded, Day Lewis welcomed the popular reception of his verse as an assuring confirmation of the social and public function of the poet, and he became an extremely accomplished and sought-after reader of poetry, his own and others', in radio broadcasts and in public performances, with the platform often shared with Jill Balcon. His poetry was autobiographically based, but public reception confirmed that it had achieved sufficient aesthetic integrity to exist independent of him, "*out there*, a piece of the Other" (1967 *Selected Poems*, x). And "out there" meant not embalmed in an aesthetic vacuum but active in other people's lives.

It may be true that in the intensity of composing, "we do not write in order to be understood; we write in order to understand" (*The Poet's Task*, 15). It may also be the case that the poet "can seldom, if ever extract the figure complete," so that "the *craft* of verse-making is the assembling and piecing-together" that only approximates "a coherent whole" (14–15).

Even so, once the finishing of the poem completes the act of understanding as effectively as the poet has the craft to manage, and once the poem then stands free as an aesthetic object, however imperfect, it lives and survives only in being "understood." Such a poetics assumes that despite the difficulties both of articulation and of interpretation the poem does attain a communicable truth: "not scientifically true, nor logically true," much less theologically true; "but sensuously, emotionally, or spiritually true" (*Enjoying Poetry*, 4). However, since "truth" and "making," for the poet, "are, in the final analysis, one and the same thing," since the poet knows by making and makes to know, "poetic truth," in counterdistinction to theological or philosophical truth, has to be understood as "the coherence, the inner and outer congruity, of the work thus composed. . . . " In the final analysis, therefore, understanding and being understood are functions of each other, for "the more successfully a poem has interpreted to its writer the meaning of his own experience, or of others' experience that imagination has enabled him to make his own, the more surely will it in the long run *be* understood" (*The Poet's Task*, 15).

Day Lewis's kind of formalism, therefore, disavows the Modernist inclination toward "autotelic" (Eliot's word) hermeticism in order to recoup something of the Romantic expectation that the made truth is an actual discovery or recovery of meaning. "Craft," after all, means not just "technical skill," but "cunning," which etymologically means "knowing." It is very indicative of Day Lewis's deeper sympathies that in *Enjoying Poetry*, a reader's guide written for the National Book League, the sources he recommends to beginners eager to learn about "the poetic mind and temperament" are all Romantic: "Keats's *Letters*[,] . . . Dorothy Wordsworth's *Journals*, the letters of Cowper and Byron, Coleridge's *Anima Poetae*, Gerard Manley Hopkins' letters and journals" (5). Day Lewis devoted most of one of the Harvard lectures to John Clare and William Barnes because their nature poetry offered modern poetry an "English" alternative to the Modernist agenda of "certain American poets," Stevens and Marianne Moore serving in this instance as the cited and deplored examples (*The Lyric Impulse*, 110–11).

The discussion of Clare and Barnes indicates how much Day Lewis would like to assent to the Romantic assumption about "an inter-animation between man and nature" (106). Is such a sense to be dismissed as merely the "pathetic fallacy"? To avoid the charge of sentimentality, Day Lewis quotes a passage from Charles Davy's *Words in the Mind*, which he was freshly aware of because Chatto and Windus published the book in the same year as the Harvard lectures; it reads in part:

> [I]t need not be a question of 'either-or'—either a projection of the poet's feelings on to a neutral nature as though onto a blank screen, or nature giving symbolic expression to some objectively real characteristic of the universe. When a poet uses images drawn from nature, he may be taking from nature's symbolic language a phrase which also expresses something he has himself felt—something which belongs to

his inner life and is not drawn directly from nature, but finds a responsive echo there.

(The Lyric Impulse, 109)

Stevens's response to the lure of the Romantic "inter-animation between man and nature" is to luxuriate in the supposition and then deconstruct nostalgic wish fulfillment. However, Day Lewis follows the sentences just cited with his endorsement: "If Mr. Davy is talking sense—and I believe he is—a considerable shift in our idea about modern nature poetry should follow" (109). The poet of the twentieth century who would write a "modern nature poetry" should therefore, in Day Lewis's view, "avoid the temptation to be 'modern' for the sake of being modern, and the vice of craving for 'originality'" (146) and instead draw on and reconstitute the pastoral poetry that is the glory of the British tradition. So the lecture on "Country Lyrics" draws a line from Pope to Wordsworth through Clare and Barnes to Hardy and that acceptably "English" American, Robert Frost, and thence, by implication, to Day Lewis.

The six lectures Day Lewis delivered as the Charles Eliot Norton Professor at Harvard in 1964 and 1965 mount an argument for the life's-blood necessity that poetry recover "the lyric impulse" eroded by the steady separation of poetry from song, especially since the Renaissance, and deliberately repressed in the Modernist rejection of Romantic subjectivity. In an anthology called *A Book of English Lyrics*, published in 1961, with an American edition under the title *English Lyric Poems*, Day Lewis's editorial intention was to include all of the "true lyric" poems composed in Britain between 1500 and 1900. The recovery of that tradition against the historical current was critical because the lyric impulse remains, as he said in several places in the Harvard lectures, "poetry's source" (117), the "ground" (139) of its "elemental forces" (133), the "essence" (133) and (Hopkins's phrase) "soul of poetry" (123). Its defining qualities are simplicity, sincerity, purity, lack of sophistication—in short "complete truth to feeling" (132), or what he described earlier as the sensuous, emotional, or spiritual truth of the poem (*Enjoying Poetry*, 4). The catastrophes of modern history have hardened the heart and, out of wounded scepticism, blocked "contact with what, in nature and human nature, is spontaneous." Whether the poem "celebrates love or loss," in either case the poem is permeated by "the element of joy"—the particular and even tragic "joy of responding to life by making patterns from a chaos" (152).

The affections are the "deepest root" of human experience and of poetry (102), and now the aging man sensed all the more urgently the need to return to sources and roots, to find again the lost child—that is to say, the "primary, instinctual self . . . from which the lyric impulse arises" (152). Moreover, it is precisely the sourcing of poetry in the poet's deepest feelings that paradoxically makes lyric expression not personal but

> impersonal, not because the poet has deliberately screened personal feelings or memories out of it, but because he has broken *through them* to

the ground of their being, a ground which is the fruitful compost made
by numberless human experiences of a like nature.

(The Lyric Impulse, 139)

The thirties' search for the Common Muse and the efforts of Auden, Day
Lewis, and others to write modern ballads, lullabies, and broadsides represented a healthy, if sometimes too modernly self-conscious, attempt to
recover something of the lost universality and popularity of those lyric
modes.

The so-called Movement poets of the 1950s—Donald Davie, Philip
Larkin, Robert Conquest—established themselves in reaction against their
immediate forebears: both what seemed to them the fuzzy-headed
posturings of the Auden group and the emotional immaturity of Dylan
Thomas and his cohorts. Davie's poem "Remembering the Thirties" became a set piece for his group because of its rueful condescension toward
the generation they wanted to displace. Day Lewis admitted that "the poets
of the Fifties" may have influenced him in the direction of making his
verse somewhat "drier" than it had been, but he found their work "aw-
fully dull" (Sean Day Lewis, 269). The Movement poets sought to avoid
sentimentality at all costs; Day Lewis's conviction that feeling was the
"deepest root" of experience and so of poetry made him willing to risk
the occasional lapse into sentimentality, when the language was not strong
enough or fresh enough to sustain the intended feeling. *The Lyric Impulse*
makes a specific response to their position. He notes the "formal elegance,
good sense, astringent irony" of the Movement poets but quotes the critic
John Press to indicate that such strategies constitute "often an elegant form
of evasion, a definitive gesture to conceal the absence of deep feeling" (133).
Later, citing Davie's contention that the modern poet "must grow ever
more self-conscious, ever more aware of his bewilderingly diverse cultural
heritage," Day Lewis takes the counterposition: the lyric poet at least may
have to leave "his cultural heritage to look after itself," to "disinvolve
himself from the intellectual subtleties and complex verbal plays" in order
"to communicate with poetry's primal sources *directly*, not through the
diverse traditions into which that source has been channelled" (145).

On the contrary, Day Lewis insisted, all the poet's disciplined training
is only his preparation to

> submit to the lyric impulse, when it comes his way—the impulse to
> grieve or to rejoice singlemindedly, to discover images and rhythms
> which convey the elemental states of mind a man shares with all other
> living men and has in common with his remotest ancestors.
>
> (The Lyric Impulse, 146)

Since this call for single-mindedness is wrung from Day Lewis's lifelong
struggle with his "divided mind," it emerges all the more poignantly and
forcefully. The source of lyricism "appears to lie somewhere in the
unconscious" (131), and the poem it shapes provides an experience of centering more enduringly realized than he had found in utopian politics or

visionary eroticism. Indeed, his instinct all along was to turn politics and erotics into a poem: *The Magnetic Mountain*, say, or "Elegy Before Death." Nevertheless, as the story of Pegasus and Bellerophon indicated, surrender to the impulse required that the poet must be *prepared* to "submit" effectively. "The Golden Bridle," the title of the last of the Harvard lectures, emphasizes the essential and requisite function of technical discipline and strategies to harness and guide the impulse: Bellerophon's training as a horseman prepared him to receive the bridle that would direct Pegasus's flight to its appointed destination:

> The nearer a poem comes to lyric, the greater his [the poet's] need for this bridle and the more skilful must be his use of it . . . . [T]he modern 'lyrical' poem, so far as it depends upon complexity of structure and irony of meaning, possesses certain built-in checks on the movement of its language. A pure lyric, on the other hand, can go in any direction. . . . For this reason, when the lyric is divorced from the music which supplied it with momentum and in a sense its *raison d'être*, poets must learn from the medium itself to educe a 'singing line'.
>
> (*The Lyric Impulse*, 132)

So when experience or reflection taps the deep sources of our being, the "singing line" is released: "haunted by the ghost of a tune, a dancing rhythm, the felt presence of that universal melody—however faint it be today—through which primitive man expressed communion with his fellows and the joy of living" (146). But, as the last sentence in the passage above indicates, the poet educes the singing line "from the medium itself"; the "built-in checks" and balances of form—meter, rhyme, stanza, sound play—provide the matrix that springs the lyric. Even so, the lift of the singing line is "not primarily a matter of discipline" (132). Meter moves the line along, but what sends it soaring, what constitutes "the magic of poetry" (*Enjoying Poetry*, 3)—indeed, its "magic as a kind of grace" (*A Need for Poetry?* 7)—is the accident or gift of words, images, rhythms that the hard work of composing the verses releases or discovers. Reflecting in "The Golden Bridle" on the reciprocity of activity and receptivity that many poets have tried to describe, Day Lewis calls it a "grace which cannot be counted on and in a sense cannot even be earned: it can only be received, though it will certainly never come unless the poet has used all his art, strenuously and truthfully, to deserve it" (131). In the previous section of the chapter we have noted passages in which the religious meaning of grace is deflected into the sense of grace as aesthetic effect, but these words of Day Lewis, almost lifted from the catechism, move here in the other direction to infuse poetic "grace" with religious charism. And Day Lewis knows how far he has come in validating the lyric impulse: "I am not arguing for a divine source of poetic inspiration, nor certainly would I dare to argue against it" (131).

At the same time, within the dynamics of the poem the earthbound, time-bound aspect of Day Lewis kept him from insisting on such large claims for the religious source of inspiration and led him to keep his poetic flights close to home in known landscapes and familiar, often domestic events. By temperament and by intellectual conviction, he remained deeply suspicious of prophetic claims and rhetorical inflation: "[M]ad dionysiac poetry (the 1940s fashion [by which he meant Dylan Thomas and his group]) has never suited me much" (Sean Day Lewis, 269). Consequently, in the actual writing of the poem, just as he relied on the prosodic restraints of meter and rhyme, so for the thematic presentation even of moments of intense lyric elevation he strategically used flat statement, colloquial rhythms, plain and even prosy phrasing as ballast to maintain contact with the ground of speech and experience. A number of Day Lewis's poems—from the last lyric in *Transitional Poem* to "The Ecstatic" in *A Time to Dance* to "A Riddle" in *Pegasus*—presents a soaring bird who, unlike Shelley's skylark, does not spiral into the empyrean but returns to the snug security of the nest. "A Riddle" asks: "What is this bird / Who . . . ," and the succession of relative clauses describes various species as different aspects of the composite bird-poet. But the riddle concludes by circumscribing and confining these flights of fancy: "This manifold one / Flies higher than rocketing hope, sings best in a cage" (498).

At the end of his inaugural lecture as Oxford Professor of Poetry, Day Lewis asked the crucial question: "Those of us who cannot accept either of the two dogmas predominant in our time, Christianity's and Communism's—how are we to help build [a life for ourselves and others]?" And the humbled response comes: by "searching patiently after the meaning of our personal experience, as it stirs, weak and inarticulate, beneath the creative heart" (*The Poet's Task*, 23). The end of the last Norton lecture at Harvard is a moving recapitulation of the agnostic's "faith" in his poetic "vocation" (he uses those words often elsewhere as well, for example in 1951 *Selected Poems*, 9–10 and in *A Need for Poetry?* 5, 6, 11):

> He may have no religious belief, may even feel no need for a god, yet he is religious in the sense that he cannot live by material values. . . . He has to make out of words an object which is distanced from his own personal experience, yet by indirections will make sense of it and communicate the feeling of it. A poem's meaning is what happens when the feeling and the sense are fused: it does not explain, it satisfies. The child, playing with stones, makes a pattern. To write a poem is an act of serious play.
>
> (*The Lyric Impulse*, 150–51)

The poem may not "explain" in the sense of providing final answers and may be, as Frost said, only "a momentary stay against confusion" (*Selected Prose*, 18), but its aesthetic pattern "satisfies" heart and mind as well as eye and ear because its momentary stay is a genuine, if improvised and provisional, clarification of our complexities.

When Day Lewis added the poem "Sheepdog Trials in Hyde Park" to the expanded American edition of *Pegasus* (it would be included also in his next British volume, *The Gate*), he paired it with "Final Instructions."

Understandably two of his favorites among his poems, they stand as excellent distillations into verse of his thinking about the difference and interdependence between form and inspiration in the finished poem. The
dedication of "Sheepdog Trials in Hyde Park" to Robert Frost is significant. Day Lewis had written a new Introduction to Penguin's *Selected
Poems* of Frost in 1955, in which he had assimilated the American into the
tradition of English pastoral and endorsed Robert Graves's view that among
the poets of this century Hardy and Frost provided the most salutary
influences. On Frost's trip to England in 1957 he had visited the Day
Lewises, and the two poets recorded for broadcast on the BBC a conversation that was warmed by their admiration for and understanding of each
other. Day Lewis's dedication also memorialized the specific occasion when
he took Frost to see the sheepdog trials in Hyde Park.

The text requires quotation in full:

A shepherd stands at one end of the arena.
Five sheep are unpenned at the other. His dog runs out
In a curve to behind them, fetches them straight to the
                                             shepherd,
Then drives the flock round a triangular course
Through a couple of gates and back to his master; two
Must be sorted there from the flock, then all five penned.
Gathering, driving away, shedding and penning
Are the plain words for the miraculous game.

An abstract game. What can the sheepdog make of such
Simplified terrain?—no hills, dales, bogs, walls, tracks,
Only a quarter-mile plain of grass, dumb crowds
Like crowds on hoardings around it, and behind them
Traffic or mounds of lovers and children playing.
Well, the dog is no landscape-fancier; his whole concern
Is with his master's whistle, and of course
With the flock—sheep are sheep anywhere for him.

The sheep are the chanciest element. Why, for instance,
Go through this gate when there's on either side of it
No wall or hedge but huge and viable space?
Why not eat the grass instead of being pushed around it?
Like blobs of quicksilver on a tilting board
The flock erratically runs, dithers, breaks up,
Is reassembled: their ruling idea is the dog;
And behind the dog, though they know it not yet, is a
                                             shepherd.

The shepherd knows that time is of the essence
But haste calamitous. Between dog and sheep
There is always an ideal distance, a perfect angle;
But these are constantly varying, so the man

Should anticipate each move through the dog, his medium.
The shepherd is the brain behind the dog's brain,
But his control of dog, like dog's of sheep,
Is never absolute—that's the beauty of it.

For beautiful it is. The guided missiles,
The black-and-white angels follow each quirk and jink of
The evasive sheep, play grandmother's steps behind them,
Freeze to the ground, or leap to head off a straggler
Almost before it knows that it wants to stray,
As if radar-controlled. But they are not machines—
You can feel them feeling mastery, doubt, chagrin:
Machines don't frolic when their job is done.

What's needfully done in the solitude of sheep-runs—
Those tough, real tasks—becomes a stylized game,
A demonstration of intuitive wit
Kept natural by the saving grace of error.
To lift, to fetch, to drive, to shed, to pen
Are acts I recognize, with all they mean
Of shepherding the unruly, for a kind of
Controlled wool-gathering is my work too.   (542–43)

"Sheepdog Trials" is an excellent example of Day Lewis's use of plain, even homely speech in the highly sophisticated elaboration of a metaphor exemplifying the making of the poem. The execution of "serious play" is here a lucid "demonstration of intuitive wit." The perfect pentameter line of five unadorned and unmodified infinitives—"To lift, to fetch, to drive, to shed, to pen"—summarizes in the last stanza the facets of the trials that the previous five stanzas have described—not in schematic lockstep, one facet per stanza, but in the constantly altering interactions and adjustments that constitute the challenge and beauty of the game.

The diction, syntax, verse rhythms and stanza pattern all serve to convey the controlled movement: a horizontal, homespun, and ground-level analogue to Pegasus's vertical flight bridled by Bellerophon. The description develops through the recurrence of a few key words—shepherd, dog, sheep, flock, drive, run, pen—in different configurations through a fast-moving, stop-and-start succession of quite short, simple clauses—overwhelmingly declarative—with few complicating subordinate clauses. The pacing of the clauses synchronizes game time to metrical time—both "of the essence" of the exercise. The commentary, voiced across heavily enjambed lines, stretches, contracts, stops in its tracks, loops back, as the timely movement follows its conventions while remaining open to "the saving grace of error": a sort of aesthetic *felix culpa*. Yet as the focus of the poet's roving eye and mind shifts to different aspects and configurations of the game's progress, the rules of the game are followed as the five-stressed verses are "gathered" into the six end-stopped stanzas.

The delightful pun on "controlled wool-gathering" in the last lines synthesizes and completes the analogy between the sheepdog trials and the composing of a poem, indeed of *this* poem. But because the analogy is realized so deftly by the example of the poem, the conceit—shepherd/poet, dog/medium, sheep/"unruly" experience—needs no heavy-handed explication. The occasional overlay of metaphor or simile onto simple description tracks the poet's mind assimilating the factual details into its own figures, at one point tentatively invoking guided missiles and radar as metaphors only to withdraw the references as too automated and mechanical for the sheepdogs' frolicsome pleasure in their expertise. All along the way, the verbal play—"plain words"/"plain of grass," the dog as "ruling idea" "shepherding" the "unruly" sheep, "angle"/"angel," "hedge"/"huge," "erratically runs"/"grace of error"—zigzags through the verses, as the running pun of "unpenned"/"penned"/"penning"/"to pen" as "unwritten"/"written"/"writing"/"to write" executes the literarily "stylized game" whose "abstract" beauty patterns the "tough, real" rush and crush of experience.

"For beautiful it is"—and "miraculous." But where "Sheepdog Trials in Hyde Park" lays out the discipline of rules and conventions prerequisite to the chance miracle, "Final Instructions" emphasizes the miraculous chance or gift over which the craftsman has no control: the inexplicable inspiration that can sometimes radiate the form with such translucent significance that it seems, perhaps not just metaphorically, a divinely conferred insight. Day Lewis frames his didactic purpose in the dramatic monologue of a wise old priest from the classical period giving a novice his "final instructions" in making a temple sacrifice. Skill in the established conventions of the ritual is presumed and necessary, but the formalities do not cause or guarantee the god's appearance: though you "lay yourself / On the altar and offer again what you have to offer," "you can neither command his presence nor explain it— / All you can do is to make it possible" (512). Craft can make the artifact but cannot make it holy—the etymological meaning of "sacrifice." On the other hand, with "luck" what the artist contributes of himself—the material substance as well as the "discipline and devotion" of the training and presentation—sometimes "catches fire of its own accord." The artist as secular priest—a vocational conception that humanists after Arnold would share—should train and practice, then, not for the narcissistic exercise of ego but for a self-sacrifice that is also a chance for self-transcendence. The elderly priest invokes the three qualities essential to successful service: "patience, joy, / Disinterestedness," with joy centered at the turn of the line, its flame the incandescence of patience and disinterestedness.

Art originates in the child's need to make patterns of stones, finds complex expression in the "serious play" of the sheepdog trials, and sometimes attains special illumination through the poet-priest's ministrations. Moreover, art is disinterested and transpersonal because it is social: expressing, satisfying, illuminating, through the poet's agency, the desires and needs of us all. The game of art plays to an audience for mortal stakes:

> [W]hat you are feeling is the touch of joy; and my play is serious. I am playing to delight and console you—myself and you. My pebbles can be a causeway, reuniting your divided self, and my own. Every good work of every artist is there to remind man of his roots, to refresh them, to satisfy—if only for a few years or hours—his perpetual need for wholeness.
>
> (*The Lyric Impulse*, 152–53)

This closing passage of *The Lyric Impulse* locates "I" and "you" as fellow travelers on the causeway of words.

The Lyric Impulse makes an aesthetic statement for Day Lewis's last decades as important as *A Hope for Poetry* was for the thirties and *The Poetic Image* for the forties. The position it stakes out is modest enough—neither original in conception nor prophetic in claim nor avant-garde in technique; but it traces the trajectory of the Western sensibility since the Enlightenment. Disillusionment with religious faith, utopian politics, and the idealization of Romantic desire has stripped him to a Hardyesque humanism infused with a modern but not Modernist reliance on words to construct an emotional or spiritual truth not wholly, he hoped, a construct of words. Through the various phases of Day Lewis's life, so dislocating that he saw them as "a series of fresh beginnings rather than a continuous line" (1951 *Selected Poems*, 7), through his engagement with politics, with erotic adventure, and now with resistance to death's silent encroachment, he learned to cling to his poetic vocation as his most reliable strategy for living in time against time's downward current.

For if time runs down, poetry rises from the deep-rooted needs and wellsprings of our nature, like the stream's resistance to its own outflow in Frost's "West-Running Brook":

> in the love of order and pattern, the desire for experience, the rhythms of fresh stimulus and familiar routine, the setting of the heart upon another human being; the simple wish to be alive rather than dead, which is the inarticulate man's form of prayer and praise, and which is felt by a poet as the lyrical impulse.
>
> (*The Lyric Impulse*, 102)

The pattern of doubling is age-old: desire going forth meets its limits in desire returning—up and down . . . and up again, out and back . . . and out another time. So the lyric impulse meets its limited form in the lyric poem. And so sometimes, in metrical time, the closure of line and stanza around a moment's circumference creates of the lyric impulse a lyric poem that holds in tense equilibrium the presence of absence and the persistence of presence, the voice of silence and the silence behind the words, the constellation of fragments and the meeting of limits, the circling of desire and the grounding of transcendence. In short, the poem comprehends the momentary single-mindedness of the divided mind.

Day Lewis, born in 1904, was a man of the twentieth century. During the decade of the sixties, in the midst of which Day Lewis turned sixty, he published three volumes of poetry in England: *The Gate* (1962), *The Room* (1965), and *The Whispering Roots* (1970); but these poems were published in the Unites States as three differently constituted volumes: *Requiem for the Living* (1964), *Selected Poems* (1967), and *The Whispering Roots* (1970). After his death in 1972 some of the poems written after *The Whispering Roots* were included in a selected *Poems of C. Day Lewis 1924–1972* (1977), edited by his friend and publishing colleague Ian Parsons, and the other last pieces were gathered by Jill Balcon in a handsome limited edition of *Posthumous Poems* (1979). These volumes are perhaps best treated together in part because they deal with the same issues of aging and dying but also because, as the staggered dates of publication above indicate, the identity of collections and the place of particular poems within a collection were blurred by the fact that British and American editions fell out of phase with each other. Readers who are not interested in those internal variances can skip the next long paragraph, which catalogues those variants in detail.

The transatlantic discrepancies began when the American *Pegasus* came out the year after its English publication in 1957 and included the following poems that would appear in *The Gate*, his next English collection: "An Episode," "A Meeting," "Edward Elgar," "Sheepdog Trials in Hyde Park," "View from an Upper Window," and the two poems for his children, "Getting Warm—Getting Cold" and "The Newborn." When *Requiem for the Living* came out in the United States two years after *The Gate*, it did not repeat the poems above that had already appeared in the American *Pegasus*; it included the other poems in *The Gate* (taking its title from the long sequence at the end of that volume) but also contained the following poems not included in *The Gate*: "The Room," "Derelict," "First School," "Elegy for a Woman Unknown," "The Fox," "The Dam," "A Course in Love," "Terns," and "Grey Squirrel: Greenwich Park." These poems would appear in the next English collection *The Room*, except for "First School" (which was also not in the *Complete Poems*), and the six-part "A Course in Love" was revised and expanded into "Seven Steps in Love." The next American volume was the new 1967 *Selected Poems*, with a Foreword by the poet, and it concluded with the following pieces left over from *The Room*: "The Way In," "Saint Anthony's Shirt," "Fishguard to Rosslare," "Pietà," "For Rex Warner on His Sixtieth Birthday," "My Mother's Sister," and "On Not Saying Everything." The American *Whispering Roots* came out in the same year as the English and was designed to bring transatlantic publication back into alignment. Its Part One and Part Two were exactly the same as the English edition (with the exception that two previously published poems, "The House Where I was Born" [from *Pegasus*] and "Fishguard to Rosslare" [from *The Room* and the American *Selected Poems*] were repeated in the title sequence of *The Whispering Roots* in the British edition but unfortunately were not repeated in the American edition of that last volume). In addition, the American *Whispering Roots* volume folded in as a third part (thus out of chronological order) all the pieces from *The Room* not previously printed in *Requiem for the Living* or *Selected Poems*: "The Passion for Diving," "The Hieroglyph," "Days before a Journey," "Seven Steps in Love," "The Romantics," "Stephanotis," "An Operation," "Who Goes Home?" "Young Chekhov," "The Widow Interviewed," "Madrigal for Lowell House," "This Loafer," "Apollonian Figure," "A Relativist," "Moral," and Day Lewis's acclaimed translation of Baudelaire's "The Voyage." Except for the chronological displacement of Part Three of *The Whispering Roots*, Day Lewis continued to attend carefully to the organization of these volumes, characteristically including one or two long poems or sequences as centers of gravity for the shorter lyrics, but the differences in the order and clustering of poems resulted in collections with differing scopes and shapes. The commentary here, therefore, will move more fluidly through these volumes in configuring the shared themes that determine Day Lewis's late work.

Religious faith, the good society, erotic desire, the poetic vocation: since *Transitional Poem* these themes have parsed out "the riddle of personal identity" (*The Poet's Task*, 10) in Day Lewis's poetry, but they assume a different configuration in the late poetry. Although less urgently and insistently than in the poetry of the middle period, the erotic theme persists. In fact, "The Disabused" and "Not Proven," two long dramatic monologues, around which the lyrics of *The Gate* and *Requiem for the Living* are grouped, harken back to the crises of the forties by telling of fatal love tragedies and can be read as two final efforts by Day Lewis to project and exorcise old guilt and remorse for the wounds given and received in the thralls of eros. In the fifties Day Lewis did not wish to vie with Dylan Thomas, the roaring sensation of reading platforms and college campuses, but he continued to think of himself as at least more dionysian than the unnamed "Apollonian Figure," a "selfpossessed master of circumspection" whose "fig leaf there, so elegantly cut" raises the question: "Just what, if anything, does it conceal?" (638).

And indeed poems from these late volumes bespeak new erotic complications: "An Episode," "The Dam," "An Operation," "Seven Steps in Love"; but they are finally peripheral to the space opened up for contemplation and reflection by his marriage to Jill Balcon, celebrated in a number of exquisite lyrics scattered through the late books. "On a Dorset Upland" (from *Pegasus* and discussed earlier in the chapter) and "An Upland Field" (from *The Gate* and *Requiem for the Living*) celebrate the happy vacations and getaways to the Dorset countryside around Dorchester for which they both had a particular love associated with their life together. "Sailing from Cleggan" (from *The Whispering Roots*) fixes on a moment of "recaptured love" ("Never could I forget it") on the first of the regular family vacations to the west of Ireland in late summer of 1964, before school resumed for Tamasin and Daniel (670). "On Not Saying Everything," one of his favorite poems and one of his best, was written in the fall of the year at Harvard, reiterating the terms of their love across the distance that then separated husband and wife.

"Fisherman and/or Fish" (from *The Gate* and *Requiem for the Living*) is a witty *ave atque vale*, at once rueful and unapologetic, to his days of erotic adventure with Billie Currall and Rosamond Lehmann and, before their marriage, with Jill Balcon:

There was a time when I,
The river's least adept,
Eagerly leapt, leapt
To the barbed, flirtatious fly.

Thrills all along the line,
A tail thrashing—the sport
Enthralled: but which was caught,
Which reeled the other in?

Anglers aver they angle
For love of the fish they play
(Arched spine and glazing eye,
A gasping on the shingle).

I've risen from safe pools
And gulped hook line and sinker
(Oh, the soft merciless fingers
Fumbling at my gills!)

Let last time be the last time
For me with net or gaff.
I've had more than enough
Of this too thrilling pastime.

The river's veteran, I
Shall flick my rod, my fin,
Where nothing can drag me in
Nor land me high and dry.   (577)

The poem deftly uses the metaphor of fishing as sexual sport to trace the speaker's transition over the years from "the river's least adept" to "the river's veteran." The sexual innuendo surrounding the poet's angling moves the poem along briskly: "Leapt / To the barbed, flirtatious fly," "thrills all along the line," "tail thrashing," "love of the fish they play," "Arched spine and glazing eye," "gasping on the shingle," "soft, merciless fingers / Fumbling at my gills," "flick my rod." But the wit operates as a ploy to lighten the veteran's grim and hard-earned lesson: fisherman and fish, angler and angled, phallic victor and hooked victim turn into each other and become indistinguishable in the violence of their play. This serious game comes to the tragic lesson Ariadne had to learn on Naxos. Here the "enthralled" angler turns into a thrall, caught by his own surrender to "too thrilling" "thrills." The grammatical apposition of "my rod, my fin" sums up the speaker's self-defeating ambiguity as "Fisherman and/or Fish," and he swears off the sport forthwith in self-preservation, relegating his old "pastime" to past time.

Politics seems even more remote from the late poetry than erotics. Social relationships have been brought down to their roots in the community of family and friends. Still, the odd poem voices the anxiety about Cold War politics in the atomic age. "The Unexploded Bomb," written for the Campaign for Nuclear Disarmament, satirizes the military and nuclear competition between the United States and the U.S.S.R. as a threat to the entire planet. "Requiem for the Living" uses the sequence of sung prayers of the Mass (Verdi's *Requiem* and Fauré's *Requiem* were two of Day Lewis's favorite musical compositions) to offer an agnostic supplication for the human vision and courage needed and perhaps lacking to avert atomic holocaust. On an entirely different level, he produced commissioned and occasional verses for public events and causes, many composed in his capacity as poet laureate: for the "I'm Backing Britain" campaign of 1968, for the investiture of Charles as Prince of Wales in 1969, for the anniversary of Oxfam, for National Library Week, for an environmental appeal, for the Florentine Flood Appeal.

The contrast between such bourgeois poems and the revolutionary poems of the thirties is obvious, but Day Lewis was not embarrassed about the discrepancy, though his critics took derisive note of it. For what they took as capitulation Day Lewis took in good cheer as the social function of the poet, especially the laureate. The poet who sought a popular audience, as he had since the thirties, could apply his verbal skills to promote worthy causes and honor notable public events without confusing the distinction between such occasional verse and poetry. Even when "Who Goes Home?" and "Pietà"—the elegies for Winston Churchill and John Kennedy, the first commissioned for broadcast on the BBC and both published in the press—brought loud sneers from the literary elite, he offered no riposte or apology and included them in his next published collection. He was always drawn to charismatic heroes, and these verses offered public speech lamenting two lost leaders, the old hero already historic, the young hero robbed of his historic opportunity. By this time Day Lewis had learned to live with the enemies—both old ones from the thirties like Geoffrey Grigson and a new, upwardly mobile generation of poet-critics hostile to and jealous of him now as the lion of the literary establishment—who seized upon these occasional poems with gleeful and self-congratulatory malice to show that the would-be radical of the thirties had capitulated to the status quo. Grigson's last attack, under the customary cover of anonymity provided by the *Times Literary Supplement*, came in 1970 after the publication of *The Whispering Roots* in the guise of a review-essay so ugly that Samuel Hynes, author of *The Auden Generation*, compared it to "a literary mugging" (Sean Day Lewis, 291).

To the end Day Lewis's actual politics remained anything but Tory-conservative. Though no longer directly involved in political activism, Day Lewis brought a commitment to democratic socialism into the postwar years, in sharp contrast to some ex-leftists of his generation whose recantation swung them into conservative, even rightwing positions. He never espoused the Tory agenda, and it was in fact his consistent support of the Labour Party and its effort to reform Britain into what the Tories denounced as the welfare state that helped to commend him to Labour Prime Minister Harold Wilson when John Masefield's death left the poet laureateship open. Looking at contemporary politics in the light of old ideals, Day Lewis could say of the Labour reforms: "Something at least of what we hoped for [in the thirties] has come true in the Welfare State; and if it is drabber than the bright new world of our visions, it is a great deal more solid" ("The Thirties in Retrospect," 25). In the wake of the Queen's official announcement of Day Lewis's appointment to the laureateship on January 2, 1968, however, his detractors old and new overlooked the irony in the fact that the honor that in their eyes marked the final sealing of Day Lewis into the establishment came about as a recognition not only of his poetic achievement but of his political adherence to the party of the British left.

Earlier chapters have associated Day Lewis's Marxist allegiance and erotic pursuits with the basically religious compulsion to heal the divided self in the transpersonal reality of the good society and consummated love, and these stirrings of religious longing intensify in the late poems. "Requiem for the Living" is the Mass of a "Churchy agnostic" and would-be believer, praying "Angels, essences of truth, enlighten us!" and addressing the "God, in whom we half believe, / Or not believe" (590, 585).

> If you exist, if heed our cares,
> If these our offerings and prayers
> Could save, if earth's entreating heirs
> Are to be born to live—
> Spirit, in whom we half believe
> And would believe,
> Free us from fear, revive in us
> A fire of love.   (586)

The transition from the first to the last stanza of the "Offertorium" of the Mass, rephrasing "half believe / Or not believe" into "half believe / And would believe," epitomizes the aspiration in many poems from the later volumes: "Christmas Eve" (from *Pegasus*), "Bread and Wine," "Wind's Eye," and "The Christmas Rose" (from *The Gate* and *Requiem for the Living*), "Ballintubber Abbey, County Mayo," and "The Whispering Roots" (from *The Whispering Roots*), "A Christmas Way" (from *Posthumous Poems*).

A combination of religious nostalgia and anxiety much like Matthew Arnold's (and Thomas Hardy's) haunts these poems, as in these lines from the "Benedictus" of the "Requiem":

Blessed who range ahead
Of man's laborious trek,
Survey marsh, desert, peak,
Signal a way to tread.

Blessed whose faith defies
The mighty, welds the weak;
Whose dreaming hopes awake
And ring like prophecies.   (588)

In fact, the three-stress meter and the slightly halting, sententious phrasing of the upbeat message recall directly Arnold's famous lines at the end of "Rugby Chapel." Even Arnold's situation parallels Day Lewis's as, almost exactly one century earlier than "Requiem," this other agnostic son recalls his clergyman father and hails the inspiration of the faithful "Servants of God":

Yours is the praise, if mankind
Hath not as yet in its march
Fainted, and fallen, and died!

See! In the rocks of the world
Marches the host of mankind,
A feeble, wavering line.
.   .   .   .
Then, in such hour of need
Of your fainting, dispirited race,
Ye, like angels, appear,
Radiant with ardour divine!
Beacons of hope, ye appear!
.   .   .   .
Ye fill up the gaps in our files,
Strengthen the wavering line,
Stablish, continue our march,
On, to the bound of the waste,
On, to the City of God.
                        (*Selected Poems*, 147–48)

At the same time, a comparison of the two passages, Day Lewis's much condensed from "Rugby Chapel," indicates that Day Lewis, even when sounding most Victorian here in his expression of religious angst, shows a rhetoric notably more restrained and pithy than Arnold's rousing drumroll.

Nor does Day Lewis settle comfortably into Arnoldian discomfort. By contrast, "Wind's Eye" is a beautifully turned lyric whose minor key develops a major theme:

Eye of the wind, whose bearing in
A changeful sky the sage
Birds are never wrong about
And mariners must gauge—

The drift of flight, the fluttered jib
Are what we know it by:
Seafarers cannot hold or sight
The wind's elusive eye.

That eye, whose shifting moods inspire
The sail and trim the sheet,
Commands me, though I can but steer
Obliquely towards it.   (570)

The trope of the mariner's voyage through life is by now a familiar one in Day Lewis's work, and it remains a major motif in the late poems. Here, as elsewhere, the voyage assumes a religious and theological resonance through the association of "wind" with "spirit" (the Latin "spiritus" means "spirit" and "wind" and "breath") and the consequent elision of "wind's eye" into God's all-seeing eye. That elision is suggested throughout the poem in the repeated inflection between short *i*'s and long *i*'s, enunciated first by the title "W*i*nd's *Eye*," and reiterated through the poem: "*Eye* of the w*i*nd," "bear*i*ng *in* / A changeful sk*y*," "dr*i*ft of fl*i*ght," "*i*t b*y*," "s*i*ght / The w*i*nd's elus*i*ve *eye*," "*eye* whose sh*i*fting moods "*i*nspire," "*I* . . . towards *i*t." Simultaneously, another elision, this time between "eye" and its pronominal homonym "I," links Creator, natural creation, and human creature. Divine providence (God's eye) blows a breath through the alternations of natural process (wind's eye) that is "changeful" and "shifting," so that the mariner's eye (I's eye) proves and maintains itself by gauging and negotiating those stormy mutabilities. As the poem moves to its conclusion, a swell of long *e* sounds emerges beneath or above the alternations of long and short *i*'s: "w*e*," "S*ea*farers," "sh*ee*t," "m*e*," "st*ee*r," "Obl*i*quely." And finally there is an echo of the traditional poetic pronunciation of "wind" as "wynd," which would elide the contrasting short and long *i*'s of "wind's eye" into the consonance of "wynd's eye."

The declension from God's eye to wind's eye to individual I returns us to "the riddle of personal identity" whose unriddling is the motivating continuity in Day Lewis's, as in most Romantic and much post-Romantic, poetry. The deracinated modern can only try to anchor its identity as center of a shifting field of circumferential—natural, personal, social, metaphysical—relations, and the dynamics of that quest move from the tentatively established center to the limits of that probe and then recoil to the fragile and uncertain center—out and back and out again for another try. We heard "Departure in the Dark" phrase the fluctuation as "the desire / Going forth meets the desire returning" (319), which meets the desire venturing forth once more. Day Lewis often expresses this dialectic of identity through the interplay of house and home. The search for a house that is a home sustains both the journey out and back.

Day Lewis's version of Baudelaire's "The Voyage" says "The soul is a three-master, Ithaca-bound" (641). The poem initiates the voyage from the void to the unknown with the opening lines: "Children, in love with maps and gravings, know / A universe the size of all they lack," and ends the periplum with these closing lines: "We wish, for our whole beings burn and burn, / To sound the abyss—heaven or hell, who cares?— / And find the secret wombed in the Unknown" (640, 645). Translating "The Voyage" allows Day Lewis to enter Baudelaire's bleak assessment, for in Baudelaire's "universe" Death's secret stays tightly "in the Unknown"—not even a stillbirth. Might a stronger sense of purpose than Baudelaire could muster make at least for a more bracing and exciting journey?

The Room ends with Baudelaire's "The Voyage," but the title poem begins the volume with a fable, dedicated to Day Lewis's friend the Greek poet-diplomat George Seferis, about the sense of center necessary for voyaging. Does Seferis offer a more centered self than Baudelaire? Day Lewis said that "The Room" evolved from the teasing insistence of the phrase "to taste myself" in his imagination and from his ruminating on Seferis's apparent success in pursuing his poetic exploration of life's voyage while also serving publicly as his country's far-flung ambassador in several European posts. The fable gives the self a royal personification and tells of the imperative need to withdraw periodically from engagement in public business to a private room all and only his own; this chamber "at the palace's / Heart" is "windowless / Though airy, bare yet filled with the junk you find / In any child-loved attic," and there, alone, the royal self can "taste himself" and "be reassured . . . he was real" (599).

The room or house is point of departure and return for the journeying self. "Ideal Home" (in *The Gate*) focuses on the elusiveness of that centering location. The breezy air of the poem, alternating unrhymed long lines with rhymed short lines within each stanza, is calculated to disguise and so to facilitate a searching act of self-examination. Each in a succession of houses (Box Cottage, Brimclose, Little Wittenham, Crooms Hill) offers to be a home, personified as a woman: "Each casts her spell. . . . Walk in, and take me. Then you shall live again." By the same magic each new lover promises to be his house and shelter ("I'll be your roof, your hearth, your paradise orchard / And treasure-trove"), and thus promises to be long-lost mother as well as wife ("Possess me. / Be born again"). But by hindsight the speaker now sees the parade of houses and lovers as merely a gauge of "Your unsuccess / In growing your self" (575–76). The last stanza undercuts the jauntiness of the earlier strutting:

> Switch love, move house,—you will soon be back where
> you started,
> On the same ground,

With a replica of the old romantic phantom
That will confound
Your need for roots with a craving to be unrooted. (576)

The speaker's sober realization that "rebirth needs more than a change of / Flesh or address" (576) matches the chastened end of that other initially jaunty poem "Fisherman and/or Fish."

"Saint Anthony's Shirt," another of the poems written during the fall of 1964 during the first part of Day Lewis's Harvard sojourn and published in *The Room* and the American *Selected Poems* of 1967, is his final and richest meditation on the rootedness and rootlessness of identity. The metaphor in the title is explicated by the epigraph, an epistolary remark from Keats to his friend Reynolds that the self is like a relic garment patched and repatched by the devoted monks "till there's not a thread of the original garment left, and still they show it for St. Anthony's shirt." Occasional words in the poem—"fabric" and "patchwork"—echo Keats's metaphor, and this conceit elides into the governing conceit of the house as the corporeal presence with an elusive ghostly occupant as the speaker self-consciously reflects once again on the continuities and discontinuities of the individual in time and place.

The "house" conceit provides the continuity of the poem's apparently meandering evolution, as the sinuous movement from line to line and from stanza to stanza traces its twists and discontinuities. Here is the poem entire:

This moving house of mine—how could I care
If, wasting and renewing cell by cell,
It's the ninth house I now have tenanted?
I cannot see what keeps it in repair
Nor charge the workmen who, its changes tell,
Build and demolish it over my head.

Ninth house and first, the same yet not the same—
Are there, beneath new brickwork, altering style,
Viewless foundations steady through the years?
Hardly could I distinguish what I am
But for the talkative sight-seers who file
Through me, the window-view that clouds or clears.

The acting, speaking, lusting, suffering I
Must be a function of this house, or else
Its master principle. Is I a sole
Tenant created, recreated by
What he inhabits, or a force which tells
The incoherent fabric it is whole?

If master, where's the master-thread runs through
This patchwork, piecemeal self? If occupant

Merely, the puppet of a quarrelsome clique,
How comes the sense of selfhood as a clue
Embodying yet transcending gene and gland?
The I, though multiple, is still unique.

I walk these many rooms, wishing to trace
My frayed identity. In each, a ghost
Looks up and claims me for his long-lost brother—
Each unfamiliar, though he wears my face.
A draught of memory whispers I was most
Purely myself when I became another.

Tending a sick child, groping my way into
A woman's heart, lost in a poem, a cause,
I touched the marrow of my being, unbared
Through self-oblivion. Nothing remains so true
As the outgoingness. This moving house
Is home, and my home, only when it's shared.   (605–6)

Bodily identity changes cell by cell and self by self, like St. Anthony's shirt or like a house undergoing continuous repair. The poet cannot answer with metaphysical and theological finality whether the body is the originary source or the function of an indwelling soul, yet he intuits his bodily identity, mortal or immortal, as individual and unique, persisting through its multiple incarnations. Thus, on an existential if not theological level, the poem comes to postulate a meeting of the desire going forth and the desire returning at the heart's hearth: "This moving house / Is home, and my home, only when it's shared."

"Days before a Journey," the poem that follows "Saint Anthony's Shirt" in *The Room*, reintroduces the counterimpulse away from home. There "[a] man begins his absence / From a loved one . . . / From a loved home" even before his actual departure, and as a result

Between staying and going
Opens the little death,
Shadowed, unformed, uncanny
And makes the real a wraith.
Oh, travelling starts many
Days before the journey.   (607)

Here "the little death" marks not consummation but separation. However, even Odysseus found the homing instinct drawing him more insistently as the lengthening years shortened the time for wandering: "The soul is a three-master, Ithaca-bound" (641). In the configuration of Day Lewis's work, therefore, the thematic importance of "Saint Anthony's Shirt" lies in the fact that the oxymoron of the "moving house" seeks to eliminate the "little death" that seems to open "between staying and going," between self and beloved. The paradox says that the very journeying brings him to wife and wife to him and that the hearth can be "shared" as they go.

The "riddle of personal identity" turns out to be that self-definition and "self-oblivion" are synonymous: "I was most / Purely myself when I became another." Day Lewis did not need Bataille to teach him that the erotic drive can be self-destructive when pushed beyond the human possibilities and limits, but, unlike Bataille, he concluded here that, domesticated within those limits, the erotic capacity for "outgoingness" can make "this moving house" "home, and my home." The seeming meandering of the poem, and of life itself, comes to cohere around this home-truth for the last leg of the journey.

• 6

Human aspiration and divine inspiration: converging lines that do not seem to intersect; but sometimes this "Churchy agnostic" sounded very Churchy. The new poet laureate preached on Whit Sunday, June 2, 1968, at Great St. Mary, Cambridge, and took as his theme "The Creative Spirit":

> X, the unknown quantity, has been called inspiration. Plato believed that poets are possessed by a god. The Neo-Platonists insisted that it is not phenomenal nature which true poets imitated, but the archetypal reality behind nature. Coleridge defined genius as "possessing the spirit, not possessed by it." There is clearly a radical change of ground here.
> ("The Creative Spirit," 1)

That radical change in the conception of the agency of the creative spirit—the poet as agent "possessing the spirit" within himself instead of being "possessed" by divine presence—begins to mark the accelerating divergence in the modern period between the poet as visionary seer and the poet as imaginative maker. Nevertheless, Day Lewis went on to say, what links both seer and maker is the awareness of the unpredictability of the creative spirit, whatever its source or agency:

> The poet knows that this spirit is a wind which bloweth where it listeth. He cannot command its presence. If he is lucky, it may whisk him aloft for a few years, or a few weeks: then it drops him, it may be for ever. But he is aware that, perhaps only once or twice in a lifetime, he has written beyond the capacity of his craft.
> ("The Creative Spirit," 1)

Consequently, even the agnostic should not make a categorical distinction between seer and poet:

> I could not possibly dismiss the belief that what is given to the artist from time to time is a form of *divine* grace. It may be convenient nowadays to speak in terms of individual psychology, or of a collective unconscious which the poet can tap to make his myths of 'archetypal reality.' But such explanations do not fully satisfy: they do not explain

the poet's conviction that, perhaps once or twice only in his life, he has come close to the Ground of Being.

("The Creative Spirit," 1)

Day Lewis did not dwell on this point in his sermon. Indeed, the empirical agnostic in him, uncomfortable as always with inflated claims of inspiration, whether Christian or Platonist, moved on to surer ground, describing inspiration from his own experience of it. Sometimes a poem would arise out of the pressures of an immediate situation, but more and more frequently from the forties on he found that inspiration involved remembering something forgotten; after all, the mother of the muses is Mnemosyne—Memory.

> Robert Frost spoke about "the surprise of remembering something I didn't know I knew". What seems to happen for a poet is that experience sinks down on to the sea-bed of the unconscious. And lying there for a length of time, it is changed: "those are pearls that were his eyes". And one day a fragment of this buried treasure floats to the surface.
>
> ("The Creative Spirit," 1)

What is more, in his experience inspiration originated not in wordless visitation from above but in mysterious phrases surfacing from deep inside:

> It comes to me, very often, in an enigmatic form—a form of words, a brief phrase, which is attended by a special feeling of anticipation, excitement. It comes, more often than not, quite unexpectedly, when the mind is neutral, or thinking of something else. I recognize in it the seed of a poem. It is, in fact, both a seed and a signpost; for it contains within it the potency of the still unwritten poem, and it points the direction that the poem should take. I meditate on this *donnée*, this riddling clue, seeking to pick out, from the many possible meanings it suggests, the right meaning—the one which should grow into the theme of the poem.
>
> ("The Creative Spirit," 1)

As seed and signpost, the embryonic phrase synecdochally contains the poem in all its potency and material realization. "The Room," we have seen, evolved from the insistent phrase "to taste myself," and Day Lewis gave other instances of the genesis of poems from such *données*. "Making a Poem," an unpublished lecture from the mid-sixties, cites the evolution of one of the sonnets of "O Dreams! O Destinations!" and thence of the whole sequence from a line that suddenly came into his head at one point during the war years: "The flags, the roundabouts, the gala day." On another occasion ruminations on the burden of possessions seemed to yield the apparently unrelated phrase "Streamlined whales and hulls," but the fragment assumed its place and significance in the poem "Travelling Light" (*The Lyric Impulse*, 147–48). Such "clue-lines" were "all that I personally understand by the word 'inspiration'" ("Making a Poem," 8–9). For, he insisted in a 1966 radio talk about "Poetic Inspiration" on the BBC, once the "clue-line" is given, the process of realization is anything but "a kind of automatic writing," as some poet-seers like Yeats liked to claim: "[T]he spirit moves the pen, and all the poet need do is sit back and let the stuff pour out." But even Yeats knew the shift from inspiration to realization, from the Romantic fixation on organic generation to the modern requirement of creative construction. Only "extremely hard work—*conscious effort*" could draw out and piece together the combination of words nascent but only latent in the seed-phrase ("Poetic Inspiration," 1). The craftsman asks: "Have I made something out of it?" ("The Creative Spirit," 2). For "the arduous, absorbed work of creating" should produce "an object which is neither the clue nor the experience" it adumbrated "but a structure of words embodying and interpreting them both. A poem" ("Poetic Inspiration," 3). This axiom was a truism for poets, but the ever-fresh challenge was to make it true.

In "Making a Poem" Day Lewis exemplified the process by analyzing the composition of a poem whose *donnée* was not a phrase but a painting by Trekkie Parsons, wife of his partner at Chatto and Windus, Ian Parsons. He found that this small landscape in subtle pastel shades "held for me a special and mysterious meaning I must try to explore through poetry," and his fascination with the painting led Jill to purchase it for him as a gift. The exploration of the image through words became the poem that turned out to be "The Gate" ("For Trekkie") and gave the title to the 1962 collection. "This poem was written more or less straight ahead" though "more often I compose a bit here, a bit there, like a painter." As a result "the first stanza objectively sets out the facts—the colour and detail of the pictured landscape" ("Making a Poem," 10–11):

> In the foreground, clots of cream-white flowers
>   (meadow-sweet?
> Guelder? Cow parsley?): a patch of green: then a gate
> Dividing the green from a brown field: and beyond,
> By steps of mustard and sainfoin-pink, the distance
> Climbs right-handed away
> Up to an olive hilltop and the sky. (538)

Since the objective facts did not unlock the mystery they portended, the observer's eye focuses in the second stanza on what struck him "subjectively" as the "dominant features" of the landscape: "my sense that the whole picture was somehow there *for the sake of* the gate, the central mystery, and my sense that the foreground flowers stood in an attentive pose, waiting for something to happen" ("Making a Poem," 12). Hence the second stanza:

> The gate it is, dead-centre, ghost-amethyst-hued,
> Fastens the whole together like a brooch.

It is all arranged, all there, for the gate's sake
Or for what may come through the gate. But those white
                    flowers,
Craning their necks, putting their heads together,
Like a crowd that holds itself back from surging forward,
Have their own point of balance—poised, it seems,
On the airy brink of whatever it is they await.   (538)

Here, at what will turn out to be the midpoint of the poem, the drama
is cast as the interaction between gate and flowers, but the character and
point of their interaction have not yet been disclosed. Having made the
flowers figuratively into a human crowd, the poet finds himself drawn into
even closer identification with the flowers, and so the third stanza poses
"a number of questions to the picture: just *what* are the flowers, and myself the outside observer, waiting for?" The queries in the first seven lines
offer "several possible answers," each "in turn rejected," but "in such a
way that their logical negatives create something emotionally positive."
As a result in the eighth and final line of the stanza the observer is able,
through a Keatsian leap of "negative capability," to move "from outside
the picture" to view the gate inside "from the flowers' point of view."
The dramatic enjambment of the third and fourth stanzas marks that imaginative leap and puts "the greatest possible emphasis" ("Making a Poem,"
12–13) on the first phrase of the new stanza:

And I, gazing over their heads from outside the picture,
Question what we are waiting for: not summer—
Summer is here in charlock, grass, and sainfoin.
A human event?—but there's no path to the gate,
Nor does it look as if it was meant to open.
The ghost of one who often came this way
When there was a path? I do not know. But I think,
If I could go deep into the heart of the picture

From the flowers' point of view, all I would ask is
Not that the gate should open, but that it should
Stay there, holding the colored folds together.
We expect nothing (the flowers might add), we only
Await: this pure awaiting—
It is the kind of worship we are taught.   (538)

"Pure awaiting": the poem has reached the limits of its "outgoingness,"
yet the observer/speaker's submission of himself to the flowers' perspective
and the consequent reflexiveness of his limited understanding infused into
the flowers (desire going forth and returning) permits closure and constellates
the picture and its poem around the flowers and the centering gate. This
clear space of "pure awaiting" offers not vision but expectancy: "[T]hey [the
flowers] (and I) are not concerned with a divine revelation (the gate opening), but only that the gate should stay there—in other words, that we should

retain the sense of some Power at the centre of things, holding them to-gether." He can only say what he can see, and he can only see what he can say. Yet, once again, as in "Final Instructions," the craftsman's patience and disinterestedness yield a muted joy. For "in my tiny way I had done what Copernicus did when, with a superb imaginative leap, leaving the earth and placing himself in the sun, he found that the orbits of the planets looked simpler from that point of view" ("Making a Poem," 12–13).

Making the place of awaiting may be the only kind of "worship" open to an agnostic. The word "worship" occurs in the last line because only when the poem had run its course did the poet realize that it had turned out to be, in its way, "a religious poem":

> It is also, obviously, the poem of an agnostic—one who is, in a sense, 'outside the picture'—but an agnostic whose upbringing was Christian: the 'olive hilltop', with its echo of Mount Olivet, may conceivably have started the poem in the religious direction which, unforeseen by me, it was to take; and the 'ghost-amethyst' colour of the gate certainly led me along to "The ghost of one who often came this way", i. e., the once-felt presence of deity in the human scene.
>
> ("Making a Poem," 13)

The gate, then, functions not just as a metaphor for an intuited or wished-for "Power at the centre of things, holding them together," but also as a metaphor for the imaginative power that crafts pictures and poems out of the inchoate welter of experience and the multivalence of language to arrive at whatever understanding of self and world, of contingencies and abso-lutes the poet can attain.

The craft of "The Gate" demonstrates the point: four stanzas, symmetri-cally arranged so that the first and last stanzas consist of six lines, all five stressed except for three stresses in the fifth line, and the middle stanzas both have eight five-stress lines. The effect is something like a double helix of sonnets, the first inverting into the second. Moreover, Day Lewis ob-served, "the rhythms are as flexible as I could make them, within a regular metre, so as to reflect the inquiring and tentative nature of the poem's thought-process" ("Making a Poem," 13). There are no end-rhymes to interfere or compete with the turns and circlings of observation and thought, but the poem is held together by three key words: "flowers," "gate," and "wait." "Flowers" is repeated four times (not counting the particular flowers mentioned and the pronominal "they" and "their"); "gate" and "wait" form internal rhymes in their repetitions and variations, with "gate" repeated six times (plus the pronoun reference "it" a couple of times) and "wait" repeated four times, counting the variations "await" and "awaiting." Just as the gate holds "the coloured folds together" spa-tially to make the picture, so the patterning and repetitions hold the ver-bal elements together temporally to make the poem.

In late 1969 Day Lewis told an interviewer from the *Observer* that he was allowing himself to feel "an old man's irresponsibility" and went on to explain what he meant: "an opting out of certain things mentally, a diminution in the urgency and importance of the general load of duties and responsibilities. . . . [I]t isn't *just* a slowing down. It is that I have decided which things are worthwhile thinking about, feeling about" (Sean Day Lewis, 285). That old man's irresponsibility is really the worshipful attendance of "pure awaiting," and the poetry of Day Lewis's last years has a concentration at once patient and urgent, deeply personal yet disinterestedly purified of ego. It is the profound engagement that only a certain disengagement can allow, an acceptance of limits devoid of sentimentality and self-pity in order to realize as intensely as possible the possibilities that remain.

From his deathbed Day Lewis took the time to respond to the inquiry of James Gibson, who was asking a number of poets to select their two favorite poems for his forthcoming anthology *Let the Poet Choose* (published the next year, 1973). Day Lewis singled out the last sonnet of "O Dreams! O Destinations!" and "On Not Saying Everything" and explained his choices on a postcard: "The sonnet because, though I wrote it 30 years ago, it still stands up and says something I feel to be truthful about the human condition: 'On Not Saying Everything' because I believe so strongly in the doctrine of limitations it speaks for—that everything, a tree, a poem, a human relationship lives and thrives by the limits imposed on it."

Day Lewis wrote "On Not Saying Everything" at Harvard in the fall of 1964, musing on the tree (actually not the linden of the poem but a New England elm) outside the desk window in his suite at Lowell House, and published it in *The Room* and the 1967 *Selected Poems*. The structure follows the outline indicated in his comment to the anthologist: the first stanza applies the doctrine of limitations to the branching of the tree; the second stanza to the evolution of poetic form; and the last three stanzas to the convolutions of the love he shared with his wife. The poem's beautifully delineated lucidity needs to be quoted in full:

> This tree outside my window here,
> Naked, umbrageous, fresh or sere,
> Has neither chance nor will to be
> Anything but a linden tree,
> Even if its branches grew to span
> The continent; for nature's plan
> Insists that infinite extension
> Shall create no new dimension.
> From the first snuggling of the seed
> In earth, a branchy form's decreed.
>
> Unwritten poems loom as if
> They'd cover the whole of earthly life.
> But each one, growing learns to trim its
> Impulse and meaning to the limits
> Roughed out by me, then modified

In its own truth's expanding light.
A poem, settling to its form,
Finds there's no jailer, but a norm
Of conduct, and a fitting sphere
Which stops it wandering everywhere.

As for you, my love, it's harder,
Though neither prisoner nor warder,
Not to desire you both: for love
Illudes us we can lightly move
Into a new dimension, where
The bounds of being disappear
And we make one impassioned cell.
So wanting to be all in all
Each for each, a man and woman
Defy the limits of what's human.

Your glancing eye, your animal tongue,
Your hands that flew to mine and clung
Like birds on bough, with innocence
Masking those young experiments
Of flesh, persuaded me that nature
Formed us each other's god and creature.
Play out then, as it should be played,
The sweet illusion that has made
An eldorado of your hair
And our love an everywhere.

But when we cease to play explorers
And become settlers, clear before us
Lies the next need—to re-define
The boundary between yours and mine.
Else, one stays prisoner, one goes free.
Each to his own identity
Grown back, shall prove our love's expression
Purer for this limitation.
Love's essence, like a poem's, shall spring
From the not saying everything.   (600–01)

Earlier in the chapter we heard Day Lewis agree with Paul Valéry that
"we use strict form in a poem so as to prevent ourselves 'saying everything' in it" ("Making a Poem," 9). From the proportions of the poem
eros seems harder than natural or aesthetic form to contain within bounds;
it takes the second half of the poem to do so. However, as in "St. Anthony's
Shirt," where Bataille would pessimistically conclude that unrestrained eros
is a death-drive that kills the lover but that domestication merely kills eros,
Day Lewis takes the counterview: eros can only survive, take root, branch
out when it does not "defy the limits of what's human." Each stanza is
developed through five couplets, each couplet yielding to the next like

the rings in a tree's trunk or the ramification of branches; then each end-stopped stanza becomes itself a ring or branch of the poem's evolving form. The poem is a serious game; the root of "illudes," the verb coined from the noun "illusion" later in the poem, is Latin "ludere, to play." The play lays one paradox over the next like so many transparencies: "continent" as a "span" yet (etymologically, the Latin "continens") "containing"; "fitting sphere" as "appropriate" but "snugly restraining"; the interface between exploring and settling, jailer or prisoner; the biological and penal sense of "cell"; definition (from Latin "finis," end) as "setting of limits" but also as the substantive "essence" of the being thus delimited; "bounds" and "boundary" as the perimeters that join and separate. These paradoxes resonate in the end-rhymes: "span/plan," "extension/dimension," "trim its/ limits," "form/norm," "cell/all," "nature/creature," "re-define/mine," "expression/limitation." The effect of the wit is to suggest vitality abounding within bounds.

For Day Lewis the "doctrine of limitations" becomes a naturalist's creed that set the terms for living within nature's cyclic course (stanza 1), within metrical time and poetic form (stanza 2), and within the human relationships that can illude two lovers into believing that for a brief moment of immortality they become "each other's god and creature" (stanzas 3 and 4). Emily Dickinson—like Frost, a staunch New England antinomian—was one of Day Lewis's favorite American poets, and all three were at times doubting Romantics and Churchy agnostics who understood the doctrine of limitations. About a hundred years before "On Not Saying Everything," Dickinson proposed, in the first stanza below, the heterodox idea that "Heaven" might be only a projection of our mortal desire for immortality, and in the second stanza went on to propose that such a seemingly disillusioning supposition can, on the contrary, actually strengthen the commitment to realizing possibilities here and now through the craft of mind and imagination:

> Heaven is so far of the Mind
> That were the Mind dissolved—
> The Site—of it—by Architect
> Could not again be proved—
>
> 'Tis vast—as our Capacity—
> As fair—as our idea—
> To Him of adequate desire
> No further 'tis, than Here—
>
> (Poem 370, *The Poems of*
> *Emily Dickinson*, I, 294)

Day Lewis would certainly have agreed with Dickinson that our "Capacity" for living in time is an extension and measure of the adequacy of our desire. "Adequate" suggests perhaps "barely sufficient" but nonetheless "sufficient." Eros, in the large sense of the drive toward fulfillment and transcendence, actually needs to be circumscribed for human survival. Nonetheless, Dickinson and Day Lewis believed, "adequate desire," thus comprehended (in the double sense of "understood" and "contained"), has the opportunity to root itself in home ground and transform "Here" into the only "Site" ("sight") of "Heaven" we may have.

• 7

In an interview Day Lewis once remarked that he had not been happy till his fifty-fifth year. That would be 1959, the year in which he was writing his autobiography. The Postscript to *The Buried Day*, which recounted his life up to the war, begins with a rumination on the life he had settled into at Crooms Hill. That passage, cited more fully in the first section of this chapter, brings us full circle here:

> Yesterday was my fifty-fifth birthday. J. [Jill] gave me a telescope. Now sitting by the Thames, I can bring . . . all the river life which, here at Greenwich, overlooked by the palace and the park, enlivens their elegance with a workaday reality. I am happy, living in this place where old and new can be focused together into a historic present. . . . [F]ortunate beyond words in my wife and children—yesterday was also the eighth anniversary of my second marriage—I shall play my luck while it lasts.
>
> (*The Buried Day*, 239)

Day Lewis had no forewarning that illness would in another five years begin to close in on home ground, but even beforehand he anticipated the end.

The invitation to be the Charles Eliot Norton Professor at Harvard for the academic year 1964–65 was a happy surprise that would take Day Lewis away from home base for a couple of months in the fall and another couple of months in the spring. He was excited about the appointment and wrote "Days before a Journey" in eager anticipation of this new adventure. During the fall's residence at Lowell House, he made new friends and enjoyed exploring New England; moreover, with the Norton lectures already written upon arrival, the unaccustomed freedom from both domestic and publishing routines allowed an extraordinary outburst of poetic energy in the course of which he wrote "St. Anthony's Shirt" and "On Not Saying Everything," along with a number of other poems to appear in *The Room*. On the platform the first batch of lectures, to be published as *The Lyric Impulse*, were beautifully delivered and enthusiastically received. However, during the holiday visit home, on the day after Christmas, he woke with a sudden and severe nosebleed that could not be stanched for days. The hemorrhage may have averted a fatal stroke, but it left him exhausted and hospitalized till mid-January. With determination to fulfill his commitments and to prove himself capable of doing so, he returned to Harvard on schedule in early February, leaving behind an anxious family. He delivered the spring lectures and completed a round of scheduled readings that took him from the east coast to California before returning to Crooms Hill, tired but pleased with his American sojourn, in early April.

A briskly descriptive article "On Being Ill," written for the American magazine *Holiday*, reported that he had not realized till after the crisis just how close to death he had come in the hospital. Though his health never recovered full vigor again, there were no serious crises till he was struck with glandular fever in June 1968, the spring after his appointment as laureate, and laid up for the summer. But the next years brought a battery of physical problems, of which the most grievous were a painful attack of gallbladder stones in the spring of 1969, a serious coronary thrombosis in June of that year, surgery to remove the bladder stones in March 1970, and more surgery in April 1971, which revealed pancreatic cancer and the prognosis—accurate, as it turned out—of perhaps a year of life left. On the doctor's advice Day Lewis was never told the diagnosis or the prognosis. Nevertheless, the truth became increasingly apparent as Jill, the family, and, most of all, the sick man himself kept up a brave and composed front during that long year, at what excruciating cost can only be imagined.

Meantime he continued his biweekly schedule at Chatto and Windus, followed through a punishing round of public appearances, lectures, broadcasts, interviews, and readings, and continued to write poems. In January and February of 1972, he and Jill filmed a series of six poetry programs for television, shown and later published under the title *A Lasting Joy* after his death in May. Day Lewis took great satisfaction in introducing poetry for the first time on BBC 2, and the poems he chose, mostly from the English tradition he knew and drew upon in his own work, were grouped under six rubrics that form something of a gloss on his own defining themes: "Childhood," "Human Heroism," "Satire and Hatred," "Love and Friendship," "Times and Seasons," "Death and Immortality."

Elegies mark the progress of Day Lewis's work. The last of the thirties poetry came in *Overtures to Death* (1938), the title poem of which was an elegy for his father, Reverend Frank Day-Lewis; and the engagement with eros in the forties climaxed in "Elegy Before Death." Not surprisingly elegies become more frequent in the later work, as time began to take its toll on him and his contemporaries. *Pegasus* paired "In Memory of Dylan Thomas" with the "Elegiac Sonnet" for friend and pianist Noel Mewton-Wood; *The Gate* paired "In Loving Memory," for E. M. Butler, with "Edward Elgar," written for his centenary; *The Room* placed "Elegy for a Woman Unknown" with the poems for the deaths of Churchill and John Kennedy, "Who Goes Home?" and "Pietà"; *The Whispering Roots*, besides the poems in the title sequence, concludes with "At East Coker," for T. S. Eliot; *Posthumous Poems* includes "Hellene: Philhellene," a double elegy written in 1971 for George Seferis and the Oxford classicist C. M. Bowra, Day Lewis's mentor during student years at Wadham.

Of these elegies the one that speaks most personally and deeply for Day Lewis himself is, oddly enough, the "Elegy for a Woman Unknown," as though the distance between poet and subject permitted special empathy. The woman was Fiona Peters, whose husband, a London pathologist named Michael Peters, made an appointment to see Day Lewis in 1961 at his Chatto and Windus office. Dr. Peters wanted to tell him that his recently dead wife had admired and drawn inspiration from his poetry during her three-years' battle with cancer and to ask him to read and advise him about the poems she had written during her illness. "Nothing," he would write in "Saint Anthony's Shirt," "remains so true / As the outgoingness"; now, years before his own diagnosis of cancer but moved by Fiona Peters's situation and response, Day Lewis set about writing her elegy. The first part memorializes her courageous spirit in affirming life against her fated end and would assume an additional poignancy in the wake of his own eventual fate.

However, stymied by the incommensurability between her spirit and her fate, the poet found it difficult to find images powerful enough to carry her tragedy through to catharsis. He would tell his Harvard audience how he had come to find what he needed:

> For some time I had wanted to write an elegy for a certain woman I had never met personally, but had heard about from her widower—a brave and fascinating woman who had died of a hideous disease. But I could not find a way into the subject. Then on the island of Delos, communing with those beautiful, weather-beaten stone lions (who, if I may say so, are now old friends of mine), I heard—almost as if the lions had spoken it out of the island's holy hush, "Not the silence after music, but the silence of no more music." To me those words had an extraordinary momentousness. I connected them at once with the dead woman; and the elegy began to get written.
>
> (*The Lyric Impulse*, 148)

The lions of Delos, seen on his second trip to Greece in the summer of 1962, seemed the perfect aesthetic embodiment of tragedy as the row of them stand in ruined majesty, their features and figures smoothed to elemental simplicity, by centuries of exposure and erosion, facing the hill of Apollo's birth with roars of rage forever stilled into stone:

> Island of stone and silence. A rough ridge
> Chastens the innocent azure. Lizards hang
> Like their own shadows crucified on stone
> (But the heart palpitates, the ruins itch
> With memories amid the sunburnt grass). Here sang
> Apollo's choir, the sea their unloosed zone.
> Island of stillness and white stone.
>
> . . . .
>
> And silence—not the silence after music,
> But the silence of no more music. A breeze twitches
> The grass like a whisper of snakes; and swallows there are,
> Cicadas, frogs in the cistern. But elusive

Their chorusing—thin threads of utterance, vanishing
stitches
Upon the gape of silence, whose deep core
Is the stone lions' soundless roar.

Lions of Delos, roaring in abstract rage
Below the god's hill, near his lake of swans!
Tense haunches, rooted paws set in defiance
Of time and all intruders, each grave image
Was sentinel and countersign of deity once.
Now they have nothing to keep but the pure silence.
Crude as a schoolchild's sketch of lions

They hold a rhythmic truth, a streamlined pose.
Weathered by sea-winds into beasts of the sea,
Fluent from afar, unflawed; but the jaws are toothless,
Granulated by time the skin, seen close,
And limbs disjointed. Nevertheless, what majesty
Their bearing shows—how well they bear these ruthless
Erosions of their primitive truth!   (625–26)

The enjambed lines move through the measured verses (five stresses tightened in the last line of the stanza to four stresses) and the stepped rhymes (a–b–c–a–b–c–c) to a closing couplet. In the last stanza above the truncation of the rhyme-word from the expected "truthless" (to rhyme with "toothless" and "ruthless") to the abrupt "truth" conveys the arrested power of those "ruthless / Erosions." The sustained gravity of the passage, visualized with almost surreal accuracy, makes it one of the most powerful in the whole of Day Lewis's work.

Sailing the stormy, windswept Aegean in 1962 with a small boatload of friends evoked the exploits of Odysseus and Aeneas and provided Day Lewis with the conceit for the third part of the "Elegy": "We did not choose to voyage. . . . But to have missed the voyage— // That would be worse." The image of the traveller as questing hero, familiar since *Transitional Poem* and *The Magnetic Mountain*, recurs again and again in the late poems: in "Moral" (*The Room*), in "Some Beautiful Morning" and "Hero and Saint" (*The Whispering Roots*), in "Hellene: Philhellene" (*Posthumous Poems*). But in the third part of "Elegy for a Woman Unknown" this motif gets its most forceful and plangent expression. The last stanza carries the mariner persona to the final shipwreck:

Whither or why we voyaged,
Who knows? . . . A worst storm blew. I was afraid.
The ship broke up. I swam till I
Could swim no more. My love and memories are laid
In the unrevealing deep . . . But tell them
They need not pity me. Tell them I was glad
Not to have missed the voyage.   (628)

Still, as Odysseus knew, even a voyage to shipwreck is driven by a homing instinct and perhaps the very prospect of disaster turns the course around, "Ithaca-bound" (641). At the end of his autobiography his sense of health and happiness did not keep him from seeing through to the end: "I have, at most, another twenty years or so to live. Extinction I do not fear; but I dread the act of dying: I hope that, when I come to die, if I have still no belief in immortality, I may at least recapture the docility of the child I once was, and go into the dark with an acquiescent murmur" (*The Buried Day*, 239). Whether or not he had in mind here Dylan Thomas's famous "Do Not Go Gentle into That Good Night," written in anticipation of Thomas's own as well as his father's impending death, Day Lewis's determination to acquiesce in mortality was as far as it could be from Thomas's violent and obsessive resistance.

Like many aging poets, Day Lewis found himself recurring to memories of home and origins for solace and a sense of completion. He remarked on a number of occasions that the threat of death during the London blitz had first summoned up long-buried childhood recollections. In the late sixties the mounting stress of mortal ills drew him irresistibly back to the boy he was and to the Ireland of his first relationships, retracing his sailing round in anticipation of the inevitable shipwreck. The annual family vacations to the home country, which began in 1964 and continued through all the physical difficulties till 1971, the summer before his death, gave rise to the long sequence of poems that provided the title and first half of the last volume published during his lifetime, *The Whispering Roots*. Some of the poems are historical, memorializing the heroes of the Irish uprising against British imperialism and remote ancestors like Oliver Goldsmith and, curiously, a Jane Eyre of Eyrescourt, County Galway. But the most resonant poems deal elegiacally with primary connections: the remote and long dead father he loved and resisted and the mother he lost before he could have memories ("The House Where I Was Born," reprinted from *Pegasus* to introduce the sequence); the aunt who became his "second mother" ("Avoca, Co. Wicklow"); the clergyman uncle whose rectory garden seemed, through the "sunshine glaze" of memory, "a land of milk and honey" ("Golden Age, Monart, Co. Wexford," 656–57); the wife of his shortening years ("Sailing from Cleggan"); his return, with Jill and his first-born Sean, to the place of his birth ("Ballintubbert House, Co. Laois").

In a number of these and other poems (as in many earlier poems, notably "Saint Anthony's Shirt") houses are extensions of the bodily selves of their occupants, and sometimes now the houses are derelict and empty. In "Near Ballyconneely, Co. Galway" the "roofless dwellings" and ruined farms of the stony, bleak Connemara countryside are the only remains of homemakers long gone (659); "A Skull Picked Clean" describes a vacant house ("Blank walls, dead grates," 678) in the metaphor of its title; and "Recurring Dream" (from *Posthumous Poems*) tells of entering a house ("Dilapidated, / Or is it only half built?") and mounting to the top of the ramshackled structure only to face a precipitous descent by a "deep staircase," with "no recollection / Where or indeed whether one egressed" (707).

Yet beyond the perils the end is also consistently experienced as a salutary return to sources and origins, not without its own rueful sweetness: "Let the waters jig / In a light glitter, / So the source run full" (658). "The Whispering Roots" begins "Roots are for holding on, and holding dear" (674) and proceeds to gather in the sequence and bring it to rest by conflating the image of the fatal voyage with the image of regression to the source:

> In age, body swept on, mind crawls upstream
> *Toward* the source; not thinking to find there
> Visions or fairy gold—what old men dream
> Is pure restatement of the original theme,
> A sense of rootedness, a source held near and dear.   (676)

"The Whispering Roots" has arrived at the point of simultaneous completion and extinction that Frost described in "Directive" as his own return upstream past the desolate cottage of childhood to the source, which is both alpha and omega: "Here are your waters and your watering place. / Drink and be whole again beyond confusion" (*The Poetry of Robert Frost*, 379).

These late poems of Day Lewis are moving because they speak about aging and dying without illusion or disillusion, without bravado or sentimentality. Some try to anticipate (in the double sense of "look ahead to" and "fend off") the moment of death. These lines are from "All Souls' Night":

> Who can know death, till he has dared to shave
> His own corpse, rubbed his nose in his own noisesome
> Decay? Oh sweet breath, dancing minds and lissome
> Bodies I've met with journeying to the grave!   (680)

All Souls' is of course the Day of the Dead, and the poet would choose living "lovers, friends," who are only "prospective ghosts," over the spirits or superstitious fantasies abroad on this haunted night. But he tries to salute his fate—whether extinction or immortality—with a bantering toast to the revenant spooks, be they real or imagined: "Welcome, invisibles! We have this in common— / Whatever you are, I presently shall be" (681). "Ass in Retirement" humorously parodies life's circumscribed round, as the verses play out the animal's lifeline, syllable by increasing syllable, and then reel it relentlessly in, syllable by decreasing syllable, to the final monosyllable and period: "dead." Here are the opening and closing lines:

> Ass
> orbits
> a firm stake:

each circle round
the last one is stamped
slow and unmomentous
like a tree-trunk's annual rings.

. . . .

. . . ignorant that he'll come in time

to the longest tether's end,
then strangle or accept
that stake. Either way
on the endless
grass one day
he'll drop
dead.   (666)

Are we tethered asses or hearty mariners? Both: asses in body, mariners in spirit. The ass's ignorance that "he'll drop / dead" spares him from playing "a tragedian, / a circumference mystic, or a treadmill hero" (666), but Day Lewis's own inveterate susceptibility to the tragic, the mystic, and the heroic doubles the irony back on itself. The posturing of consciousness before its tethered fate is at once asinine and ennobling; it manifests both the absurdity and the glory of the human condition. "Some Beautiful Morning" invokes again the mariner trope to hail the last voyage out, even for those not "fortunate" enough to "read / Their sailing orders as a firm *God-speed, / This voyage reaches you beyond the horizon*" (678). "Harebells over Mannin Bay" reads the blooming of all those frail, tiny flowers, undaunted by the immensity of sea and sky and "grave mountain faces," as an emblem of mortal resistance made all the more moving by its unassuming modesty: "I like / These gestures of the ephemeral / Against the everlasting" (668).

Acquiescence to death, however, need not mean blind and abject surrender. The "pure awaiting" he sought fused acceptance and resistance in living the given moments to the realizations, however small, that time allows. The imaginative energy and technical resources of the late poems are concentrated on allowing tragedy to reach catharsis in an everyday kind of heroism in an humbled attendance upon mystery. "A Privileged Moment" tells of a brief euphoria, after returning home "only half alive" from the hospital in January 1965, when the familiar, simple objects on the bedroom mantlepiece and the raindrops on the windowpane shone with a preternatural clarity: "It was enough. He'd seen what he had seen" (684). "Tenure" relinquishes any specious claims of permanence to commit time to living: "I would live each day as if it were my last and first day" (690). "A Tuscan Villa," like "Time To Go" and *An Italian Visit*, broods on the unavoidable departure from another Italian scene, this time after an almost Edenic period of convalescence at the home of friends; the meditation concludes that we learn to seize those precious moments in order to release them freely from our grasp: "If we are quick and catch them,

/ We shall not grudge to let them fly. / ... Today, be glad it is ours"
(686).

The title of "Merry-go-round" becomes a metaphor for the circle of
life: in the first stanza the boy's sense of life as an endless carousel ride, in
the second stanza the aging man's sense of life's swirling suck down the
spout into time's vacuum:

Here is a gallant merry-go-round.
The children all, entranced or queasy,
Cling to saddlebows, crazily fancy the
Circular tour is a free and easy
Gallop into a world without end.
Now their undulating time is up.
Horses, music slow to a stop.

Time's last inches running out,
A vortex, only guessable
Before by the circus ring of bubbles
Sedately riding, now turns visible—
A hole, an ulcer, a waterspout.
Bubbles twirl faster as closer they come
To the brink of the vacuum.

And my thoughts revolve upon death's
Twisted attraction. As limbs move slower,
Time runs more quickly toward the undoer
Of all. I feel each day devour
My future. Still, to the lattermost breath
Let me rejoice in the world I was lent—
The rainbow bubbles, the dappled mount.   (686–87)

The enjambed lines turn and turn through the rhyme-words (a–b–b–b–
a–c–c), rounded off in each stanza by the concluding couplet. But the flow
and movement of lines and rhymes is somewhat countered and slowed by
the stop-and-start of short, declarative sentences: "Now their undulating
time is up. / Horses, music slow to a stop"; "I feel each day devour / My
future." The images of carousel and vortex fuse into a jaunty apocalypse:
"Still, to the lattermost breath / Let me rejoice in the world I was lent—
/ The rainbow bubbles, the dappled mount."

At the end of *The Whispering Roots*, Day Lewis placed an epithalamion
and an elegy, and the conjunction stands as a summary of the volume and
of a lifetime's concerns. "A Marriage Song" was written on his visit to La
Jolla, California, in April 1965, for the June wedding of two friends of
his Harvard sojourn, my wife Barbara and me. The pastoral epithalamion
is infused with the impressions of a lush California spring, measured and
rounded out by the mounting exclamatory refrain: "start the dancing ...
oh start the dancing ... start the dance." Eliot's death in January 1965
came only days after Day Lewis's near-fatal hemorrhage, and during the

busy spring term at Harvard he was also able to write the second part of his elegy, "At East Coker." The first part waited till Day Lewis's return to England and was completed after a visit to the ancestral town of the Eliots and to the old stone church where Eliot's ashes had been interred. Day Lewis had no way of knowing then that he would himself be buried in Dorset earth at Stinsford, just east of Dorchester as East Coker stood north and west; his grave, in the churchyard of the old and weathered Romanesque church of St. Michael's, lies under a slate headstone close by the plot that holds the heart of Thomas Hardy, the poet for whom he felt the most abiding affinity.

After *The Whispering Roots*, despite the painful, debilitating infirmities and despite numerous public engagements and his regular editorial duties at Chatto and Windus, Day Lewis still managed to write not just several occasional pieces as laureate but the poems that make up the end of Ian Parsons's *Selected Poems* and Jill Balcon's edition of *Posthumous Poems*. He wrote about small epiphanies. He wrote about poetry's sublime and tragic calling: "Poet seer / Summon a rainbow from the cataract's wrath, / Image the faith by which we steer" (705). He wrote about Masaccio's depiction of the expulsion from paradise: "the hour when the animal knew that it must die / And with that stroke put on humanity" (700); the poem appeared in a Festschrift for Auden's sixty-fifth birthday in 1972. He wrote of the recent deaths of George Seferis and C. M. Bowra, in the double elegy "Hellene: Philhellene." He wrote the last of his Christmas poems: "One way's still open. Return to the child / *You* were on Christmas Eve" (705).

And, most movingly perhaps, he wrote to his own children in valediction. Years before, "Walking Away" (from *The Gate* and the American *Pegasus*) had turned the seemingly prosaic moment when his first son, Sean, turned away from his father toward his teammates on the football field into a small epiphany of "nature's give-and-take," measured here by the rhymes "so/show/go":

> I have had worse partings, but none that so
> Gnaws at my mind still. Perhaps it is roughly
> Saying what God alone could perfectly show—
> How selfhood begins with a walking away,
> And love is proved in the letting go.   (546)

Now in *Posthumous Poems* "Remembering Carrownisky" hankers back to his daughter Tamasin's initial testing of her selfhood at age thirteen at a horse race on the west coast of Ireland. And "Children Leaving Home" is a farewell to the now adolescent Tamasin and Daniel from a father who knew but could not say that it was he, not they, who would soon be gone. Again, the prosiness of family memories and of the father's plea for forgiveness and for their own self-forgiveness ends with a blessing: "Go forth and make the best of it, my dears" (713). A blessing characteristically measured in form and intent: the completed iambic pentameter acknowledges to his "dears" that it requires all the will and skill we can muster to "make" from living in time "the best" of our limited capacities and opportunities: not the absolute and perfected "best," admittedly not the Platonic ideal, but still no mean feat.

Early in April of 1972, a year after the discovery of the cancer, the Day Lewises accepted the invitation of their old friends, Elizabeth Jane Howard and Kingsley Amis, to spend what was euphemistically called a "holiday" at Lemmons, their house at Hadley Common in the north of London. There was plenty of room, with a nurse already in attendance on their friend's invalid mother, and the arrangement would permit Jill to film her scenes for a television movie at a nearby studio without requiring hospitalization for the failing patient. Though the ruse of a holiday maintained the decorum of his final illness, in which no public notice of the desperate situation was given or received, the decorum deceived none of those involved and surely made these final weeks all the more heartbreaking. But the plan made practical sense, and Jill drove them on April 6 from Crooms Hill to Lemmons. After the filming was done, the Amises suggested that the Day Lewises remain as long as they wished, and they agreed because the loving and caring ambiance of Lemmons gave them the support and comfort that they each desperately needed in their different but mutual suffering.

By the end life had come, in a sense, full term. Throughout the fifties and well into the sixties there had been regular lunches with Mary Day Lewis when she came to London from Brimclose, and there had been a final meeting with Billie Currall some months earlier. Rosamond Lehmann had sent a letter of reconciliation to Crooms Hill. Three of the children were nearby in these agonizing weeks: Tamasin among the first women preparing to enter King's College, Cambridge, Daniel a student and already a brilliant actor at Bedales, Sean a journalist living with his family in London. Nicholas, who had emigrated to South Africa in the fifties, had recently returned for a final visit. Now there was only the terrible waiting for the end. As loved ones and friends visited and read to him, Day Lewis was, by all accounts, unfailingly composed and uncomplaining, resolutely considerate and appreciative in his responses to their efforts to help him die at peace. Jill was there throughout the long wait. On May 21 he lapsed into a coma, and Daniel was summoned from school as Jill kept vigil with Tamasin and two close friends. The next morning Daniel and Sean arrived, and Day Lewis slipped away without regaining consciousness.

The companionship at Lemmons included, besides Kingsley Amis and Elizabeth Jane Howard, her brother, the painter Colin Howard, and Sargy Mann, an inventor: "This moving house / Is home, and my home, only when it's shared" (606). Day Lewis's response to the invitation to remain at Lemmons and spend his last days in their company was completely characteristic. He asked Jill for a notebook to try to compose a poem of thanks, and in ten days he had painfully completed "At Lemmons," with a dedication "For Jane, Kingsley, Colin, Sargy with much love":

Above my table three magnolia flowers
Utter their silent requiems.
Through the window I see your elms
In labour with the racking storm
Giving it shape in April's shifty airs.

Up there sky boils from a brew of clouds
To blue gleam, sunblast, then darkens again.
No respite is allowed
The watching eye, the natural agony.

Below is the calm a loved house breeds
Where four have come together to dwell
—Two write, one paints, the fourth invents—
Each pursuing a natural bent
But less through nature's formative travail
Than each in his own humour finding the self he needs.

Round me all is amenity, a bloom of
Magnolia uttering its requiems,
A climate of acceptance. Very well
I accept my weakness with my friends'
Good natures sweetening every day my sick room.   (713–14)

This final poem is his own modest, understated elegy before death, and it represents the ultimate refinement of the strategy of "not saying everything." Verses in the second stanza declare that "No respite is allowed / The watching eye, the natural agony"; but the resonance of the entire poem—not just its "amenity" but its almost preternatural serenity, at once embodied and disembodied—declares that the eye watching the natural agony amidst the flowers' "silent requiems" had attained, in this loving company, "a climate of acceptance," the worshipful condition of "pure awaiting." He had written years before: "Oh, travelling starts many / Days before the journey" (607). Now, however, "At Lemmons" observes, with exquisite tact and restraint, the end of restless journeying and the end of a lifetime's song. Then there fell "not the silence after music, / But the silence of no more music."

AFTERWORD

EVEN AFTER THE explicitly political thirties, C. Day Lewis believed that poetry has an essential moral and psychological function in a society, and with that conviction he won and held a broad reading and listening public that was sometimes the envy of his peers and would-be peers. As we have seen, he had his detractors, but at the same time he always had strong and vocal admirers. The poet L. A. G. Strong told him that "his work says more than that of any poet since Yeats." Charles Causley, a poet of the generation after his, called him "the greatest lyric poet of the century, and this is including Yeats and Hardy" (Sean Day Lewis, 262, 241). Kenneth Hopkins summed up his place in British poetry trenchantly:

> C. Day Lewis was the most important English poet to be born in the years 1900–1914, which produced the generation of writers who composed the characteristic poetry of the mid-century. There may be readers who will question this, in particular with reference to W. H. Auden, whose influence was probably wider. I believe Auden's overall achievement as a poet—impressive as it is—is too much of its time to be wholly accepted as time passes. There is an essence of poetry in the work of Day Lewis which is as timeless as . . . that marvelous lyric heritage, which the centuries have left us. He accepted the tradition, and enlarged it.
>
> (*The Poets Laureate*, 201)

In his own critical remarks Day Lewis ranked Yeats, Hardy, and Auden as greater poets than himself, but he also wisely questioned the authority and usefulness of such rankings, citing more than once (the last time in his elegy

219

for Eliot) the phrase from *East Coker*: "but there is no competition" (*Collected Poems*, 189). And indeed one does not have to play that shifty game to acknowledge Day Lewis as one of the great and important poets of the century: a historical and literary judgment that this study has sought to substantiate.

At the end of his booklet *C. Day Lewis* Clifford Dyment wrote that by 1963 he was beginning to make out the developing design of the poet's work (47). Keats said that a writer figures his experience into "allegory" (*Letters*, 2:67) and it is the intention of this study to discern the allegorical design that gives Day Lewis's work—735 pages in the *Complete Poems*—its coherence. Day Lewis thinks and feels and speaks as a modern when he takes as his primary task the reconciling of the violent divisions in himself and in the world outside his consciousness, and he speaks as a modern poet when he makes language the site and ground of such contention and resolution. With the loss of religious faith in a heavenly paradise where the dislocations of mortality would be transcended, he sought an alternate vision of a paradise recoverable here and now—first in a utopian collectivity of comrades and lovers, then in the sublime reaches of erotic desire that intimated individual fulfillment in cosmic harmony. When experience taught him that both visions of an earthly paradise eluded—and deluded—the limits of human attainment, he was left with the chastening recognition that, in the words of the epigraph for this book, "for certain temperaments the only Paradise is Paradise Lost" (*The Buried Day*, 234).

Emily Dickinson located the life of consciousness in the initiating awareness of bereavement: "A loss of something ever felt I" (*Poems*, II, 694–95). And like her Day Lewis took that aboriginal loss not as the end but as the beginning of the human—and so poetic—task. Living within the bounded flux of time required a quiet heroism, which refused a solipsistic and incapacitating retreat into reverie for the lost or unattainable, and instead focused whatever could be reclaimed from memory of the past on the lifetime of the moment, wherein on certain happy occasions we lose and find ourselves in fleeting, transfiguring oneness with the frail existences we love. Day Lewis's enduring place in the long history of poetry in English is assured by the large body of poems, many of which are discussed in these pages, that articulate such hard-earned, epiphanal moments.

For too long the poets of the "MacSpaunday" group have been bracketed as thirties poets, and for too long Auden has overshadowed the others in critical discussion and literary histories. Perhaps only now can we begin to assess more accurately the very different careers and qualities of Day Lewis, Spender, and MacNeice. When the Spenders brought Auden for a final lunch with Day Lewis at Crooms Hill on October 31, 1971, it was a historic and inescapably nostalgic occasion that evoked both their old association and their subsequent divergence. MacNeice had been dead since 1963; a year after the luncheon Spender attended Day Lewis's memorial service, and in the next year Auden too would be dead. Before Spender's death in the summer of 1995, this youngest and surviving member of the group prefaced his last book, *Dolphins* (1994), with a dedication "Remembering Earliest Friends and Colleagues: W. H. Auden, Cecil Day Lewis, Louis MacNeice, Christopher Isherwood" and added the verses: *"The Yesterdays that were the Nows / Are buried under the Tomorrows."*

Undoubtedly Day Lewis was deeply gratified by a 1963 letter from Auden that took a long and positive view of his career since "Mac-Spaunday": "I've always been meaning to write to you about your *Selected Poems*, to tell you how delighted I was to find your later poetry so much finer than your earlier. The critics, of course, think our lot stopped writing twenty-five years ago. How silly they are going to look presently" (Sean Day Lewis, 252). Without underestimating the thirties poetry, Dyment also found the later work finer, because in becoming more personal it had become more universal:

> More and more [Day Lewis] has been looking into himself and seeing others; more and more he has been looking into others and seeing himself. If the high spirits of the early work have gone, so has the cock-sureness: in their place are humility, understanding, wisdom. . . . In speaking, in his poetry, of the clash of irreconcilables in himself C. Day Lewis is speaking to and of us all.
>
> (47–48)

Day Lewis's poetry became finer because, for all his responsiveness to other poets—Yeats, Auden, Hopkins, Hardy, Frost—he achieved a voice and register distinctly his own. In Kenneth Hopkins's words, "the originality in this poetry far outweighs its echoes, and at the same time the echoes enhance its music" (*The Poets Laureate*, 198). Over the decades the virtuosic inventiveness and control of metrical form—always functional, never facile—fitted themselves more and more surely to the needs and intentions of the poem.

Because Pound the American Modernist and Day Lewis the British anti-Modernist conceived such different roles for the modern poet, they would not have read each other with much appreciation (though in fact *The Draft of XXX Cantos* was on the shelf in Day Lewis's study). Though both honored Eliot, in many ways the pivotal figure in modern poetry, Pound singled out *The Waste Land* as Eliot's masterpiece, but Day Lewis instead singled out *Four Quartets*. Such differences in assumption and judgment serve to delineate the historical and critical differences between British and American poetry in the twentieth century, and to place Day Lewis centrally in the British tradition. For a generation or two trained in Modernism and now in Postmodernism, I want to extend to Day Lewis Pound's terse imperative about Eliot: "READ HIM" (*Selected Prose*, 464).

WORKS CITED

Arnold, Matthew. *A Selection of His Finest Poems*, ed. Miriam Allot. Oxford: Oxford University Press, 1995.

Auden, W. H. *Collected Poems*, ed. Edward Mendelson. London: Faber & Faber, 1976.

———. *The English Auden: Poems, Essays and Dramatic Writings, 1927–1939*, ed. Edward Mendelson. New York: Random House, 1977.

Auden, W. H., and C. Day-Lewis, eds. *Oxford Poetry 1927*. Oxford: Basil Blackwell, 1927.

Authors Take Sides on the Spanish War. London: Left Review, n. d.

Bataille, Georges. *Erotism: Death and Sensuality*, tr. Mary Dalwood. San Francisco: City Lights Books, 1986; first published as *L'Erotisme*. Paris: Les Editions de Minuit, 1957.

Bowen, Elizabeth. *The Heat of the Day*. New York: Alfred A. Knopf, 1949.

Campbell, Roy. *Talking Bronco*. London: Faber & Faber, 1946.

Caudwell, Christopher (Christopher St. John Sprigg). *Illusion and Reality: A Study of the Sources of Poetry*. London: Lawrence & Wishart, 1977; first published 1937.

———. *Collected Poems*. Edited and with an Introduction by Alan Young. Manchester: Carcanet Press, 1986.

Crossman, R. H. S., ed. *The God That Failed*. London: Hamish, 1950.

Cunningham, Valentine. *British Writers of the Thirties*. Oxford: Oxford University Press, 1988.

Davie, Donald. *Thomas Hardy and British Poetry*. New York: Oxford University Press, 1972.

———. *Collected Poems*. Manchester: Carcanet Press, 1984.

Davy, Charles. *Words in the Mind*. London: Chatto & Windus, 1965.

Day Lewis, C. *Beechen Vigil and Other Poems*. London: Fortune Press, 1925.

———. *Country Comets*. London: Martin Hopkinson, 1928.

———. *Transitional Poem*. London: Hogarth Press, 1929.

———. *From Feathers to Iron*. London: Hogarth Press, 1931.

———. *The Magnetic Mountain*. London: Hogarth Press, 1933.

———. "Letter to a Young Revolutionary" in *New Country*, ed. Michael Roberts. London; Hogarth Press, 1933.

———. *A Hope for Poetry*. Oxford: Basil Blackwell, 1934, 1936.

———. *Collected Poems 1925–1933*. London: Hogarth Press, 1935.

———. *A Time to Dance and Other Poems*. London: Hogarth Press, 1935.

———. *Revolution in Writing*. London: Hogarth Press, 1935.

———. *Noah and the Waters*. London: Hogarth Press, 1936

———. (with L. Susan Stebbing) *Imagination and Thinking*. Life and Leisure Pamphlets: No. 4. London: British Institute of Adult Education, 1936.

———. "Surrealists Get the Bird." *New Verse*. No. 21 (June–July 1936), 20–21.

———, (editor). *The Mind in Chains: Socialism and the Cultural Revolution*. London: Frederick Muller Ltd., 1937.

———. *Overtures to Death and Other Poems*. London: Jonathan Cape, 1938.

———. *The Georgics of Virgil*. London: Jonathan Cape, 1940.

———. *Poems in Wartime*. London: Jonathan Cape, 1940.

———. Edited with L. A. G. Strong. *A New Anthology of Modern Verse 1920–1940*. London: Methuen, 1941.

———. *Word Over All*. London: Jonathan Cape, 1943.

———. *Short Is the Time: Poems 1936–1943*. New York: Oxford University Press, 1945.

———. *The Poetic Image*. London: Jonathan Cape, 1947.

———. *Enjoying Poetry: A Reader's Guide*. Published for the National Book League. Cambridge: Cambridge University Press, 1947, 1951.

———. Introduction. *Modern Love*, by George Meredith. London: Rupert Hart-David, 1948.

———. *Poems 1943–1947*. London: Jonathan Cape, 1948.

———. *Selected Poems*. Harmondsworth: Penguin Books, 1951; revised and enlarged 1969.

———. *The Poet's Task*. An Inaugural Lecture Delivered Before the University of Oxford on July 1, 1951. Oxford: Clarendon Press, 1951.

———. *An Italian Visit*. London: Jonathan Cape, 1953.

———. "The Lyrical Poetry of Thomas Hardy." The Warton Lecture on English Poetry. *Proceedings of the British Academy*. Volume 37, 155–74. London: Geoffrey Cumberlege, 1953.

———. *Notable Images of Virtue: Emily Brontë, George Meredith, W. B. Yeats*. The Chancellor Dunning Trust Lectures Delivered at Queen's University, Kingston, Ontario, 1954.

———. *Collected Poems*. London: Jonathan Cape, 1954.

———. *The Poet's Way of Knowledge*. The Henry Sidgwick Memorial Lecture, 1956. Cambridge: Cambridge University Press, 1957.

———. *Pegasus and Other Poems*. London: Jonathan Cape, 1957.

———. *The Buried Day: A Personal Memoir*. New York: Harper & Brothers, 1960.

———. *The Gate and Other Poems*. London: Jonathan Cape, 1961.

———. *The Eclogues of Virgil*. London: Jonathan Cape, 1963.

———. "Oration" for the Quartercentenary Celebration of the Birth of William Shakespeare. *Westminster Abbey Occasional Paper No. 13*, August 1964.

———. *Requiem for the Living*. New York: Harper and Row, 1964.

————. *The Lyric Impulse*. The Charles Eliot Norton Lectures, 1964–1965. Cambridge, Mass.: Harvard University Press, 1965.

————. *The Room and Other Poems*. London: Jonathan Cape, 1965.

————. "Making a Poem." Typescript of a lecture in the possession of Jill Balcon.

————. "Poetic Inspiration." Typescript of a radio broadcast on the British Broadcasting Corporation on April 7, 1966, in the possession of Jill Balcon.

————. *Selected Poems*. New York: Harper & Row, 1967.

————. "The Thirties in Retrospect." Typescript of an unpublished lecture given at the University of Hull, 1968, in the possession of Jill Balcon.

————. "The Creative Spirit." Typescript of a sermon given on June 2, 1968, Church of Great St. Mary's, Cambridge, in the possession of Jill Balcon.

————. *A Need for Poetry?* Hull: University of Hull, 1968.

————. *The Whispering Roots and Other Poems*. London: Jonathan Cape, 1970.

————. *On Translating Poetry*. The Second Jackson Knight Memorial Lecture Delivered at the University of Exeter, March 7, 1969. Abington-on-Thames: Abbey Press, 1970.

————. "On a Tilting Deck: C. Day Lewis Talks to Hallam Tennyson About His Life and Work." Typescript of an interview broadcast on British Broadcasting Corporation Radio 3 on June 16, 1972, in the possession of Jill Balcon.

————. *A Lasting Joy: An Anthology Chosen and Introduced by C. Day Lewis*. London: George Allen Unwin, 1973.

————. *Posthumous Poems*, ed. Jill Balcon. Manor Farm, Andoversford, Gloucestershire: The Whittington Press, 1979.

————. *Poems of C. Day Lewis 1925–1972*, Chosen & with an Introduction by Ian Parsons. London: Jonathan Cape & Hogarth Press, 1977.

————. *The Complete Poems*, ed. Jill Balcon. London: Sinclair-Stevenson, 1992; Stanford, Calif.: Stanford University Press, 1992.

Day-Lewis, Sean. *C. Day Lewis: An English Literary Life*. London: Wiedenfeld & Nicholson, 1980.

Dickinson, Emily. *The Poems of Emily Dickinson*, ed. Thomas H. Johnson. Cambridge, Mass.: Harvard University Press, 1955.

Dyment, Clifford. *C. Day Lewis*. London: Longmans, Green & Co. for the British Council and the National Book League, 1955; revised 1963.

Eliot, T. S. *Collected Poems 1909–1962*. New York: Harcourt, Brace & World, 1970.

Faulkner, William. *Light in August*. New York: Random House, 1932.

Fitzgerald, F. Scott. *The Great Gatsby*, ed. Matthew J. Bruccoli. Cambridge & New York: Cambridge University Press, 1991.

Frost, Robert. *The Poetry of Robert Frost*, ed. Edward Connery Latham. New York: Holt, Rinehart & Winston, 1969.

————. *Selected Prose of Robert Frost*, ed. Hyde Cox and Edward Connery Latham. New York: Holt, Rinehart & Winston, 1969.

Gibson, James, ed. *Let the Poet Choose*. London: Harrap, 1973.

Grigson, Geoffrey. "Two Whiffs of Lewisite." *New Verse*. No. 19 (February–March 1936), 17–19.

————. "New Verse Goes Trotskyite?" *New Verse*. No. 23 (Christmas 1936), 24.

————. "Day Lewis Joins Up." *New Verse*. No. 25 (May 1937), 23–24.

Handley-Taylor, Geoffrey, and Timothy d'Arch Smith, eds. *C. Day-Lewis The Poet Laureate: A Bibliography*. Chicago & London: St. James Press, 1968.

H. D. (Hilda Doolittle). *Helen in Egypt*. New York: New Directions, 1974; first published New York: Grove Press, 1961.

Hewison, Robert. *Under Siege: Literary Life in London 1939–1945*. New York: Oxford University Press, 1977.

Hopkins, Kenneth. *The Poets Laureate* (3rd edition). New York: Barnes & Noble, 1973.

Hynes, Samuel. *The Auden Generation: Literature and Politics in England in the Thirties.* New York: Viking Press, 1977.

Isherwood, Christopher. "Some Notes on Auden's Early Poetry." *New Verse.* No. 26–27 (Auden Double Number, November 1937), 4–9.

Keats, John. *The Letters of John Keats 1814–1821,* ed. Hyder E. Rollins. Cambridge, Mass.: Harvard University Press, 1958.

Lawrence, D. H. *Complete Poems,* ed. Vivian de Sola Pinto and F. Warren Roberts. New York: Viking Press, 1964.

Lehmann, Rosamond. *Rosamond Lehmann's Album.* London: Chatto & Windus, 1965.

————. *The Swan in the Evening: Fragments of an Inner Life.* London: William Collins, 1967; London: Virago, 1977, 1982.

MacNeice, Louis. "A Statement." *New Verse.* Nos. 31–32 (Autumn 1938), 7.

————. *I Crossed the Minch.* London: Longmans, Green, 1938.

————. *Collected Poems,* ed. E. R. Dodds. London: Faber & Faber, 1966, 1979.

M[arsh], E[dward]. *Georgian Poetry 1911–1912.* London: Poetry Bookshop, n.d.

M[arsh], E[dward]. *Georgian Poetry 1913–1915.* London: Poetry Bookshop, 1915.

Muggeridge, Malcolm. *The Thirties: 1930–1940 in Great Britain.* London: Collins, 1967; first published, London: Hamish Hamilton, 1940.

O'Neill, Michael, and Gareth Reeves. *Auden, MacNeice, Spender: The Thirties Poetry.* London: Macmillan, 1992.

Osborne, E. A., ed. *In Letters of Red.* London: Michael Joseph, 1938.

Pound, Ezra. *The Cantos.* New York: New Directions, 1972.

————. *Selected Prose 1909–1965,* ed. William Cookson. New York: New Directions, 1973.

Pound/Zukofsky: Selected Letters of Ezra Pound and Louis Zukofsky, ed. Barry Ahearn. New York: New Directions, 1987.

Ransom, John Crowe. *Selected Poems.* New York: Alfred A. Knopf, 1969.

Reeves, Gareth. *T. S. Eliot: A Virgilian Poet.* New York: St. Martin's Press, 1989.

Roberts, Michael, ed. *New Signatures: Poems by Several Hands.* London: Hogarth Press, 1932.

————. *New Country: Prose and Poetry by the Authors of* New Signatures. London: Hogarth Press, 1933.

Robinson, Edwin Arlington. *Collected Poems.* New York: Macmillan, 1945.

Sartre, Jean Paul. *Black Orpheus,* tr. S. W. Allen, in the series Présence Africaine. Doullens: Dessaint, n. d. Translated from "Orphée noir," *Anthologie de la nouvelle poésie nègre et malgache de langue française,* ed. Leopold Sedar-Senghor. Paris: Presses Universitaires de France, 1948.

Spender, Stephen. "Oxford to Communism." *New Verse.* Nos. 26–27 (Auden Double Number, November 1937), 9–10.

————. *The Still Centre.* London: Faber & Faber, 1939.

————. *World Within World.* London: Hamish Hamilton, 1951.

————. *The Thirties and After: Poetry, Politics, People 1933–1970.* New York: Random House, 1978.

————. *Dolphins.* London: Faber & Faber, 1994.

Stevens, Wallace. *The Necessary Angel: Essays on Reality and the Imagination.* New York: Alfred A. Knopf, 1951.

————. *Collected Poems.* New York: Alfred A. Knopf, 1954.

Stonier, G. W. "Mr. Day Lewis." *New Statesman and Nation.* Volume 26 (November 6, 1943), 306.

Symons, Julian. *The Thirties: A Dream Revolved.* London: Cresset Press, 1960.

Tate, Allen. "A New Artist." *New Verse.* No. 3, May 1933, 21–23.

Underhill, Hugh. *The Problem of Consciousness in Modern Poetry.* Cambridge: Cambridge University Press, 1992.

Welty, Eudora. *The Golden Apples.* New York: Random House, 1948.

Williams, William Carlos. *Collected Poems*, ed. A Walton Litz and Christopher MacGowan, New York: New Directions, 1986, 1989.

Woolf, Virginia. "The Leaning Tower." *Collected Essays.* Volume 2. New York: Harcourt, Brace & World, 1967; first published in *Folio of New Writing* (Autumn 1940), 11–33.

INDEX

1940 and, 8–9; *Poems 1920*, 8; *Prufrock*, 3, 8; "Tradition and the Individual Talent," 6; "Virgil and the Christian World," 83; *The Waste Land*, 7–9, 16, 33, 76–77, 123–24, 221

Emerson, R. W., 6, 18, 112
Engels, F., 70; *The Communist Manifesto*, 56–57
Enlightenment, 35, 112, 155, 188
epiphanies, 34, 42, 215
Eros, 110, 115, 130, 160–61
eroticism, 105–15, 120–21, 126, 143–44, 176, 190; Bataille on, 106, 108–9, 111, 116, 119, 120, 129, 142–43; in CDL's *An Italian Visit*, 139–45; in CDL's late poetry, 190–92; CDL's "On Not Saying Everything" and, 205–7; in CDL's *Pegasus and Other Poems*, 160–62, 171; in CDL's *Poems, 1943–1947*, 106, 129–37, 151; in CDL's *The Poetic Image*, 116, 143; in CDL's *Transitional Poem*, 25–26, 30; in CDL's *Word Over All*, 98–116, 118–29, 131, 161–62; of creation, 177; and death, 57, 106–9, 121, 129–31, 140–43, 148, 205; of image, 105–6, 116, 118; imagination and, 112–13; as life force, 57, 148; and lyricism, 182–83; and marriage, 49, 63–66, 120, 134, 148; Meredith and, 153; and poetic energy, 107–8, 188; and politics, 29, 48, 49, 50, 55, 68, 105–6; and religion, 106, 111, 155, 193, 220; and violence, 66, 108, 109–11, 113–14, 115; and war, 79–80, 82, 94–95, 98–101, 109. *See also* love; sexuality; women in CDL's life
escapism, aesthetic, 42, 43, 68
ethics, 9, 33, 70, 150, 154; morality plays, 56–59; poetry reconciling conflicts in, 17–18, 19, 59

faith, 18–19, 184, 190; and CDL-father relationship, 168–69; hero worship and ancestor worship, 155; Marxism as substitute, 34, 48, 70, 77, 111, 155, 193, 220; secular, 34, 48, 118. *See also* agnosticism; religion; vision
farmer-poet, 87–88, 89, 91
fascism, 60–62, 79; T. E. Lawrence and, 46, 47; leftists vs., 77, 80; of Modernists, 74; Pound's, 88; Spain, 40, 43, 60–62, 69, 71; Spender vs., 40, 60–61; Yeats and, 154. *See also* Nazis
Faulkner, William, *Light in August*, 159
Fitzgerald, F. Scott, *The Great Gatsby*, 129, 133
flyers: as heroes, 45–46, 53. *See also* bird imagery
Ford, Ford Madox, 7
forgiveness, 158, 159, 168
formalism, 9, 21–22, 33, 180. *See also* poetic form and technique
Forster, E. M., 153
Franco, Generalissimo Francisco, 60–61, 71
Freud, Sigmund/Freudianism, 41, 77, 104–6, 108, 111
From Feathers to Iron, 27–30, 34, 41, 69; dedication "To the Mother," 64, 130; pastoral in, 28–29, 88; politics in, 29–30, 35, 79; sexuality in, 28, 29, 35, 65, 92–93
Frost, Robert, 6, 21, 185, 206, 221; in CDL's "The Creative Spirit," 200; CDL's *Enjoying Poetry* on, 9; CDL's *An Italian Visit* and, 138; CDL's "Sheepdog Trials in Hyde Park" dedicated to, 185; country lyrics, 86; "Directive," 212; and form, 7, 125; and imagination, 112; and nature, 24, 181; and pastoral tradition, 15; "The Road Not Taken," 166; *Selected Poems*, 125, 185; *Selected Prose*, 170, 184; "West-Running Brook," 188; and wit, 102

traveler, 124, 165–66, 168, 210. *See also* flyers; train; voyage
Tucker, Sophie, 30

Underhill, Hugh, 21
Upward, Edward, 30
utopia: CDL's disillusionment with, 188, 220; CDL's lyricism and, 182–83; CDL's *The Magnetic Mountain* and, 35–36, 38; CDL's *Overtures to Death* and, 62–6; and love, 111; Machine Age and, 29; pastoral and, 58; Roberts's, 33

Valéry, Paul, 171, 172, 178, 205; "Le Cimetière Marin," 136–37
violence: CDL's "The Image" and, 111, 113; in CDL's *Noah and the Waters*, 57, 58; CDL's *Word Over All* and, 108, 109–11, 113–14, 115; eros and, 66, 108, 109–11, 113–14, 115; in myth, 158, 159. *See also* war
Virgil, 83–92, 104–5; CDL's "O Dreams! O Destinations!" and, 128; CDL's translation *The Aeneid of Virgil*, 156–57; CDL's translation of *The Georgics*, 57, 83, 84–88, 156–57
virtu, 150, 151, 153–54
vision, 70–71, 199–200, 220. *See also* eroticism; prophetic vision; secular vision; spiritual vision; utopia
vocation, poetic, 184, 187, 190
voyage: trope of, 35–36, 195, 196, 210–11, 213. *See also* road; train; traveler

war: American Civil, 99; in CDL's poetry, 58, 61, 192 (*see also under* World War II); Cold, 97, 192; eroticism and, 79–80, 82, 94–95, 98–101, 109; marriage and, 131; as obsessive trope, 77; pastoral and, 86; Roman, 85–86; Spanish

Civil, 40, 43, 60–62, 71; stress of, 100; World War I, 13–14. *See also* class war; World War II
Warner, Rex, 22, 30, 37, 59
Waugh, Evelyn, 37, 60
Welty, Eudora, *The Golden Apples*, 158, 159
The Whispering Roots (CDL), 189–90, 192–93, 211–15; "All Souls' Night," 212–13; "At East Coker" (Eliot elegy), 208, 215, 219–20; "Avoca, Co. Wicklow," 211; "Ballintubber Abbey, County Mayo," 193; "Ballintubbert House, Co. Laois," 211; "Golden Age, Monart, Co. Wexford," 211; "Hero and Saint," 210; "The House Where I Was Born," 211; "A Marriage Song," 214; "Merry-go-round," 214; "Near Ballyconneely, Co. Galway," 211; "A Privileged Moment," 213; "Recurring Dream," 211–12; "Sailing from Cleggan," 190, 211; "A Skull Picked Clean," 211; "Some Beautiful Morning," 210, 213; "Tenure," 213; "A Tuscan Villa," 213; "The Whispering Roots," 193, 212
Whitman, Walt, 4, 6, 89, 90, 112; *Drum Taps*, 99, 100; "Reconciliation," 99, 100, 101; "Sea Drift," 135; "Song of Myself," 27, 135
wholeness, 19, 77, 118. *See also* "central mind"; synthesis
Williams, Raymond, 58
Williams, William Carlos, 4, 7, 22, 89; on creative process, 177–78; and imagination, 112; "A Sort of Song," 170; *Sour Grapes*, 8
Wilson, Edmund, 9
Wilson, Harold, 193
wit, 23, 28, 102, 169
women: in CDL's *The Magnetic Mountain*, 37, 64; in Lehmann's novels, 95. *See also* sexuality; women in CDL's life

Friends of the
Houston Public Li...

humca   821
                             .91209
                             D33G

GELPI, ALBERT
LIVING IN TIME : THE POETRY
    OF C.DAY LEWIS

HUMCA   821
          .9120
          9
          D3G

HOUSTON PUBLIC LIBRARY
CENTRAL LIBRARY

MAR 99

1/09